Developing Extensions for Joomla! 5

Extend your sites and build rich customizations with
Joomla! plugins, modules, and components

Carlos M. Cámara Mora

BIRMINGHAM—MUMBAI

Developing Extensions for Joomla! 5

Group Product Manager: Alok Dhuri

Publishing Product Manager: Kushal Dave

Associate Project Manager: Deeksha Thakkar

Senior Content Development Editor: Rosal Colaco

Technical Editor: Maran Fernandes

Copy Editor: Safis Editing

Indexer: Tejal Daruwale Soni

Production Designer: Nilesh Mohite

DevRel Marketing Coordinators: Deepak Kumar and Mayank Singh

Business Development Executive: Mayank Singh

First published: November 2023

Production reference: 2281123

Published by Packt Publishing Ltd.

Grosvenor House

11 St Paul's Square

Birmingham

B3 1RB, UK

ISBN 978-1-80461-799-1

www.packtpub.com

To my parents, who gave me the push that got me farther in my life. To my beloved wife, the perfect companion for our crazy trip in life. To my wonderful sons, you are the reason I work hard every day.

– Carlos Cámara

Foreword

For nearly two decades, hundreds of individuals worldwide have generously dedicated their time, energy, and expertise to create, share, and enhance the web content management system known as Joomla! We engage in this endeavour, entirely without compensation, because we believe in the significance of Open Source and the collective power of collaboration to achieve something greater than individual efforts. Carlos, our author, stands among those who, throughout his extensive involvement in what we fondly refer to as the Joomla Community, has made many diverse contributions. Sharing his Joomla knowledge through this book is yet another manifestation of his commitment to this truly exceptional software phenomenon.

This book is crafted for three categories of individuals. Firstly, it caters to those who do not intend to develop their own Joomla extensions, offering them a deeper insight into website construction with Joomla. Similarly, if you are contemplating building your inaugural Joomla extension but are apprehensive about the process, this book is tailored for you. I recommend reading it twice – first without opening your computer, and then again, seated in front of your computer, coding as you read.

Lastly, if you are among those with prior experience in building a Joomla extension, I believe this book will be a valuable supplement, propelling you further by imparting best practices and elucidating how to leverage the latest functionality.

Constructing a website with Joomla is just the beginning. This book illustrates the techniques necessary to craft your own customised Joomla components, modules, and plugins. Armed with this knowledge, you will have an advanced understanding of the possibilities Joomla offers for website development. Joomla's applications are boundless, and with this book, your potential will be boundless as well.

Brian Teeman,

Co-Founder Joomla!

Contributors

About the author

Carlos M. Cámara Mora is a Joomla! expert and cofounder at Hepta Technologies, a web development company, with a focus on developing long-lasting websites and applications that help businesses own their logic and data. As a Joomla! Expert, Carlos has helped site owners around the world to develop the right solution for their business, using Joomla! and developing custom solutions.

I would like to first and foremost thank my loving and patient wife and sons for their continued support, patience, and encouragement throughout the long process of writing this book. Also, thanks to Joomla! volunteers all around the world. You made a difference and helped me develop wonderful solutions for lots of people! I hope this book gives back a bit of what I received from you.

About the reviewer

Peter Martin, from Nijmegen, Netherlands, is a tech enthusiast with a passion for, and sharing knowledge on, information technology. He holds a bachelor's degree in economics and a master's degree in mass communication. He moved into the tech world and, since 2005, has specialized through his company, db8.nl, in crafting optimized Joomla! websites and developing custom web applications.

Since 2005, Peter has actively contributed to the Joomla! community, as a Global Forum Moderator, in the Community Leadership Team, as an Operations Department Coordinator, on the Board of Directors, and as a mentor for **Google Summer of Code (GSoC)**.

Peter fosters tech communities by organizing: Joomla! User Group Arnhem-Nijmegen, Linux Usergroup Nijmegen, and Open Coffee Nijmegen.

Table of Contents

Preface   xv

Part 1: Developing Components

1

Planning Your Component   3

Understanding what a Joomla!   Adding extra information columns to tables   13
component is   4   Reflecting relationships in the database   14
Translating your problem into an   Creating tables in the database   16
application   5   **Adding mock data to your database**   **18**
Identifying your elements   5   Defining the content of our mock data   18
A real-world example   6   Automating mock data generation   19
                                                    Importing mock data into the database   21
Defining your component database
structure   10   **Summary**   **22**
A quick look at the Joomla! database   11   **Further reading**   **23**
Adding database tables for entities   12

2

Developing the Backend of a Basic Joomla! Component   25

Technical requirements   **26**   **Developing a list view for a component 35**
Component file architecture   **26**   Adding the view for projects data   35
Building a component's backend   26   Adding a model to the projects view   36
Creating our component repository structure   31   Showing the list of projects   40
Creating a manifest file   **32**   **Developing an edit item view for**
Testing a minimum component on Joomla!   34   **our component**   **41**

Creating a Project view   42
Adding a model to retrieve and save data   44
Adding a controller to our Project entity   48
Creating a layout for our edit project view   48

Changes to our manifest file   49
Testing the component   51

Summary   **51**
Further reading   **51**

3

Developing the Frontend of a Basic Joomla! Component   53

Technical requirements   **54**

**Developing a frontend list view for
our component**   **54**
Coding the list view   55

Adding CSS and JS to our component   **61**
Adding our own styles and JavaScript to
our component   63
Joomla's Web Asset Manager   64
Loading assets with HtmlHelper   67

**Developing a frontend item view
for our component**   **68**

Adding the model for the frontend item view   69
Adding the layout for the item detail   72
Adding a menu item for our views   73

**Adding friendly URLs to
our component**   **77**
Translating parameters into a friendly URL   80
Translating SEF URLs into variables for
our component   81

Summary   **82**
Further reading   **82**

4

Creating Forms in Joomla!   83

Technical requirements   **83**

Defining forms in Joomla!   **84**
Adding general options to our extensions   84
Adding search and filter capabilities to our
listings   86
Editing or adding individual items   89

Using standard Joomla! Form fields   **90**
Using the Editor form field type   91
Using the accessiblemedia field type   92

Creating select options from database tables   92

Defining custom form field types   **93**
How to use the subform field type   **95**
**Validating user input on the
client side**   **97**
**Validating user input on the
server side**   **99**
Summary   **101**
Further reading   **102**

5

Harnessing the Power of Joomla! in Your Component   103

Technical requirements	104	using Joomla! categories	112
Reviewing what Joomla! features you can use in your component	104	Using our categories' custom properties	113
		Adding ACL to our component categories	117
Adding an ACL to our component	105	**Introduction to Joomla! custom fields**	**117**
Setting up Joomla! user groups and viewing access levels	105	Using custom fields in our component	118
Adding the permissions configuration	106	Showing custom fields in our views	120
Honoring the permissions in our extensions	108	Adding an ACL to the custom fields	122
Defining custom actions for our component	109	**Using Joomla's multilingual capabilities in our component**	**124**
Using Joomla! categories in our component	**110**	Adding complex translations	126
Customizing our component categories	112	**Summary**	**127**
Exploring the benefits and limitations of		**Further reading**	**128**

6

Adding a Web Service API to Your Component   129

Technical requirements	130	Using createCRUDRoutes() to add our Web Service endpoints	138
What is a Web Service API?	130		
How to consume any Web Service API	131	Adding custom endpoint requests to our Web Service	139
How can I use the Joomla! Web Service API?	**132**	Handling the request in our component	140
Authorization for the API	**134**	**Reading data from your Web Service – adding a GET endpoint to your component**	**141**
Basic authorization	134		
Joomla! token authorization	134		
Web Services API permissions	**135**	**Writing data from your Web Service – adding a POST endpoint to your component**	**142**
Adding a Web Service API to your component	**136**		
Developing the Web Service plugin	136	**Summary**	**144**
		Further reading	**144**

Part 2: Developing Modules and Plugins

7

Developing a Module   147

Technical requirements	148	Using module configuration parameters	154
Understanding the module file structure	148	Adding an Advanced tab to our module configuration	157
Creating the provider code	148	Caching Joomla! modules	158
Using module helpers	150	Using saved parameters in your code	159
Adding the layout for the module	152	Summary	162
Writing the manifest for our module	152	Further reading	162

8

Developing a Joomla! Plugin   163

Technical requirements	164	Creating the manifest file for our plugins	168
What is a plugin in Joomla!?	164	Creating a content plugin	170
Calling Joomla! plugins from our component	165	Adding plugins to our component	178
Understanding Joomla's plugin file structure	168	Creating our customer's plugin	180
		Summary	183
		Further reading	183

9

Adding a CLI to Your Extension   185

Technical requirements	186	Introducing Joomla! CLI commands	188
What is a CLI?	186	Introducing generic options for Joomla! CLI	189
What is a Cron Job?	186	Adding a Joomla! CLI command to Joomla!	189
How to use Joomla! CLI	187	Exploring SymfonyStyle methods	194

What Symfony console output tags can we use? 194

How to internationalize CLI messages   195

Adding parameters to your CLI

command   199

Summary   202

Further reading   203

Part 3: Extending Templates

10

Creating Unique Web Applications with Template Overrides   207

Technical requirements   208

What is a Joomla! template?   208

What are template overrides?   209

Creating a template override for
Joomla! views   210

Creating a template override for a
component view   210

Creating a template override for a module   212

Creating a template override for a plugin   212

Creating alternative layouts   213

Adding an alternative menu item for a
component view   213

Adding an alternative layout for a module   214

Overriding CSS and JS   215

Overriding assets with the Web
Assets Manager   215

Adding new assets to our overrides   216

Disabling assets in our overrides   216

Summary   217

Further reading   217

11

Creating a Child Template in Joomla!   219

Technical requirements   219

Why do we need child templates?   220

Creating a child template   220

Creating a child template directly in
our repository   221

Creating a child template using the Joomla!
template manager   223

Overrides in child templates   224

Adding a new module position to
the template   226

Using different styles for the module   227

Reusing child templates on
different sites   229

Adding parameters to a child template   231

Adding language files to our child template   232

Summary   233

Further reading   233

Part 4: Distributing Your Extensions

12

Testing Your Extensions 237

Technical requirements	237	Installing Codeception	247
Do I need tests?	238	Testing accessibility in our extensions	251
Including unit testing in Joomla!	238	Testing accessibility with your browser	252
What is TDD?	239	Summary	254
Installing PHPUnit	240	Further reading	254
How to add system testing in Joomla!	246		

13

Security Practices in Joomla! 255

Technical requirements	255	Preventing SQL injection	262
Fetching data from forms	256	Securing your assets for the future	264
Filtering input data before saving it to a database	258	Hardening access to your files	265
Preventing cross-site request forgery (CSRF) attacks in forms	260	Using the JED Checker extension	265
		Summary	267
Preventing cross-site scripting (XSS) attacks	261	Further reading	268

14

Distributing Your Joomla! Extensions 269

Technical requirements	270	How to manage database changes on your extensions	276
Creating a package for your extensions	270	How to change your database structure by updating your extensions	278
Managing versions in your extension	273	Cleaning the database on uninstall	280
Packaging all the extensions into one file	274		
		How to execute advanced tasks on extension install	280

Setting up an update server   284

Adding a paywall to your
extension download   287

Summary   288

Further reading   288

Index   289

Other Books You May Enjoy   298

Preface

Joomla! is one of the most popular **Content Management Systems (CMS)** around. What started in 2005 as a fork of Mambo, now has nothing to do with it and has evolved to a great standard of security, efficiency, and usability. In all these years Joomla! API has grown to a stable and functional framework, and it embraces the modern PHP development standards. This book is about the latest Joomla! architecture and how to develop extensions that take advantage of it. The 14 chapters are grouped into 4 sections, each of which can be read individually, but if you are not familiar with Joomla! development, I recommend following the chapters sequentially.

Part 1 covers all topics related to component development and provides a full vision of the current Joomla! architecture that will be used in the other parts of the book.

Part 2 of the book explores module and plugin development and introduces the Joomla! Command Line Interface. This part will settle your understanding of Joomla's new architecture.

Part 3 of the book covers template development. We go first through template overrides to understand how a template works and we then introduce Joomla! child templates. When you know how to develop a child template, developing a parent template is just a matter of adding the remaining files.

Finally, in the last part of the book, we explore what we need to take into account before distributing our extensions. We cover testing, security practices, and of course how to package and distribute our extensions.

Who this book is for

This book is for Joomla! users and web designers who want to extend the functionalities of Joomla! and find awesome ways to extend and customize their content management systems, ecommerce websites, business websites, and so on.

What this book covers

Chapter 1, Planning Your Component, introduces the problem we want to solve and provides a simple methodology to plan the development for our extension. It also defines the database architecture that we are going to use in the book.

Chapter 2, Developing the Backend of a Basic Joomla! Component, starts the development of the backend part of a Joomla! component. It introduces Joomla! 5 MVC architecture and the new Joomla! development paradigm.

Chapter 3, Developing the Frontend of a Basic Joomla! Component, shows how to develop the frontend area of our component. It introduces Joomla! Routing and how to use Joomla! Web Assets Manager to add Styles and JavaScript to our component.

Chapter 4, Creating Forms in Joomla!, provides an overview of using forms in Joomla!. It shows how to create our forms using Joomla! API methods. It also covers Joomla! standard form fields and how to develop our own form fields. Finally, it shows how we can add server-side and client-side validation to our forms.

Chapter 5, Harnessing the Power of Joomla! in Your Component, provides a guide on the Joomla! core features we can use in our developments. It shows how to add Joomla! core permissions to our component using Joomla! ACL, it covers how to add Joomla! Categories to our component. This chapter also demonstrates how to integrate Joomla! custom fields in our extension and how to use the Joomla! translation system.

Chapter 6, Adding a Web Service API to Your Component, introduces Joomla! Web Service API. It also shows how to develop a Web Service endpoint for our extensions.

Chapter 7, Developing a Module, shows how to develop a Joomla! module using the new Joomla! architecture. It also introduces module helpers to develop more complex modules.

Chapter 8, Developing a Joomla! Plugin, introduces Joomla! plugins and shows the new plugin architecture. It explains how to trigger plugin events and covers how to develop plugins for our component.

Chapter 9, Adding a CLI to Your Extension, introduces Joomla! Command Line Interface usage. It also covers how to develop a console command for Joomla!, style its output, and include parameters in the command.

Chapter 10, Creating Unique Web Applications with Template Overrides, shows how to change any Joomla! template to meet your design specifications using template overrides. It also explains how to expand components by adding extra views.

Chapter 11, Creating a Child Template in Joomla!, introduces Joomla! template development through the new child template feature.

Chapter 12, Testing Your Extensions, shows how we can include PHP unit testing in our Joomla! extensions. It introduces Test Driven Development paradigm. It also covers how to create integration tests for your Joomla! component using Codeception. Finally, it explains how to test accessibility in your developments.

Chapter 13, Security Practices in Joomla!, covers Joomla! measures to secure your developments and provides useful tips to avoid common exploits. It also introduces the JED Checker tool for further checks.

Chapter 14, Distributing Your Joomla! Extensions, explains the manifest files for our extensions and it shows how to create a package for them. It also covers how to include an update server for our extensions. Finally, the chapter describes the mechanism built in Joomla! to allow updating extensions that are behind a paywall.

To get the most out of this book

You will need to know some basic PHP coding and of course HTML, CSS, and JavaScript coding. You will also need an operational version of Joomla! 5 installed, functional and accessible. All the code examples have been tested in **Joomla! 5** and **PHP 8.2**.

If you are using the digital version of this book, we advise you to type the code yourself or access the code from the book's GitHub repository (a link is available in the next section). Doing so will help you avoid any potential errors related to the copying and pasting of code.

Disclaimer

Packt Publishing Ltd. is not affiliated with or endorsed by The Joomla! Project™. Use of the Joomla!® name, symbol, logo and related trademarks is permitted under a limited license granted by Open Source Matters, Inc.

Download the example code files

You can download the example code files for this book from GitHub at https://github.com/PacktPublishing/Developing-Extensions-for-Joomla-5. If there's an update to the code, it will be updated in the GitHub repository.

We also have other code bundles from our rich catalog of books and videos available at https://github.com/PacktPublishing/. Check them out!

Conventions used

There are a number of text conventions used throughout this book.

`Code in text`: Indicates code words in text, database table names, folder names, filenames, file extensions, pathnames, dummy URLs, user input, and Twitter handles. Here is an example: "In PHP, the values that are passed via a form are stored in the $_POST global variable, but we do not use it."

A block of code is set as follows:

```
$search = $this->getUserStateFromRequest(
            $this->context . '.filter.search',
            'filter_search');
```

When we wish to draw your attention to a particular part of a code block, the relevant lines or items are set in bold:

```
<field
     name="customer"
     type="text"
     label="COM_SPM_INVOICE_CUSTOMER"
     filter="int"
     />
```

Any command-line input or output is written as follows:

```
$userid = $_POST['userid'];

$query = "SELECT * FROM users_table WHERE userid = $userid";
```

Bold: Indicates a new term, an important word, or words that you see onscreen. For instance, words in menus or dialog boxes appear in **bold**. Here is an example: "Create the package and click on **Submit**."

> **Tips or important notes**
> Appear like this.

Get in touch

Feedback from our readers is always welcome.

General feedback: If you have questions about any aspect of this book, email us at customercare@ packtpub.com and mention the book title in the subject of your message.

Errata: Although we have taken every care to ensure the accuracy of our content, mistakes do happen. If you have found a mistake in this book, we would be grateful if you would report this to us. Please visit www.packtpub.com/support/errata and fill in the form.

Piracy: If you come across any illegal copies of our works in any form on the internet, we would be grateful if you would provide us with the location address or website name. Please contact us at copyright@packt.com with a link to the material.

If you are interested in becoming an author: If there is a topic that you have expertise in and you are interested in either writing or contributing to a book, please visit authors.packtpub.com.

Share Your Thoughts

Once you've read *Developing Extensions for Joomla! 5*, we'd love to hear your thoughts! Scan the QR code below to go straight to the Amazon review page for this book and share your feedback.

https://packt.link/r/1804617997

Your review is important to us and the tech community and will help us make sure we're delivering excellent quality content.

Download a free PDF copy of this book

Thanks for purchasing this book!

Do you like to read on the go but are unable to carry your print books everywhere?

Is your eBook purchase not compatible with the device of your choice?

Don't worry, now with every Packt book you get a DRM-free PDF version of that book at no cost.

Read anywhere, any place, on any device. Search, copy, and paste code from your favorite technical books directly into your application.

The perks don't stop there, you can get exclusive access to discounts, newsletters, and great free content in your inbox daily

Follow these simple steps to get the benefits:

1. Scan the QR code or visit the link below

https://packt.link/free-ebook/9781804617991

2. Submit your proof of purchase
3. That's it! We'll send your free PDF and other benefits to your email directly

Part 1: Developing Components

The king of extensions in Joomla! is the component. With components, we can create tables in our database and we can offer views to manage the information in this table. Also, understanding components gives you a full view of the Joomla! 5 architecture as modules and plugins will use the same paradigm.

This part has the following chapters:

- *Chapter 1, Planning Your Component*
- *Chapter 2, Developing the Backend of a Basic Joomla! Component*
- *Chapter 3, Developing the Frontend of a Basic Joomla! Component*
- *Chapter 4, Creating Forms in Joomla!*
- *Chapter 5, Harnessing the Power of Joomla! in Your Component*
- *Chapter 6, Adding a Web Service API to Your Component*

1
Planning Your Component

Joomla! is an extensible **Content Management System (CMS)**. For years, people have used Joomla! to build great websites, such as company websites, sites for associations, niche social networks, blogs, and school websites.

Joomla's popularity stems from the plenty of features and functionalities it comes with – content and user management, custom fields to expand your articles and create directories, and built-in search, among others.

Even so, despite all these great features, it does not solve all the problems you may face when building a web application. In this book, you are going to learn how to use Joomla! to build solutions while leveraging the Joomla! Framework™ to make your work easier. Throughout this book, we will explore how to code our components, modules, plugins, and even templates to develop an integrated and portable solution to our technical problems.

The first step to solving a technical problem is always to write a good plan. The planning process provides a better understanding of the problem. In this chapter, we will go through the process of identifying our problem and writing a plan to solve it.

We will identify which parts of our problem correspond to which technical entities. After that, you will see how easy it is to define the basic architecture of your project. Finally, we will add some mock data that will be helpful when we start testing our work.

In this chapter, we are going to cover the following main topics:

- Understanding what a Joomla! component is
- Translating your problem into an application
- Defining your component database structure
- Adding mock data to your database

By the end of this chapter, you will be able to design and plan the development of a Joomla! component that solves a problem in the real world.

Technical requirements

You do not need special software to develop a Joomla! extension. A text editor should do that, but using the right tools will help you develop quicker. Also, all the tools we recommend are free and are available for several operating systems:

- A Joomla! website. We recommend using a free site from `https://launch.joomla.org`. It's perfect for testing purposes, and it has all the server tools we need. For development purposes, it's better to use a local LAMP stack because you have better and faster access to all files.

- **Visual Studio Code** as your code editor. You may download it from `https://code.visualstudio.com/`.

- **PhpMyAdmin** as a database client to edit the database structure of your site. It is included in the server tools of the Joomla! Launch server panel.

You can find the code files for this chapter on GitHub: `https://github.com/PacktPublishing/Developing-Extensions-for-Joomla-5/tree/chapter01`

Understanding what a Joomla! component is

In Joomla!, we have several types of extensions – components, modules, plugins, templates, libraries, packages, and languages. All of these have a specific purpose in the system, but due to Joomla's flexibility, in some cases, it can get difficult to choose one type over the other. Should I use a module to include content at the end of my articles, or is it better to use a content plugin? Do I use a custom user plugin to add fields to my user profile, or should I use Joomla! Custom Fields capabilities? After reading this book, you will be able to choose the option that best fits your project.

The main and most complete extensions in Joomla! are **components**. We can think of Joomla! components as small web applications on their own. Components do not need to be supported by any other parts of your Joomla! site. They can work isolated from the rest of your site, and they complete the scope of your website.

In any case, you will get the most from any component when they team up with other Joomla! parts, such as modules or plugins.

Your website is formed by lots of pages, and every page has a URL. In Joomla!, every time you access a URL, you are inside a Joomla! component. So, components have their own page requests, and no other components of the site can affect them when you load their URL. Despite this isolation, they can communicate with other components using their code.

Some characteristics of a Joomla! component are as follows:

- Joomla! components offer a secure entry point for your requests. With them, you may create webhooks for external services or receive data from forms.

- Components usually have a backend and a frontend. The backend is usually restricted to managers and administrators of the site and is used to manage the data.

- In most scenarios, your component will have to store data in the database. For instance, if you want to create a component to track your projects' progress, you need to store the names of your projects, their statuses, and probably more information in the database. For this reason, components install new tables in your database to store information.

- Components automatically add themselves to Joomla's backend menu, and they install new menu item types on your site to show their data on the site's frontend.

In fact, in Joomla!, you are always working with components as every page (backend or frontend) of your site is a component view.

Now that we know some characteristics of a component, let's see how we can use them to solve real-world problems.

Translating your problem into an application

Whenever your customers demand a new feature for their website, you need to think of how to put it in place. Most of the design process consists of understanding your client's needs and being able to translate them into all the entities that conform to your web application.

Modeling applications into coding elements is a complex subject that involves lots of research. In this book, we will take a practical approach and make a visual and simplified architecture for our data.

In any case, you need to plan your extension properly, and for that, you need to translate your customer's words into coding blocks.

Identifying your elements

In any problem you want to solve, you can identify different elements that form part of your problem:

- **Entities**: An entity is an element of your problem with which other elements can interact. For instance, it could be a company, a user, a task, or an invoice. Also, an entity implies data that needs to be stored in the database.

- **Relationship**: A relationship relates entities to one another with no action between them. For instance, a customer will have a company.

A real-world example

In this book, we will be solving a real-world problem. We need to develop a project management tool that allows us to do the following (these are also the requirements to solve the problem):

- Store customer data

- Generate invoices

- Create tasks for the project

Now, let's begin by defining entities for this problem.

Defining your entities

Data entities are one of the most important parts of our project. They correspond to the data we need to store for our project. Data entities will be the tables in our database where we store our component information.

Some of these data entities are easy to recognize. For instance, if your project has users, then the user will correspond to a data entity.

Finding entities

In our project management tool project, we can see several entities at a glance:

Figure 1.1 – Entities we identify in our problem

In this figure, we can see the following entities:

- **Customers**: This represents our customers and will have enough information to identify them – Firstname, Lastname, Email, Company name, Company ID, Company Address, and Phone.

- **Invoices**: This involves the invoices we may send to our customers. Our invoicing system will be quite simple; it will just need the Customer data, Services provided, and Amount fields.

- **Projects**: Projects are entities in our problem as they represent the service our customer has requested. In our case, projects will just have a name, description, and deadline.

- **Project category**: We want to be able to differentiate several categories in our project, and an easy way of doing so is by adding categories to our projects. Our project categories will need just a name.

- **Tasks**: Tasks are the jobs we have to do for our project, so it makes sense to think of them as entities in our requirements. In our scenario, a task will have a name, a description, a state, and a deadline.

What actions can we find in our problem?

Not only do we need to define the entities that form our system, but we also need to identify the actions that can be applied to all of them. Actions are the tasks we can perform on our entities. In our extension, for instance, we can create new projects, or edit existing customers. So, **Create** and **Edit** are the actions of our component.

Some types of actions are common to all entities, and you should count on them every time:

- **Create entity**: This action allows us to add data to our database. Any time you create an entity, a row is added to its table in the database.

- **Edit entity**: This action allows us to modify the data we previously added to the database. When you edit an entity, no extra row is added to the database.

- **Remove entity**: This action removes data we previously added to the database. When you remove an entity, you remove at least one row from the database. Or move it to the trash first and remove it from the trash later.

- **Show entity**: This action allows you to show the data of your entity. No data is changed in your database when you use this action.

And, of course, every project will have its own needs and can have several actions not shown in this book. For our real-world project, we have identified the following actions for each of our entities:

- **Customer**: For our Customer entity, we can find the following actions:

  - Create customer

  - Edit customer

  - Archive customer

  - Remove customer

- **Invoice**: For the Invoice entity, we can define the following actions:

  - Create invoice

  - Edit invoice

  - Send invoice

  Please be aware that we have omitted the *removed* action from invoices. Most countries do not allow you to remove invoices, so it makes sense not to consider this action in our project. You need to find a solution for changing or deleting customer data. An invoice should always contain the original data.

- **Project**: For the Projects entity, we define the following actions:

  - Create project

  - Edit project

  - Archive project

  - Remove project

- **Project category**: For the Project category entity, these are the actions we can add:

  - Create a project category

  - Edit project category

  - Remove project category

- **Task**: For the Task entity, we find these actions:

  - Create task

  - Edit task

  - Archive task

  - Remove task

Defining relationships

Our entities are not isolated; they need to be connected to have some functionality. For instance, a task must belong to a project, and a customer might have several invoices.

It is important to define the relationships between all our entities to be able to devise the database tables.

In our example, we can find the following relationships:

- Customer:

  - Our customers can be in a project

  - Our customers might have multiple invoices (hopefully tons of them!)

- Invoice:

  - For any invoice, we must have just one customer

  - Any invoice is related to a service provided, so it must have at least one project, but it might have more

- Project:

  - Our projects will only be in one category

  - We will only have one customer per project

  - Any project is composed of multiple tasks

- Task:

  - Every task will be assigned just to one project

These relationships are illustrated in the following figure:

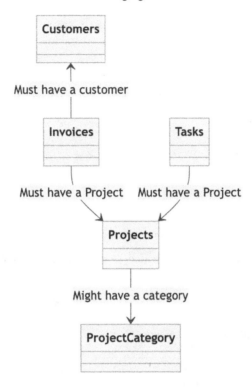

Figure 1.2 – Graphical representation of our relationships

The arrows in the figure show the entities' relationships. When we create our database tables in the following sections, these arrows will represent a field that relates to two tables. For instance, in the **Invoices** table, we will have an **id_customer** field that shows the relationship between the customer and the invoice.

Once we have translated our problem into entities and their relationships, we can define the database structure for our component.

Defining your component database structure

Our component needs to store information in the Joomla! database. So, we need to identify all the tables and columns we need for our component. Once we have identified all the elements of our problem, it is easy to write down the table's structure.

We will take the following approach to write the table's structure:

- Add database tables for entities

- Add extra information columns to tables

- Reflect relationships in the database

- Create tables (What kind of tables? We already added database tables for entities (see the first item))

Let's start by taking a quick to the Joomla! database's default tables before adding our tables.

A quick look at the Joomla! database

After installing Joomla!, your database will be populated with several tables. These tables are part of Joomla! Core.

If you log in to PhpMyAdmin, you may see something like this:

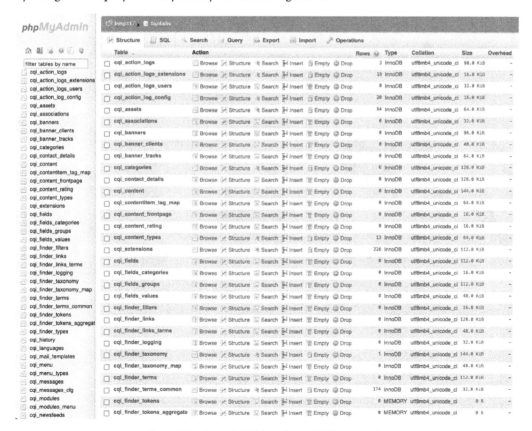

Figure 1.3 – Joomla! tables after installing Joomla!

Here, you can see some tables that come with Joomla!. You should not change these tables or edit their content directly in the database unless you know what you are doing.

One thing you may have noticed is that my installation table names are different from yours. In my case, all the tables start with the **cqi_** prefix; in your installation, you will find a different prefix.

This is a security measure that has come with Joomla! since Joomla! 1.0. Adding this prefix prevents possible attackers from knowing the exact name of the tables, thus preventing them from planning a direct attack on your database.

This also makes it impossible for us to know the exact table names when we are creating our extensions. To overcome this problem, in Joomla!, we can use the #__ prefix for table names in the code of the extension. You will also find this convention in this book when referring to database tables.

If you want to know the exact database prefix of your Joomla! installation, access the backend of your site and go to **System**. In the **Information** panel, click on the **System Information** link. Then, go to the **Configuration File** tab; you may find it next to the **dbprefix** setting.

Adding database tables for entities

As a rule of thumb, we will have one table per entity in our problem, so we can start representing our tables as per this schema:

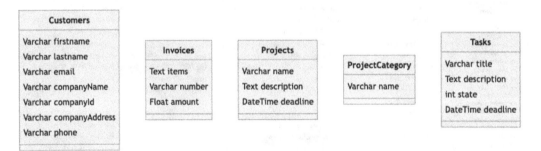

Figure 1.4 – Representation of our tables with their fields

This simple scheme covers all the tables with their fields. Even so, you may notice we have not added any customer data to the invoice. You need to add Customer data to the invoices because when you delete customers, you will lose the Customer data on your invoice! That is because we have just added fields that hold unique and independent information, and now, we are going to add the fields that relate one table with another. Consider the following schema:

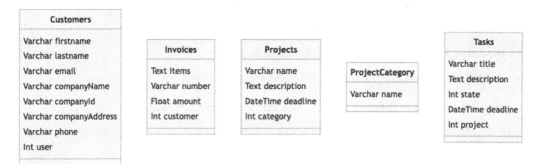

Figure 1.5 – Representation of our tables after adding related fields

Our tables are now complete as they define all the fields and relationships we specified in the previous sections.

Adding extra information columns to tables

Even though we have completed our database structure, it will be a poor database definition if we do not add some extra columns to our definition. For instance, we could add a column registering the creation date of an invoice. Also, it might be interesting to know if an invoice has been modified after creation.

Finally, how do you relate the **customer** field in the **Invoices** table with the **Customers** table? We can do this by adding **metadata** to our component.

You will want to add some metadata columns to all your tables. These metadata fields give you information about when a new row was added to your table or the last user who modified it. Therefore, these are the common fields you will add to your tables:

- **id**: It's used to refer to the specific entity

- **modified**: Represents the date when the entity was edited

- **created**: Represents the date when the entity was created

- **modified_by**: Links to the user who edited the entity

- **created_by**: Links to the user who created the entity

The database should generate the **id** column value automatically when each entity is created:

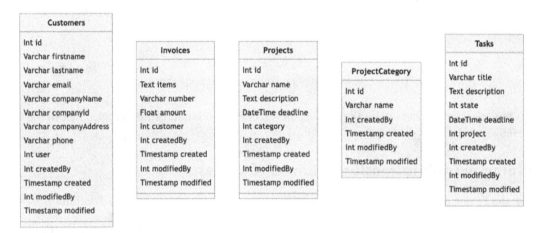

Figure 1.6 – Representation of our tables after adding metadata fields

Reflecting relationships in the database

The last step to having a good visual representation of the project is adding relationships to our diagram.

After adding the extra information fields, our relationships have grown – now, every table is related to the Joomla! **User** table via the **modified_by** and **created_by** fields.

Even though we do not need to create the Joomla! User table, it is a good idea to include a representation of this table in our diagram. We do not need to cover the whole table; just showing the fields we use is enough:

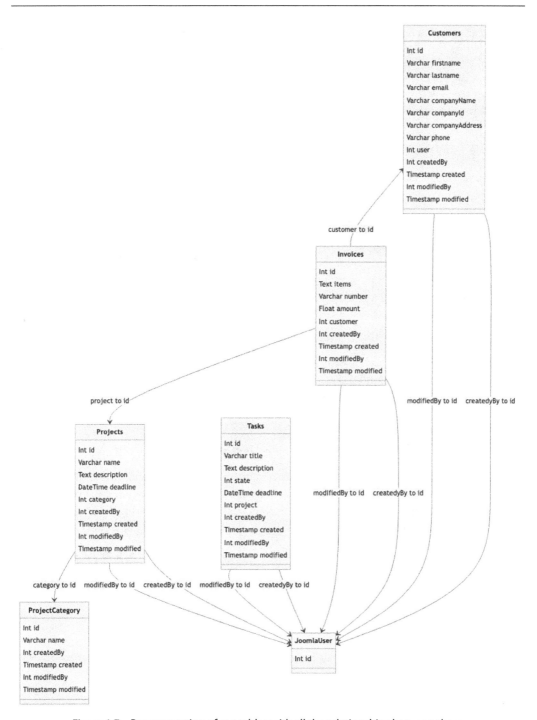

Figure 1.7 – Representation of our tables with all the relationships between them

Here, you can see a full representation of our tables, with arrows representing how they are related.

As you can see, every table links to the Joomla! User table. This is because we have different fields such as **modified_by** or **created_by**, which relate to the **id** field in the Joomla! User table. Besides that, we can see how our tables are related graphically so that we can represent all the relationships we defined in the previous section.

Creating tables in the database

Once we have a clear representation of our tables, we can generate the code to create the tables in our database.

You can use the following code to create the projects table:

```
CREATE TABLE IF NOT EXISTS '#__spm_projects' (
    'id' int(11) UNSIGNED NOT NULL AUTO_INCREMENT,
    'name' VARCHAR(255) NOT NULL,
    'alias' VARCHAR(255) NOT NULL,
    'description' TEXT,
    'deadline' DATETIME,
    'category' INT(11),
    'created' DATETIME DEFAULT NOW(),
    'modified' DATETIME DEFAULT NOW(),
    'created_by' INT(11)  NOT NULL ,
    'modified_by' INT(11)  NOT NULL ,
    PRIMARY KEY ('id')
    ) ENGINE=InnoDB;
```

This SQL code will create our projects table. To ensure our tables are unique, and we do not clash with other extensions using similar table names, we can use an extra prefix with the name of our component. In our case, we will use #__spm_projects. Also, remember that before using this code to create your database, you need to replace #_ with your database prefix, as explained in the previous section.

Finally, note the change of casing in the field names. Though MySQL allows you to use caps in the field names, historically, database fields are all in lowercase. So, for our SQL code, we are replacing and renaming our fields from **modifiedBy** to modified_by and so on. So, why did I mention "modifiedBy" earlier? You can leave that out to make it less confusing.

To create the tasks table, we will use this code:

```
CREATE TABLE IF NOT EXISTS '#__spm_tasks' (
 'id' int(11) UNSIGNED NOT NULL AUTO_INCREMENT,
    'title' VARCHAR(255) NOT NULL,
    'alias' VARCHAR(255) NOT NULL,
    'description' TEXT,
```

```
'deadline' DATETIME,
'state' INT(3) NOT NULL,
'project' INT(11),
'created' DATETIME DEFAULT NOW(),
'modified' DATETIME DEFAULT NOW(),
'created_by' INT(11)  NOT NULL ,
'modified_by' INT(11)  NOT NULL ,
PRIMARY KEY ('id')
) ENGINE=InnoDB;
```

In this SQL code, we are using an INT type for the project field. This indicates that the project field will store the value of the id field from the #__spm_projects table.

For our customers table, we use a similar code:

```
CREATE TABLE IF NOT EXISTS '#__spm_customers' (
    'id' int(11) UNSIGNED NOT NULL AUTO_INCREMENT,
    'firstname' VARCHAR(255) NOT NULL,
    'lastname' VARCHAR(255) NOT NULL,
    'email' VARCHAR(255) NOT NULL,
    'company_name' VARCHAR(255) NOT NULL,
    'company_id' VARCHAR(255) NOT NULL,
    'company_address' VARCHAR(255) NOT NULL,
    'phone' VARCHAR(25) NOT NULL,
    'user' INT(11),
    'created' DATETIME DEFAULT NOW(),
    'modified' DATETIME DEFAULT NOW(),
    'created_by' INT(11)  NOT NULL ,
    'modified_by' INT(11)  NOT NULL ,
    PRIMARY KEY ('id')
    ) ENGINE=InnoDB;
```

In this case, we use an INT field to store the id value of our user from the #__users table in the user field.

Finally, we will create our invoices table using this code:

```
CREATE TABLE IF NOT EXISTS '#__spm_invoices' (
    'id' int(11) UNSIGNED NOT NULL AUTO_INCREMENT,
    'items' TEXT NOT NULL,
    'number' VARCHAR(25) NOT NULL,
    'amount' FLOAT DEFAULT 0.0,
    'customer' INT(11),
    'created' DATETIME DEFAULT NOW(),
    'modified' DATETIME DEFAULT NOW(),
```

```
    'created_by' INT(11)  NOT NULL ,
    'modified_by' INT(11)  NOT NULL ,
    PRIMARY KEY ('id')
) ENGINE=InnoDB;
```

Once we have the code to create our tables, we can access our database and create them. So, go to your server hosting tools and access your database client. I recommend using **phpMyAdmin**, but other tools, such as **dbadminer**, are also an excellent choice. Once you are connected to your database, just execute the preceding SQL code.

After that, all your tables will be created and you will be ready to start adding data to your tables.

Adding mock data to your database

Sample data is a key part of any development process. The benefits of using mock data in our application are clear:

- It provides a better overview of the application
- It saves testing time as you do not need to introduce the data yourself in the app
- It helps you identify errors in your application as you will see the application working sooner
- When you release the app, you can use this mock data to feed your test environments

As mock data does not need to be real or accurate, you may just create some random sentences and copy them into a .csv file. Still, there is a better alternative and you should aim to have useful mock data. Here are some tips you may follow:

- Try to find data that makes sense to your context. For instance, if you have to fill in a phone number, do not add random numbers. Instead, use a number with 9 digits that match your phone number format.
- Do not use real information as your mock data. It might be leaked and you do not want to expose your family and friends.
- Try to automate the process as much as possible.
- You probably need as many types of mock data, as entities you have.

So, keeping these tips in mind, we are going to create a little script that helps us generate our mock data.

Defining the content of our mock data

For each of our entities, we'll generate a CSV file with sample data. We will import this data into our recently created tables, so we need it to have a specific structure.

For each entity, we will have the following columns (one per field):

- **Customers**: Firstname, lastname, email, company name, company ID, company address, and phone
- **Invoices**: Services provided and amount
- **Projects**: Name, description, and a deadline
- **Tasks**: Name, description, state, and deadline

Automating mock data generation

It's a good idea to have more than one sample item per entity in our component. The more items you have, the more cases you can test and notice when developing your component. Also, having random items helps you discover issues and errors in an early phase. You may create sample items one by one by hand, but that will be a repetitive, boring task prone to human error. Instead, we are going to automate the creation of sample data using a simple PHP script.

As we are developing for Joomla! and we love PHP (also, since most of the Joomla! coding is done in PHP, it makes sense not to introduce another language), we are going to code a small PHP script. This script will use a **Faker PHP library** to automate the process of creating the data. You can find more information about Faker in the *Further reading* section at the end of this chapter.

The Faker PHP library can create fake data for several type fields and it's very popular in the PHP community.

Let's create a folder in our repository called Mock and copy this composer.json file:

```
{
    "name": "project-manager/mock-data",
    "description": "A script to generate mock data for the
        project",
    "type": "project",
    "license": "GPL v2",
    "autoload": {
        "psr-4": {
            "Carcam\\MockData\\": "src/"
        }
    },
    "require": {
        "fakerphp/faker": "^1.19"
    }
}
```

This `composer.json` file defines our project and tells Composer that we want to use the Faker PHP library in it. After that, we must execute `composer install` in our folder and create the `create-mock-customers.php` script. In this file, we start loading the Composer autoloader file. This allows us to use namespaces in our script. If you are not familiar with Composer, I recommend that you check out the relevant link in the *Further reading* section of this chapter:

```php
<?php

require_once 'vendor/autoload.php';
```

Then, we must define the headers of the CSV file and the number of lines of data we want to create.

> **How much fake data should I create?**
>
> For the number of lines in our CSV, we use a number bigger than 20. In Joomla!, by default, we have 20 items per page, so this helps us show at least two pages of items in the listings.

We must also define the path to save the resulting file before we create the data:

```php
$headers = ['firstname', 'lastname', 'email',
    'company_name', 'company_id', 'company_address',
        'phone'];

$totalLines = 30;
$filepath = './data/customer.csv';
```

Once we have set up the script, we must initialize the `Faker` class and start creating our CSV file in a `for` loop. Inside this `for` loop, we must initialize an array to store each column and add the values obtained from the `Faker` class. Finally, we must assign the `$data` array to the CSV line:

```php
$faker = Faker\Factory::create('en_US');

$csv[0] = $headers;
for ($line = 0; $line < $totalLines - 1; $line++) {
    $data = array();
    $data[] = $faker->firstName();
    $data[] = $faker->lastName();
    $data[] = $faker->email();
    $data[] = $faker->company();
    $data[] = $faker->ein();
    $data[] = $faker->address();
    $data[] = $faker->phoneNumber();
```

```
    $csv[$line] = $data;
}
```

As soon as we finish adding the lines to the data array, we must create the file that will store this data. First, we must create and open the file; then, we must go through our $csv array with a loop to write down every line of the .csv file:

```
if (!file_exists(dirname($filepath))) {
    mkdir(dirname($filepath), 0755);
}

$file = fopen($filepath, 'w');

foreach ($csv as $row) {
    fputcsv($file, $row);
}

fclose($file);
```

The process for creating the other entities' mock data files is similar, so I leave it up to you to check the code in this book's GitHub repository.

Importing mock data into the database

Once we have created our mock data, we need to add it to our database to be able to use it or retrieve it from our component.

At this point, we are going to import the data manually. However, later in this book, we will learn how we can include it in the installation files, though I do not recommend this approach.

> **Note**
>
> Adding sample data in your installation files will install this data every time your user installs the component. This might be interesting for first-time users, but it is annoying for users who are already acquainted with the component.

To begin importing, follow these steps:

1. To import data into your database, you need to access phpMyAdmin or a similar tool and go to the **#__spm_customers** table we created in the previous section.

2. Then, click on **Import**, add your CSV file, and click on **Import**:

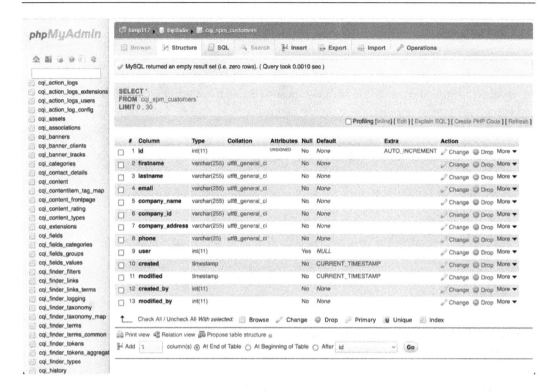

Figure 1.8 – The #__spm_customers table with the Import button at the top right

Now, our database is full of mock data and we are ready to start coding our component to see the results of this import.

Summary

In this chapter, we showed you all the possibilities we have when using a Joomla! component. We also presented a real-world problem, and we started planning a solution for it. Having a development plan helps us understand the problem and allows us to envision all the possible approaches we might take to solve the problem. Finally, we created the database structure and the fake data we are going to use to test it.

You are now ready to translate a real-world problem into a coding problem. You also know how to create a database structure for your component and how to fill it with test data.

In the next chapter, we will code the backend for our component and interact with our new tables from it.

Further reading

- You can read about SemVer at `https://semver.org/`.

- W3Techs is the site of reference for the CMS market. You can view Joomla! usage and trends worldwide at `https://w3techs.com/technologies/details/cm-joomla`.

- The `FakerPHP` library offers lots of possibilities for creating fake data. You can find more information about it at `https://fakerphp.github.io/`.

- Composer is the de facto dependency manager standard for PHP and it helps you create featured-rich applications using third-party libraries. You can read more about it at `https://getcomposer.org/`.

- Joomla! relies on namespaces to work. Namespaces in PHP solve lots of issues when using different libraries in your code. You can read more about namespaces in the PHP manual at `https://www.php.net/manual/en/language.namespaces.rationale.php`.

2

Developing the Backend of a Basic Joomla! Component

One of the benefits of using Joomla! is that it actually has two applications in place – Joomla! frontend and Joomla! backend. Joomla's backend is used for site configuration and data management, and its components reflect this architecture. This separation allows for more secure and scoped applications, where you handle data management and administration in the backend, while you leave user interaction for the frontend. This is why there is a dedicated area in the Joomla! backend for management. In this area, users can see private data and configure the behavior of a component.

A component's backend covers all the data entities we described in our component plan in the previous chapter. Each entity is usually provided with a listing view and an edit view. Additionally, in the backend, we also find the configuration page of the component.

In this chapter, we will work with minimum code to create a Joomla! component. We will discover the file architecture we need to create for a standard Joomla! component.

Once we have our code, we will see how to create a manifest file for our component, and we will install it on a Joomla! site.

Finally, we will add some code to add a list view and an edit item view to our component, which will allow us to modify and add data to our database.

In this chapter, we will cover the following topics:

- Component file architecture
- Creating a manifest file for our component
- Developing a list view for our component
- Developing an edit item view for our component

Technical requirements

To go through this chapter, we need to edit code and test it on a Joomla! site. So, you will need the following:

- Visual Studio Code (or your preferred code editor)
- The Joomla! site we installed in the previous chapters

You can find all the code files used in this chapter on GitHub: `https://github.com/PacktPublishing/Developing-Extensions-for-Joomla-5/tree/chapter02`

Component file architecture

We can create a Joomla! component using almost any folder architecture you can imagine. However, if we want to take advantage of Joomla! libraries, we need to follow some rules. In this section, we will create a file and folder structure to follow Joomla! standards and use it to our benefit.

When installing a component on your Joomla! site, Joomla! automatically moves all different parts of your component to the right location.

A basic component will have at least an `admin` folder and a `site` folder. These folders host the files for the backend and the frontend of our component, respectively. Let's continue to work in our development folder and create two folders – `admin` and `site`:

- **admin**: This folder will contain all the files and folders that belong to the backend of our component. It will be responsible for component interaction in the Joomla! Administrator.
- **site**: This folder will contain all the files and folders that conform to the frontend or public part of our component.

We will see the contents of the `site` folder in the next chapter. For now, we will start considering what is inside the `admin` folder for a basic component with minimum code.

Building a component's backend

The main folder of the backend of our component contains all the logic it needs to work in the backend of our Joomla! site. It also contains some files used in the component installation.

To start coding our component, we will need to create a basic folder structure for the backend. We will start with minimum code, and we will grow from it. As a starting point, let's create the following folders:

- `services`
- `src`
- `tmpl`

The services folder

The `services` folder's purpose is to host the `provider.php` file – it registers all the services our component will use. However, our components also need to define the services they use from Joomla!. To make it easier for us, Joomla! 4 introduced the **Dependency Injection Container**. This is a design pattern that aims to simplify dependency management and create a more robust platform.

To add the `services` folder to the backend of our component, we will add the `services/provider.php` file with the following code:

```php
<?php

use Joomla\CMS\Dispatcher\ComponentDispatcherFactoryInter
  face;
use Joomla\CMS\Extension\ComponentInterface;
use Joomla\CMS\Extension\Service\Provider\ComponentDispatcherFactory;
use Joomla\CMS\Extension\Service\Provider\
  MVCFactory;
use Joomla\CMS\MVC\Factory\MVCFactoryInterface;
use Joomla\DI\Container;
use Joomla\DI\ServiceProviderInterface;



use Piedpiper\Component\Spm\Administrator\Extension\
  SpmComponent;

return new class implements ServiceProviderInterface
{
    public function register(Container $container)
    {
        $container->registerServiceProvider(new
          MVCFactory('\\Piedpiper\\Component\\Spm'));
        $container->registerServiceProvider(new
          ComponentDispatcherFactory('\\Piedpiper\\
            Component\\Spm'));

        $container->set(
            ComponentInterface::class,
            function (Container $container)
            {
                $component = new SpmComponent($container->
                get(ComponentDispatcherFactoryInter
                  face::class));
```

```
                        $component->setMVCFactory($container->
                            get(MVCFactoryInterface::class));

                        return $component;
                }
            );
        }
    };
```

Although this might look a bit like boilerplate code, the purpose of it is to implement the dependency injection container pattern. The interesting part of this code is the highlighted block. In this block, we start to register the services our component is about to use.

One of these services is MVCFactory. In Joomla!, the **Model-View-Controller** (**MVC**) implementation is provided as a service. This means that we need to call the MVCFactory service in this file. Another service that we must call is ComponentDispatcherFactory. It is responsible for dispatching our components and needs to be used in every component.

In the highlighted block, you can see that we call the $pm class, which we will define later in the following sections. Other services we will add in future chapters are RouterFactory and CategoryFactory, but right now, we'll keep it simple.

The src folder

Once our dependencies are set, we can explore the src folder. This folder contains the basic MVC model for our component. It also contains the following subfolders:

- Controller
- Extension
- Model
- Table
- View

If you are familiar with Joomla! 3 development, you may recognize all of these subfolders, except the Extension folder. Actually, these folders host the classes that complete the MVC model of our component.

Namespaces in Joomla!

In Joomla!, every library has a namespace, and we use namespaces to load classes in our component. So, our component should also have a namespace. This namespace has the form ROOT_NAMESPACE\ TYPE_OF_EXTENSION\ALIAS, where ROOT_NAMESPACE is a unique starting name. It could be the name of your company, your name, or any word that has some meaning to you. Then, we add the type of extension – in this case, it is `Component`. Finally, we include `ALIAS`, which is the name or the alias you've chosen for your component – in this case, we use `Spm` as our alias (an acronym of **Simple Project Manager**). So, we get our final namespace as `Piedpiper\Component\Spm`.

Every subfolder inside the `src` folder starts with an uppercase letter. This helps the autoloader to find the different classes using their namespaces. For folders outside `src`, we use lowercase letters, as Joomla! will look for filenames in this format.

The Extension folder

The `Extension` folder holds the boot file. This will be the entry point for the backend. This file will be named as our component in the form `COMPONENT_ALIAS_Component`. So, let's create in the `admin/src/Extension/` folder the `SpmComponent.php` for our component in the following code block:

```php
<?php

namespace Piedpiper\Component\Spm\Administrator\Extension;

use Joomla\CMS\Extension\BootableExtensionInterface;
use Joomla\CMS\Extension\MVCComponent;
use Psr\Container\ContainerInterface;

class SpmComponent extends MVCComponent implements
  BootableExtensionInterface
{
    public function boot(ContainerInterface $container)
    {
    }
}
```

At this moment, this file is not very impressive. We just call the `boot()` method with the container from the dependency injection configured in the `providers.php` file. However, this file is the starting point for our component, so it needs to be there.

We will add some extra code to this file in future chapters in any case.

The Controller folder

In this folder, we will place all the controllers for the backend of our component. Our first controller will be `DisplayController.php`. This file is the first file the Joomla! MVC checks after the component bootup. In this file, we will define the default view for our component in the backend.

Let's create this file inside this `Controller` folder:

```php
<?php

namespace Piedpiper\Component\Spm\Administrator\Controller;

use Joomla\CMS\MVC\Controller\BaseController;

class DisplayController extends BaseController
{
        protected $default_view = 'cpanel';
}
```

In this code block, the `DisplayController` class extends Joomla's `BaseController`, and we define the default view for our component, which is the view called `cpanel`. We will create it in the next section.

In the `spm` component, we will create a control panel view where our users will have easy access to all the entities in our component, so it makes sense that we use this as the default view. In any case, you can also assign any other views of your component as the default view.

The View folder

In the `View` folder, we store all the views of our component. In our first component, we will start to add the control panel view so that we can install the component as soon as possible.

Each view has to be installed in its own folder, so we will create the `admin/src/View/Cpanel/HtmlView.php` file in the following code block:

```php
<?php

namespace Piedpiper\Component\Spm\Administrator\
  View\Cpanel;

use Joomla\CMS\MVC\View\HtmlView as BaseHtmlView;

class HtmlView extends BaseHtmlView
{
    public function display($tpl=null): void
    {
        parent::display($tpl);
    }
}
```

In this code block, the `HtmlView` class extends Joomla's `HtmlView` class, and to avoid a name clash, we need to set an alias (`BaseHtmlView`) for it when using the namespace.

For this class, we just define the `display()` method that will call the `tmpl` file with our content.

The tmpl folder

Our views call a template file with the HTML code needed to display our data. These files are stored inside the `tmpl` folder. To differentiate between templates from different views, we need to create one folder per view.

So, we will create the `default.php` file inside the `tmpl/cpanel` folder with really simple content:

```php
<?php

echo 'Simple Project Manager Control panel'
```

This code will just show the message `Simple Project Manager Control panel` on our screen.

So far, we have created all the files needed for a functional component in the backend. We have set up the basic code to follow Joomla! standards, and we have even created a simple view that shows a message. In the next sections, we will see how to create a package with this code to install it on our Joomla! site.

Creating our component repository structure

We have been through the basic files and folder architecture of the backend of our component, so now it's a good time to create the file structure on our computer to expand this project and create a repository for it.

There are some things we need to consider while creating the repository structure to hold our extension code:

- The repository structure should reflect the final structure of our component. This will help us create the installation package for our extension at any time.

- It should hold all the code related to the project.

- Throughout this book, we will also develop a module and some plugins for our project, so let's create a repository where we can keep adding things to the project.

- In the following chapters, we will also cover some testing techniques, so creating a repository will keep those techniques in mind.

Having said that, let's start creating our local repository with the following two folders:

- The `src` folder: This folder will hold all our component files

- The `scripts` folder: This folder will hold any supporting script for our project – for instance, the mock data creator we developed in *Chapter 1, Planning Your Component.*

Creating a manifest file

To install an extension, Joomla! follows the directions in the manifest file of the component. The manifest file is an `xml` file with basic information about your extension. In this file, we must specify the final destination of each file. Also, it must have the same name as your component alias. So, in our case, as our component is `com_spm`, the manifest file will be `spm.xml`.

Locally, we need to place the manifest file inside the main folder of our component.

So, we will start to write our manifest file like this:

```xml
<?xml version="1.0" encoding="utf-8"?>
<extension type="component" method="upgrade">
    <name>COM_SPM</name>
    <author><![CDATA[Carlos Cámara]]></author>
    <authorEmail>carlos@hepta.es</authorEmail>
    <authorUrl>https://extensions.hepta.es</authorUrl>
    <creationDate>2022-07-21</creationDate>
    <copyright>(C) 2022 Piedpiper Inc.</copyright>
    <license>GNU General Public License version 2 or later;
        see LICENSE.txt</license>
    <version>0.1.0</version>
    <description><![CDATA[COM_SPM_DESCRIPTION]]></
      description>
    <namespace path="src">Piedpiper\Component\
      Spm</namespace>
    <administration>
        <files folder="admin">
            <folder>services</folder>
            <folder>src</folder>
            <folder>tmpl</folder>
        </files>
        <menu link="option=com_spm" img="class:default">
          COM_SPM_MENU_BACKEND</menu>
    </administration>
</extension>
```

First of all, you may notice that we declared the XML syntax of the document with xml version and file encoding.

Immediately after that, in *line 2*, we start our manifest declaration indicating we are installing an extension. We also indicate the type of the extension (component, in this case) and the method to install it. The method could be install or upgrade. If you choose the install method, you could only install this extension version on sites where it has not been installed yet. If you choose the upgrade method, you can install the same version as many times as you want, overwriting previous extension files every time.

Lines 3 to *9* are the metadata of the extension. We define our name and email, and we can specify its license of use.

After that, we can have some real fun, where we define some technical aspects of our extension. Let's go through the following subsections.

- <version>: This defines the version of our extension. Joomla! uses it to know whether it needs to track extension updates, and we might use it when installing the extension to perform custom changes.

  In Joomla!, it is a common practice to follow the **Semantic Versioning Specification** (https:// semver.org), where you use three numbers to specify the version of each component.

- <description>: In this tag, we add a description of our extension. In this case, we use a key string to specify the description – COM_SPM_DESCRIPTION. This will help us offer translated versions of our descriptions.

> **Using non-ASCII characters in XML**
>
> If you are not familiar with the XML syntax, it might seem weird to see the key string wrapped in the [CDATA[]] definition. This is an escape command that allows us to use non-ASCII characters and other forbidden characters in XML.

- <namespace>: This tag defines the namespace of our extension, as we saw in previous sections of this chapter.

- <administration>: This section of the XML file allows us to define some stuff from our extension for the Joomla! backend. Here, we define the files and folders that are moved to the backend of the component. We can also define the menus we want to include in the backend of the site.

- `<files>`: Inside the `<administration>` section, we define the `<files>` section, which tells Joomla! where in the backend to store the files of the package we install.

  The `<files>` section can be used outside of the `<administration>` section, and if so, it represents the location of the files that need to be installed in the component's frontend area.

  In our manifest file, the `<files>` section also includes a `folder` attribute. This attribute is used to specify the name of the folder in our package that contains the files and folders we are about to instruct. The `<files>` section allows two tags – `<folder>` and `<filename>`. The former represents a full folder that needs to be placed, as it is in the component's backend folder, and the latter represents the individual files we want to include.

- `<Menu>`: In this section, we define the link we will add to Joomla's main backend menu for our component. We fill in some properties as follows to define the menu:

  - `link`: Here, we set the target URL of our component. Actually, Joomla! will figure out the URL; we just need to add its parameters. In our case, the parameter is `option=com_spm`.

  - `img`: We can use this to add an image to our menu entry in the backend. Nevertheless, in the Joomla! Administrator default template, this image is not shown.

Showing icons for menus in the backend

In Joomla's default backend template, the icons in menu items are not shown. In this case, you will want to provide an image for users that use a different backend template; the best option is to do it using CSS. The standard method is to fill in this attribute with the `css` class of the icon prefixed with `class:`. So, in our code, we could use `<menu link="option=com_spm" img="class:book">COM_SPM_MENU_BACKEND</menu>`. This will show a book icon in capable backend templates.

To render these icons, Joomla! uses the **FontAwesome** free icon library (`https://fontawesome.com`).

This covers our minimum manifest file, and we can now create a Joomla! package with our minimum component and try to install it on a Joomla! site.

Testing a minimum component on Joomla!

We are ready now to install our minimum component on a Joomla! site. If you haven't already created your Joomla! website, now is the time to do it.

There are lots of options to start a Joomla! site, and for this book, we will use the **Launch Joomla!** service. For this, just go to `https://launch.joomla.org`, fill in the form, and within minutes, you will have a Joomla! website up and running.

Before installing our extension, we need to create a ZIP package that contains it. If you followed our directory structure in the previous sections, you can easily create it by making a .zip file that contains the component folder. The name of the package is not relevant, but I recommend naming it com_spm_TIMESTAMP.zip, where you replace TIMESTAMP with the current time and date. This name also has a timestamp, so you can easily identify the package.

After logging in to your Joomla! backend, go to the extension installer and upload the package.

Once you install it, you will see a success message and an info box with the content of the <description> tag of our manifest file.

Also, when you now click on the **Components** section of the side menu, you will see there is a new menu entry with the text **COM_SPM_MENU_BACKEND**. If you click on that link, you will go to your component and see the content of the control panel view we created.

Developing a list view for a component

Hooray! We have created our first Joomla! component, and it's installed in the backend of our site! However, we must admit that it does not do much yet. Let's make it a bit more useful.

In the previous chapter, we installed some sample data for the database in the tables of our component. Let's create a list view for the project's data.

Adding the view for projects data

We will start by adding a folder named Projects inside the src/component/admin/src/View folder.

Inside this folder, we also add our HtmlView.php file, but now, this file will have some code to call the model and get the data before passing it to the template:

```php
<?php
namespace Piedpiper\Component\Spm\Administrator\View\
  Projects;
use Joomla\CMS\MVC\View\GenericDataException;
use Joomla\CMS\MVC\View\HtmlView as BaseHtmlView;

class HtmlView extends BaseHtmlView
{
    public $filterForm;
    public $state;
    public $items=[];
    public $pagination;
    public $activeFilters=[];
```

```
public function display($tpl=null): void
{
    $this->state       = $this->get('State');
    $this->items       = $this->get('Items');
    $this->pagination  = $this->get('Pagination');
    $this->filterForm    = $this->get('FilterForm');
    $this->activeFilters = $this->get('ActiveFilters');

    if (count($errors = $this->get('Errors'))) {
        throw new GenericDataException(implode('\n',
            $errors), 500);
    }

    parent::display($tpl);
}
}
```

The new code gets some variables that we need in the list view. First of all, we get the state of the session in the state property. This state provides information about the state of the request. It usually stores information about which filters are in place, how many items you need to show in the listing, and any other non-persistent information about a user browsing a page.

After getting the state, we request the items to show by calling the $this->get('Items') method. This method directly calls the getItems() method in the model, which retrieves the items from the database. In this case, it will retrieve the list of projects in our database.

Finally, we get the $pagination variable and the form to provide a filter for the listing, and discover which filter fields are in place on this request.

If any errors occur when fetching the data, we catch them, and we throw a PHP exception, including an error message. In this case, our error message is just the list of errors in the $errors variable. Joomla! automatically detects the exception and handles showing the error to the user.

As you can see, we are not doing much work; we just request data using the $this->get() method. This method is a getter for the model, so let's see what happens when we request the data.

Adding a model to the projects view

As we use the MVC pattern, we will add a model to our component. This model is responsible for retrieving data from the database. To create the model, we also extend one of the already existing model classes in Joomla!. This guarantees we abide by the Joomla! standards, but it avoids extra work for us.

You can find all the possible models you can extend in your Joomla! installation in the `libraries/src/MVC/Model` folder. For our backend model, we will focus on these ones:

- `BaseModel`: This is the most basic model from which every other model inherits basic state management. However, it does not implement a database connection. Unless you create a very basic model, you probably don't want to use it.

- `BaseDatabaseModel`: This inherits from `BaseModel`, so it provides state management, but it also provides methods to query the database.

- `ListModel`: This class inherits from `BaseDatabaseModel`, and besides a database connection, it provides some functions to help us create a list of items. For example, it provides a standard way to implement filtering in our lists and lets us query the database to obtain a list of items.

You will use these models most of the time when developing your component's backend. However, this does not mean you cannot use them in the frontend.

As we are developing a list of items, we will use `ListModel`, so we will create the `ProjectsModel.php` file inside our `src/component/admin/src/Model`. We will start defining our namespace and what other namespaces we will use in this file:

```php
<?php

namespace Piedpiper\Component\Spm\Administrator\Model;

use Joomla\CMS\MVC\Model\ListModel;
use Joomla\CMS\Factory;
```

In this case, we need to declare the `ListModel` namespace that contains the class definition we will extend in our model. Now, we can add the class:

```php
class ProjectsModel extends ListModel
{
}
```

Inside our `ProjectsModel` class, we will start adding the `__construct` method with this code:

```php
public function __construct($config = [])
{
    if (empty($config['filter_fields']))
    {
        $config['filter_fields'] = [
            'id', 'a.id',
            'name', 'a.name',
        ];
```

```
    }

        parent::__construct($config);
}
```

This is the class parent constructor. It receives a configuration array. If you examine the parent class, you can see all the options you can set in this configuration array. However, in our code, we will only add the name of the id field and name field. These will be the only two fields that we will allow to rule how we order our list of projects.

In a Joomla! model following the Joomla! MVC, we need to define the populateState() method, so we will add it next:

```
protected function populateState($ordering = 'name',
    $direction = 'ASC')
{
    $app = Factory::getApplication();
    $value = $app->input->get('limit', $app->get('
      list_limit', 0), 'uint');
    $this->setState('list.limit', $value);


    $value = $app->input->get('limitstart', 0, 'uint');
    $this->setState('list.start', $value);


    $search = $this->getUserStateFromRequest($this->context .
'.filter.search', 'filter_search');
    $this->setState('filter.search', $search);


    parent::populateState($ordering, $direction);
}
```

The populateState() method is important because it gets all the information submitted in the user request and recreates the state of the application. This way, our list of projects will show the requested number of items or keep the same ordering or filters when searching through pages of data.

In the previous code, we got the total number of projects we wanted to display per page (limit), which is the first project we have to show (limitstart), along with whether the user has added any search filters (search).

Finally, the last method we need is getListQuery(). This method creates the query we use to get the list of items from the database.

In this method, we use the `$db` object to define all parts of the query that Joomla! will translate into SQL and send to the database. Note that there is no direct call to the database in this method. We just provide all the information we want to extract and let the `ListModel` parent class handle the rest:

```
protected function getListQuery()
{
    $db    = $this->getDatabase();
    $query = $db->getQuery(true);
    $query->select(
        $this->getState('list.select',
            [
                $db->quoteName('a.id'),
                $db->quoteName('a.name'),
                $db->quoteName('a.deadline'),
            ]
        )
    )->from($db->quoteName('#__spm_projects', 'a'));

    $search = $this->getState('filter.search');

    if (!empty($search))
    {
        $search = $db->quote('%' . str_replace(' ', '%',
            $db->escape(trim($search), true) . '%'));
        $query->where('(a.name LIKE ' . $search . ')');
    }

    $orderCol  = $this->state->get('list.ordering',
        'a.name');
    $orderDirn = $this->state->get('list.direction',
        'ASC');

    $query->order($db->escape($orderCol) . ' ' . $db->
        escape($orderDirn));

    return $query;
}
```

This is a simple model that queries the database and returns a list of results. We have only added three methods to the model, and it gives us lots of features.

Working with different types of SQL systems

One cool feature of using the Joomla! Db class is that it automatically translates your query into **MySQL** or **PostgreSQL**. So, if you aim to develop an extension that can work in both types of database servers, you do not need to worry about it.

With this minimum model, our view can get all the data it needs to show a list of projects, so let's see how we can put all this information together in the template to show our listing in the next section.

Showing the list of projects

Once we have created the model and the view, we just need to make it pretty by adding the template file. To add the template file, we need to create the `src/component/tmpl/projects/` folder, and we can create the `default.php` file inside using the following code:

```php
<?php

use Joomla\CMS\Language\Text;
use Joomla\CMS\Router\Route;
use Joomla\CMS\HTML\HTMLHelper;

$listOrder = $this->escape($this->state->get('
  list.ordering'));
$listDirn  = $this->escape($this->state->get('
  list.direction'));
?>
```

As usual, we declare the namespaces we need to support our code.

Finally, we define a couple of variables to keep track of the ordering.

After this block, we can add the HTML for our template:

```
<form action="<?php echo Route::_('index.php?option=
  com_spm&view=projects'); ?>" method="post" name="
    adminForm" id="adminForm">
    <div class="table-responsive">
        <table class="table table-striped">
            <caption><?php echo Text::_('COM_SPM_PROJECTS
              _LIST');?></caption>
            <thead>
                <tr>
                    <td><?php echo Text::_('COM_SPM_
                      PROJECTS_LIST_ID');?></td>
                    <td><?php echo Text::_('COM_SPM_
```

```
                        PROJECTS_LIST_NAME');?></td>
                    <td><?php echo Text::_('COM_SPM_
                        PROJECTS_LIST_DEADLINE');?></td>
                </tr>
            </thead>
            <tbody>
                <?php foreach ($this->items as $item) : ?>
                    <tr>
                    <td><?php echo $item->id; ?></td>
                    <td><?php echo $item->name; ?></td>
                    <td><?php echo $item->deadline; ?></td>
                    </tr>
                <?php endforeach;?>
            </tbody>
        </table>
    </div>

    <?php echo $this->pagination->getListFooter(); ?>

    <input type="hidden" name="task" value="">
    <?php echo HTMLHelper::_('form.token'); ?>
</form>
```

In the template, we add a table with three columns – id, name, and deadline – to show data from our projects.

If you take a closer look at the code, you can see that we include the table inside an HTML form. We need to do this to activate pagination and other actions that we will add throughout this book. This form action just routes to the Projects view of our component.

After dealing with our table, you can see that we have added a call to the pagination object. This method will show the pagination in the tfooter position of our table.

So far, we have learned how to show a list of items in our component and how Joomla! implements the MVC pattern. Furthermore, we have also discovered some useful Joomla! libraries to reduce the code we have to write. Let's go to the next section to see how we can edit our items.

Developing an edit item view for our component

Besides listing projects from the database, our component is a tool to manage them. As a project manager, you need to be able to edit your projects. Let's see how we can edit our projects in this section.

To add an edit screen for our projects, we will create an edit view for our projects. To do this, we need the following:

- A `Project` view inside our `View` folder
- A model to get the data or our project from the database and to save our changes
- A layout file inside the `tmpl` folder to show our edit form
- A `ProjectController` field inside our `Controller` folder

Let's start our first edit item view.

Creating a Project view

A single-item view looks quite like the list view in Joomla!, but there are some important changes we need to be aware of. To add this view, create the `src/component/admin/src/View/Project/HtmlView.php` file and then the `HTMLView` class extending it, as we did in the previous section when creating the list view. So, let's start with the following code:

```php
<?php
namespace Piedpiper\Component\Spm\Administrator\View\
    Project;
use Joomla\CMS\Factory;
use Joomla\CMS\Helper\ContentHelper;
use Joomla\CMS\Language\Text;
use Joomla\CMS\MVC\View\HtmlView as BaseHtmlView;
use Joomla\CMS\MVC\View\GenericDataException;
use Joomla\CMS\Toolbar\Toolbar;
use Joomla\CMS\Toolbar\ToolbarHelper;
class HtmlView extends BaseHtmlView
{
    public $form;
    public $state;
    public $item;
}
```

Inside our class, we have to declare the `display()` method that will request the data to the model and pass it to the template. So, we will keep adding this code:

```php
public function display($tpl=null): void
{
    $this->form     = $this->get('Form');
    $this->state    = $this->get('State');
    $this->item     = $this->get('Item');
    if (count($errors = $this->get('Errors')))
```

```
    {
        throw new GenericDataException(implode("\n",
            $errors), 500);
    }
    $this->addToolbar();
    parent::display($tpl);
}
```

In this code block, we removed `Pagination` and `Filter` from the list view from the previous section, as we do not deal with a list of items anymore. Instead, we added a `Form` property, which will retrieve the HTML form definition that we will show to our users in the template.

We also added a new method called `addToolbar()`. This method helps us to add the **action buttons**, **Save**, **Apply**, and **Cancel**, with the code Joomla! already provided for it. We can define this method like this:

```
protected function addToolbar()
{
    Factory::getApplication()->input->set('hidemainmenu',
        true);
    $isNew = ($this->item->id == 0);
    $canDo = ContentHelper::getActions('com_spm');
    $toolbar = Toolbar::getInstance();
    ToolbarHelper::title(
            Text::_('COM_SPM_PROJECT_TITLE_' . ($isNew ?
                'ADD' : 'EDIT'))
    );
    if ($canDo->get('core.create'))
    {
        if ($isNew)
        {
            $toolbar->apply('project.save');
        }
        else
        {
            $toolbar->apply('project.apply');
        }
        $toolbar->save('project.save');
    }
    $toolbar->cancel('project.cancel', 'JTOOLBAR_CLOSE');
}
```

In this method, we use the `Toolbar` and `ToolbarHelper` classes from the Joomla! code base to create the action buttons, using the `apply()`, `save()`, and `cancel()` methods.

The value we use for these methods is the name of the controller and the task that needs to be executed. So, for instance, for our **Save** button, we initialize the toolbar with the `project` controller and the `save` task.

In the code of the view, you can see that we also perform some access level or permission checks to decide which action buttons to show. To do this, we simply check what actions can be performed according to the user permissions. These user permissions are configured using Joomla's **Access Level Configuration (ACL)**.

We will go into more detail in *Chapter 5*, but for now, we can define standard ACL easily. We just need to add a new file called `access.xml` to the main folder of the backend of our component. Inside this file, we will define different actions that we can take.

So, create the `access.xml` file inside the `src/component/admin` folder with the following code:

```xml
<?xml version="1.0" encoding="utf-8" ?>
<access component="com_spm">
    <section name="component">
        <action name="core.admin" title="JACTION_ADMIN" />
        <action name="core.options" title="JACTION_
          OPTIONS" />
        <action name="core.manage" title="JACTION_
          MANAGE" />
        <action name="core.create" title="JACTION_
          CREATE" />
        <action name="core.delete" title="JACTION_
          DELETE" />
        <action name="core.edit" title="JACTION_EDIT" />
    </section>
</access>
```

With this simple file, we add basic ACL capabilities to our component, and we can use global ACL to manage access to our extension.

Adding a model to retrieve and save data

For a model of the item view, you will see that it's quite different from the list view if you abide by Joomla! MVC. Let's create the `ProjectModel.php` file inside `src/component/admin/src/Model/` with the following code:

```php
<?php
namespace Piedpiper\Component\Spm\Administrator\Model;
use Joomla\CMS\Factory;
use Joomla\CMS\MVC\Model\AdminModel;
```

```
class ProjectModel extends AdminModel
{
}
```

To make things easier, we will extend the `AdminModel` class from the Joomla! MVC library, which makes our file small. In this file, we do not need to remember the state or add pagination to the view, so all those methods are not included in the model. What we do need is the form we will use to send changes. To retrieve the form, we have to define the `getForm()` method using the following code:

```
public function getForm($data = array(), $loadData = true)
{

    $form = $this->loadForm(
        'com_spm.project',
        'project',
        [
            'control' => 'jform',
            'load_data' => $loadData
        ]);
    if (empty($form)) {
        return false;
    }
    return $form;
}
```

This method encapsulates some magic that makes our life easier. In the first parameter, we pass the `com_spm.project` string. This instructs the method to look for the `project.xml` file inside the `forms` folder of the backend of our component.

This `loadForm()` method also calls the `loadFormData()` method, which we can define like this:

```
    protected function loadFormData()
    {
        $app = Factory::getApplication();
        $data = $app->getUserState(
            'com_spm.edit.project.data',
            []
        );
        if (empty($data)) {
            $data = $this->getItem();
        }
        return $data;
    }
```

The `loadFormData()` method populates the form with the values from the database or the request. To do this, it uses the `getItem()` method. We can define it, but as the item data is in just one table of our database, we can use the `getItem()` method provided in the `AdminModel` class we extend.

Creating the forms folder

We will see the benefits of Joomla! forms in *Chapter 4*, but let's create our first form now to be able to edit our projects:

1. Create the `forms` folder inside `src/component/admin/`. This will be the place where we will create all forms.

2. Inside this folder, we will add all the form definitions we need for the backend of our component.

    To define a form in Joomla!, we will use a `.xml` file, where we provide instructions for the fields of our form. For our edit project form, we will create the `src/component/admin/forms/project.xml` file and fill it with this code:

    ```xml
    <?xml version="1.0" encoding="UTF-8"?>
    <form>
        <field
            name="name"
            type="text"
            label="COM_SPM_PROJECT_NAME"
            required="true"
            />
        <field
            name="alias"
            type="text"
            label="COM_SPM_PROJECT_ALIAS"
            required="false"
            />
        <field
            name="description"
            type="text"
            label="COM_SPM_PROJECT_DESCRIPTION"
            required="false"
            />
        <field
            name="deadline"
            type="text"
            label="COM_SPM_PROJECT_DEADLINE"
            required="false"
            />
    ```

```
    <field
        name="created_by"
        type="user"
        label="COM_SPM_PROJECT_CREATED_BY"
        filter="unset"
        />
</form>
```

To make things simpler at this stage, we will use a simple Text field for all the fields. In *Chapter 4*, we will learn how to use other field types and develop our own fields.

Getting project data from the database

To get data from the database, the loadFormData() method calls the getItem() method, which is already defined in the AdminModel class, and we do not need to create it.

However, to use the standard way of getting (and saving) data for an item, Joomla! uses the Active Record design pattern. This means we need to create a new folder in our MVC structure – src/component/admin/src/Table.

Inside this new folder, create the ProjectTable.php file with the following code:

```php
<?php
namespace Piedpiper\Component\Spm\Administrator\Table;
use Joomla\CMS\Table\Table;
use Joomla\Database\DatabaseDriver;
class ProjectTable extends Table
{
    public function __construct(DatabaseDriver $db)
    {
        parent::__construct('#__spm_projects', 'id', $db);
    }
}
```

In this code, we take full advantage of Joomla! libraries and extend the Joomla! Table class. The Table class implements the so-called **Active Record** pattern, which allows us to treat our database records as programming objects. To relate this class with the database table, we pass the name of the table, the name of the primary key of the table, and the $db object.

Adding a controller to our Project entity

We need to add a controller to control which actions are performed for our data. However, as usual, Joomla! handles most of the work if we follow its standards, so we just need to create the `ProjectController.php` file inside the `src/component/admin/src/Controller` folder with this minimum code:

```php
<?php
namespace Piedpiper\Component\Spm\Administrator\Controller;
use Joomla\CMS\MVC\Controller\FormController;
class ProjectController extends FormController
{
}
```

Because we extend the `FormController` class, the `save`, `apply`, and `cancel` methods are already implemented, so we do not need to do anything.

Creating a layout for our edit project view

Once we have added all the code and files needed to edit a project, we just need to create a layout for our edit project view.

As we did with the `Projects` view, we need to create the layout with the user interface for our edit form. So, inside our `src/component/admin/tmpl/` folder, we create the `edit.php` file with the following code:

```php
<?php
use Joomla\CMS\HTML\HTMLHelper;
use Joomla\CMS\Router\Route;
HTMLHelper::_('behavior.formvalidator');
HTMLHelper::_('behavior.keepalive');
?>
<form action="<?php echo Route::_('index.php?option=
  com_spm&view=project&layout=edit&id=' . (int) $this->
    item->id); ?>" method="post" name="adminForm" id="
      project-form" class="form-validate">
    <div>
        <div class="row">
            <div class="col-md-9">
                <div class="row">
                    <div class="col-md-6">
                        <?php echo $this->form->
                            renderField('name'); ?>
                        <?php echo $this->form->
```

```
                            renderField('alias'); ?>
                    <?php echo $this->form->
                        renderField('description'); ?>
                    <?php echo $this->form->
                        renderField('deadline'); ?>
                </div>
            </div>
        </div>
    </div>
</div>
<input type="hidden" name="task" value="">
<?php echo HTMLHelper::_('form.token'); ?>
</form>
```

In this code, we add a form element, using the `form` object we obtained in the view, to render our fields, using the `renderField()` method. This way, it's Joomla! that creates the fields from our definition, and it takes care of all the properties and HTML needs for our forms. For instance, it takes care of setting the `required` attribute to the HTML field.

At the beginning of the code, we also call two helpers:

```
HTMLHelper::_('behavior.formvalidator');
HTMLHelper::_('behavior.keepalive');
```

These include some helpful JavaScript on the page. The first one provides JavaScript validation, so it detects and informs about errors in the form, and the second one helps keep the session active while filling up a form.

Another interesting fact is that you must include the `name=adminForm` property to your forms so that the toolbar buttons we added from the view work out of the box (otherwise, you need to add your own JavaScript to make them work).

At the end of the form, we define a hidden field called `task`. This field is also required to use the toolbar buttons, and Joomla! uses it to know what you are trying to do in your request.

The last line before closing the form is also required in Joomla!. This line adds another hidden field to our form with a random key that protects our site from **Cross-Site Scripting (XSS)** attacks.

Changes to our manifest file

As we have added some new folders to our component structure, we need to reflect these in the manifest file. Otherwise, Joomla! will not install them. So, we will open our manifest and add the new folders to the `files` section, and we include the `access.xml` file too.

At this point, we can also include a direct link in the menu for the projects view so that we can easily access it. For this, we will use the submenu tag and define the menu link there.

Our final manifest file looks like this:

```xml
<?xml version="1.0" encoding="utf-8"?>
<extension type="component" method="upgrade">
    <name>COM_SPM</name>
    <author><![CDATA[Carlos Cámara]]></author>
    <authorEmail>carlos@hepta.es</authorEmail>
    <authorUrl>https://extensions.hepta.es</authorUrl>
    <creationDate>2022-07-21</creationDate>
    <copyright>(C) 2022 Piedpiper Inc.</copyright>
    <license>GNU General Public License version 2 or later;
      see LICENSE.txt</license>
    <version>0.1.0</version>
    <description><![CDATA[COM_SPM_DESCRIPTION]]></description>
    <namespace path="src">Piedpiper\Component\
      Spm</namespace>
    <files folder="site">
    </files>
    <administration>
        <files folder="admin">
            <folder>forms</folder>
            <folder>services</folder>
            <folder>src</folder>
            <folder>tmpl</folder>
            <file>access.xml</file>
        </files>
        <menu line="option=com_spm" img="class:default
          ">COM_SPM_MENU_BACKEND</menu>
        <submenu>
            <menu link="option=com_spm&amp;view=projects"
              img="default">
                    COM_SPM_PROJECTS
            </menu>
        </submenu>
    </administration>
</extension>
```

Testing the component

At this point, we have finished our edit project controller, and now seems a good time to check how it works. So, create a new `.zip` file with the content of your `src/component` folder and install it on your Joomla! site.

After a successful installation, you will see that the main component link in the sidebar has changed to a dropdown, which shows the `Projects` link after we click on it.

Also, we can see our edit/new project view using this URL:

`/administrator/index.php?option=com_spm&view=project&layout=edit`

We have finished the edit view and all the other parts of the MVC needed to edit our projects. We are now ready to show our data in the frontend part of our development.

Summary

We have started the development of our component. So far, we have added just the minimum code to make it work and added some functionalities.

In this chapter, you learned what the architecture of a Joomla! component is, how to add different views to your component, and of course, how to allow the items in your database to be edited. In this journey, we learned about some Joomla! classes that can work for us, minimizing the code we need to add to connect to the database.

We will keep adding new features in the following chapters, and we will create another type of extension to add even more functionalities to the project.

In the next chapter, we will develop the frontend part of our component.

Further reading

- If you are new to Joomla! development, you can read this introduction to Joomla! components in the official documentation: `https://docs.joomla.org/Absolute_Basics_of_How_a_Component_Functions#Introduction_to_MVC`

- You can learn more about the `Table` class in Joomla's official documentation: `https://docs.joomla.org/Using_the_JTable_class`

3

Developing the Frontend of a Basic Joomla! Component

In the previous chapter, we developed the backend for our component. However, most of those components will need a frontend area where our users can interact with our component.

In this chapter, we will develop the frontend part of our component. We will create a project list that will show our current projects. Then, we will code a project detail view that will show the details of each project. By developing these new views, we will learn how to create menu items for our components. We will also learn how to add options to our menu items.

When coding for the frontend, we need to be careful and improve the user experience, so we need to create friendly URLs for our component. In the frontend, we want to offer an awesome experience, so we will learn to add CSS styles and interaction with **JavaScript (JS)** to our component.

So, in this chapter we'll cover the following:

- Developing a frontend list view for our component
- Developing a frontend item view for our component
- Adding friendly URLs to our component
- Adding CSS and JS to our component

By the end of this chapter, you will be able to offer a functional frontend to your users, where they can see a list of items and a customized detail view of each item.

Technical requirements

To go through this chapter, we need to edit code and test it on a Joomla! site. Therefore, you will need the following:

- Visual Studio Code (or the code editor of your preference)
- The Joomla! site we installed in the previous chapters

You can find the code files for this chapter on GitHub at `https://github.com/PacktPublishing/Developing-Extensions-for-Joomla-5/tree/chapter03`.

Developing a frontend list view for our component

Using Joomla's **Model-View-Controller** (**MVC**) pattern simplifies extension development in Joomla!. The file structure for the frontend is like the one for the backend, with just a few minor changes.

We will start with the frontend area of our component, by recreating the folders inside the `site` folder, as shown in the following figure:

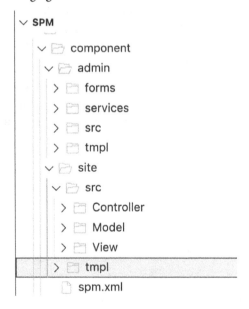

Figure 3.1 – The folder structure for the frontend part of our component

We are coding in the frontend part of our component, so we will store our files inside the `src/component/site/` folder. And, as with the backend, we have the following folders:

- `src`
- `tmpl`

In the `src` folder, we repeat the same folder structure as in the backend:

- `Controller`
- `Model`
- `Service`
- `View`

The files and their content are also like the ones in the backend. Let's start adding the files for the list view.

Coding the list view

Even though the Joomla! backend and frontend are two separate applications, the file architecture and the coding patterns are the same in both cases. So, for the list view in the frontend, we also need to add the file with the main `DisplayController` class, which handles the display of our component in the frontend.

Adding DisplayController

In the frontend of our component, we will create the `src/component/site/src/Controller/DisplayController.php` file with the following code:

src/component/site/src/Controller/DisplayController.php

```php
<?php
namespace Piedpiper\Component\Spm\Site\Controller;
defined('_JEXEC') or die;
use Joomla\CMS\MVC\Controller\BaseController;

class DisplayController extends BaseController
{
    protected $default_view = 'Projects';
    protected $app;
}
```

In this code, the first thing you may notice is that the namespace for our class has changed. As we are in the frontend now, our namespace path changes to `Piedpiper\Component\Spm\Site`.

After that, we extend the `BaseController` class from Joomla! MVC, exactly as we did for the `DisplayController.php` file in the backend.

To create the list of projects in the frontend, we need to set up the MVC folders in the same way we did in the previous chapter for the backend.

Adding the view for our list of projects

In Joomla! MVC, the view requests the data for the model, so let's see what data we need for our view.

Let's start creating our view file at `src/component/site/src/View/Projects/HtmlView.php` with the following code:

---

src/component/site/src/View/Projects/HtmlView.php

```php
<?php
namespace Piedpiper\Component\Spm\Site\View\Projects;

\defined('_JEXEC') or die;

use Joomla\CMS\MVC\View\HtmlView as BaseHtmlView;

class HtmlView extends BaseHtmlView
{
    public $state;
    public $items=[];
    public $pagination;

    public function display($tpl=null): void
    {
        $this->state      = $this->get('State');
        $this->items      = $this->get('Items');
        $this->pagination = $this->get('Pagination');

        parent::display($tpl);
    }
}
```

The first thing we can see is that the namespace for this code is in the `site` folder:

```
namespace Piedpiper\Component\Spm\Site\View\Projects
```

Then, we will extend `HtmlView` from Joomla! MVC, and we will alias it to avoid clashing with our class name.

For the view, we need to implement the `display` method, where we ask the model for the state, pagination, and item data.

As our model is the class in charge of providing all this data, let's see how we can add it to our frontend.

Getting the data to show – adding the model

To add a model to our `Projects` view, we will create the `src/component/site/src/Model/ProjectsModel.php` file. We will start defining our namespace and adding the class we are creating:

---

src/component/site/src/Model/ProjectsModel.php

```php
<?php

namespace Piedpiper\Component\Spm\Site\Model;

defined('_JEXEC') or die;

use Joomla\CMS\Factory;
use Joomla\CMS\MVC\Model\ListModel;

class ProjectsModel extends ListModel
{
}
```

The namespace for this model uses the `site` folder of our namespace:

```
namespace Piedpiper\Component\Spm\Site\Model
```

Also, it extends the `ListModel` class from Joomla! MVC to simplify the development.

When extending the `ListModel` class, we need to implement our own method for `populateState` to reflect the variables we need to get from the current user interaction. Therefore, we will add this method to the class:

```
protected function populateState($ordering = 'name', $direction =
'ASC')
{
    $app = Factory::getApplication();
    $value = $app->input->get('limit', $app->get('list_lim
      it', 0), 'uint');
    $this->setState('list.limit', $value);
    $value = $app->input->get('limitstart', 0, 'uint');
    $this->setState('list.start', $value);
    parent::populateState($ordering, $direction);
}
```

In this method, we will get the number of projects to display (represented by the `list_limit` variable) and determine where our pagination starts (represented by the `limitstart` variable).

To get these variables, we will use the built-in `$app->input-get()` method. This method gets the specified variable from the form request. Besides the variable name as the first parameter, the method accepts a second parameter, which will be returned if the requested variable has no value. Lastly, it accepts a third parameter with the type of filtering we want to apply to the variable. We will learn more about form filtering in *Chapter 4* and *Chapter 13*.

Finally, we will call the parent method to finish all the other tasks that Joomla! takes care of for us.

In the Joomla! `ListModel`, we will get the items using `getListQuery`. In this method, we will create the query to use against a database. This method is specific to our database structure, and in our Projects listing, we will use this code:

```
protected function getListQuery()
{
    $db    = $this->getDatabase();
    $query = $db->getQuery(true);
    $query->select(
        $this->getState(
            'list.select',
            [
                $db->quoteName('a.id'),
                $db->quoteName('a.name'),
                $db->quoteName('a.deadline'),
            ]
        )
    )->from($db->quoteName('#__spm_projects', 'a'));
```

```
    $orderCol   = $this->state->get('list.ordering',
       'a.name');
    $orderDirn = $this->state->get('list.direction',
       'ASC');
    $query->order($db->escape($orderCol) . ' ' . $db->
       escape($orderDirn));
    return $query;
}
```

In this method, we will use the database object to generate our query. This object is part of the listModel object, and we get it with the getDatabase() method. Finally, we will include the ordering data from the state to respect the user's decision on ordering.

Once we have requested the data, the view passes all the information to the template layout file, so let's now see how to show this data.

Adding the template to lay out data

The template layout defines how we show the data we got in the view. We will create this file at src/ component/site/tmpl/projects/default.php, and we will define the namespaces we are using at the beginning of the document in a PHP block:

src/component/site/tmpl/projects/default.php

```
<?php
\defined('_JEXEC');
use Joomla\CMS\Router\Route;
use Joomla\CMS\HTML\HTMLHelper;
use Joomla\CMS\Factory;
?>
```

After the PHP block, we will start our markup for the projects list:

```
<form>
    <div class="items-limit-box">
        <?php echo $this->pagination->getLimitBox(); ?>
    </div>
</form>
```

In this code, we are adding the HTML markup for our projects list, but we need to wrap the listing inside a form tag to allow filtering interaction. Inside the form, we will add a request to the $this->pagination->getLimitBox() method. This will show a select box to choose the number of projects we want to see per page.

After the limit box, we will create our list of projects, adding the following `div` just after the previous / `div`:

```
<div>
    <?php foreach ($this->items as $item) : ?>
    <div>
        <h2>
            <?php echo $item->name; ?>
        </h2>
        <div id="project-id">
            <?php echo $item->id; ?>
        </div>
        <div id="project-deadline">
            <?php echo $item->deadline; ?>
        </div>
    </div>
    <?php endforeach;?>
</div>
```

In this HTML, we will go through all our items using a `foreach` loop. In the frontend, we will use a `div` block instead of a table to lay out the data and make it a bit more attractive.

Finally, we need to consider that we may have more than one page of items in this list, so we have to provide a way to change the page. We will do this by using the pagination object once more. So, we will add this code just below our last `div` container:

```
<div><?php echo $this->pagination->getResultsCounter();
    ?></div>
<?php echo $this->pagination->getListFooter(); ?>
<input type="hidden" name="task" value="projects">
```

Also, as we will see in the next chapter, in Joomla! forms, we need to pass a security token as a hidden value, so we will add it on the line before closing the form:

```
<?php echo HTMLHelper::_('form.token'); ?>
```

You can find more information about the **pagination object** in the *Further reading* section of this chapter.

Now that we have completed all the MVC files, we can create our package by zipping all the files and installing them on our test site.

After installing the package on your site, go to `yourtestsite.joomla.com/index.php?option=com_spm&view=projects`, where you will see your list of projects, as shown in the following screenshot:

Figure 3.2 – The list of projects in the frontend of our component

In the preceding figure, you can see a list of five projects from your database. At the top, you will find the limit box to change how many projects you can see, and a list of pages to check the rest of the projects.

Some standard parts of the listing look good, such as the limit box and the pagination, but we can do better styling for the list of projects. In the following section, we will see how to add CSS and JS files to improve the interface of our component.

Adding CSS and JS to our component

Joomla! comes with the popular frontend toolkit **Bootstrap 5**. This toolkit provides several CSS classes and JavaScript files to add common features and styles to our component.

We can use Bootstrap CSS classes directly in our component by just adding them to the markup of the file. Let's transform our list of projects in a grid by simply using Bootstrap classes. Edit the `src/component/site/tmpl/projects/default.php` file, and add the class attribute to the div elements containing the elements, as per the following code:

src/component/site/tmpl/projects/default.php

```php
<div class="cards row row-col-3">
<?php foreach ($this->items as $item) : ?>
    <div class="card col m-1">
        <h2>
            <?php echo $item->name; ?>
        </h2>
        <div id="project-id">
            <?php echo $item->id; ?>
        </div>
        <div id="project-deadline">
            <?php echo $item->deadline; ?>
        </div>
    </div>
<?php endforeach;?>
</div>
```

We have added the `row` and `row-col-3` classes to the `div` element that contains the projects, and to every `div`, we have added the `col` and `m-1` classes.

With this simple change, our listing now looks like this:

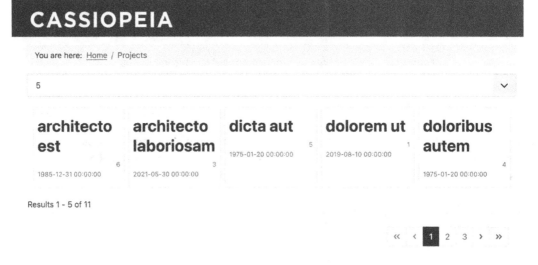

Figure 3.3 – The grid for our list of projects

In this screenshot, we can see the result of adding the bootstrap classes. In place of a simple list with no spacing or styling, we now have a nice grid of projects, in which there are five projects per row.

Bootstrap 5 is a powerful tool, and it's useful to build nice layouts. Even so, let's see how we can add our own CSS using Joomla's **Web Asset Manager** to customize the user experience.

Adding our own styles and JavaScript to our component

In Joomla!, we use the `media` folder to store public assets for our components. This is a good practice because the `media` folder will be publicly accessible for your user's browser, and they will be able to check the files inside it. However, the `media` folder is not directly accessible to a regular administrator of your site. The standard way of doing this is to create a folder for your extension, and inside it, you place `css`, `js`, and any other folders you may need. For instance, you could add an `img` folder for your extension images.

Right now, we will add a file with our own styles to the component.

First, we need to create our CSS file, so let's go to our component structure and create the `src/component/media/css/projects.css` file with the following content:

src/component/media/css/projects.css

```
.cards {
    padding: 1rem;
    flex-wrap: wrap;
}

.card{
    padding: 1rem;
}

.meta {
    color: #666;
    font-size: .8rem;
}

#project-id{
    text-align: right;
}
```

With this CSS, we will add a bit more padding to the projects, and we will make the font size for the project ID and the deadline date a bit smaller. Also, the project ID will move to the right of the card.

Now, we have to instruct Joomla! to create a folder for our component inside the `media` folder when installing the component. To do this, we will edit the manifest file of our `src/component/spm.xml` component, and we will add the following lines just before the closing `</extension>` tag:

src/component/spm.xml

```
<media folder="media" destination="com_spm">
    <folder>css</folder>
</media>
```

This code is the `media` tag, which has two attributes:

- `folder`: This indicates where the files and folders are in our package
- `destination`: This indicates the name of the subfolder inside the Joomla! `media` folder in which our files will be stored

Our `media` tag has one child, of type `folder`, which indicates the name of the folder that needs to be installed.

So, basically, this will tell Joomla! to install the `css` folder, which is inside the package's `media` folder, in a folder called `com_spm`, which is inside Joomla's `media` folder.

You can now create a new installation package for your component and install it on your testing site. After that, you can check with an FTP client, or with your hosting file browsing tool, that Joomla! has created the `media/com_spm` folder and that it contains our `css` folder with the `projects.css` file inside.

This is great, but if you load the project's view, you will notice that our new styles have not loaded yet. In the following section, we will instruct Joomla! to load the new CSS file when loading our project's view, using the Web Asset Manager.

Joomla's Web Asset Manager

Web Asset Manager was introduced in Joomla! 4 to manage CSS and JS assets and improve site performance. To use Web Asset Manager, we need to register the assets we are going to use in our extension. We will do this by declaring a file called `joomla.asset.json` with a specific format.

Using Joomla's Web Asset Manager provides some interesting advantages to our code:

- It prevents us from loading the same asset file twice
- It helps us to load dependencies in JS files
- It prevents conflicts when different extensions try to load the CSS and JS files with the same names

So, let's see how we can use Joomla's Web Asset Manager to add our CSS to this component.

Registering all our assets using a JSON file

Registering our assets in the component will allow our users to override them if they need to perform customizations or overrides.

Also, registering your assets using a JSON file will allow you to keep track of all your styles. It's a more organized way of managing your assets.

To use this asset file, we need to create `joomla.asset.json` inside the `src/component/media/` folder with the following content:

---

src/component/media/joomla.asset.json

```
{
    "$schema": "https://developer.joomla.org/schemas/json-
        schema/web_assets.json",
    "name": "com_spm",
    "version": "1.0.0",
    "description": "Simple Project Manager component assets",
    "license": "GPL-2.0-or-later",
    "namespace": "Piedpiper\\component\\Spm",
    "assets": [
        {
            "name": "com_spm.projects",
            "type": "style",
            "uri": "com_spm/projects.css"
        }
    ]
}
```

This is a JSON object in which we declare all the assets of our component. In the first property, we will declare the $schema property. This property declares the type of structure we will abide by. This is always the same and points to a URL on the Joomla! developer network website.

After that, we must declare the name, version, and description properties, and finally, an array of our assets.

Each asset definition is also an object for which we must declare name, type, and uri:

- The name property of the asset is what we will use to include our asset when we need to. It should be unique so that we do not override another asset. So, in our case, we will add the name of the extension as a suffix.

- The `type` property establishes which kind of asset we are loading. For the purpose of this book, we can use `style` to load a CSS file or `script` to load a JS file. Please refer to the *Further reading* section for more information about Web Asset Manager.

- The `uri` property tells Joomla! where to find the asset we are declaring. The path here is relative to the `media` folder, where we will store our assets.

Once we have created our `joomla.asset.json` file, we have to register it in the manifest file, so please update your manifest file, adding the new file inside the `media` tag as follows:

```
<media folder="media" destination="com_spm">
    <folder>css</folder>
    <filename>joomla.asset.json</filename>
</media>
```

This new manifest file adds the `filename` tag inside the `media` tag to tell Joomla! that it needs to install the file in the `css` folder.

Once our `joomla.asset.json` file is in place, we are ready to load our new CSS styles in our component.

Loading projects.css using joomla.assets.json file

After registering our styles using `joomla.asset.json`, we can use the Web Asset Manager to load our styles in the projects view. Edit the `src/component/site/tmpl/projects/default.php` file and replace it with the following content:

src/component/site/tmpl/projects/default.php

```php
<?php

\defined('_JEXEC');

use Joomla\CMS\Router\Route;
use Joomla\CMS\HTML\HTMLHelper;
use Joomla\CMS\Factory;

$wam = Factory::getApplication()->getDocument()->
    getWebAssetManager();

$wam->useStyle('com_spm.projects');

?>
<form>
<div class="items-limit-box">
```

```php
        <?php echo $this->pagination->getLimitBox(); ?>
    </div>
    <div class="cards row">
    <?php foreach ($this->items as $item) : ?>
        <div class="card col m-1">
            <h2>
                <?php echo $item->name; ?>
            </h2>
            <div id="project-id" class="meta">
                <?php echo $item->id; ?>
            </div>
            <div id="project-deadline" class="meta">
                <?php echo $item->deadline; ?>
            </div>
        </div>
    <?php endforeach;?>
    </div>
    <p><?php echo $this->pagination->getResultsCounter();
      ?></p>
    <?php echo $this->pagination->getListFooter(); ?>
        <input type="hidden" name="task" value="projects">
        <?php echo HTMLHelper::_('form.token'); ?>
    </form>
```

In this code, you can see how, after getting the Web Asset Manager inside $wam, we use it to load our style, calling it by the name we assigned it in the joomla.asset.json file.

Besides using joomla.asset.json to register our styles and scripts, we can also add styles using the HtmlHelper class.

Loading assets with HtmlHelper

In Joomla!, it is also possible to add your style sheet files without using the Web Asset Manager. This is not recommended, as you will lose all the benefits of using the Web Asset Manager, but it might be helpful in some scenarios.

For instance, assets loaded with the HtmlHelper class are loaded after Web Asset Manager. This allows you to override specific styles of your CSS without overriding the whole style sheet file.

Let's say we want to change the color for the deadline date and ID of the project. We would create the src/component/media/css/projects-override.css file with the following content:

src/component/media/css/projects-override.css

```
.meta {
    color: #666;
}
```

As the file is already in the `css` folder inside our `media` folder, it will be added to our Joomla! site on the next package installation, and its final path will be `media/com_spm/css/projects-override.css`.

To use this override in our template, we will modify the `src/component/tmpl/projects/default.php` file to place this code before initializing the `$wam` variable:

```
HTMLHelper::_(
    'stylesheet',
    'com_spm/projects-override.css',
    ['version' => 'auto', 'relative' => true]
);
```

If you package and install your component now, you will see how the deadline date shows a different color.

It's interesting to note that we have included the `HtmlHelper` class before calling the Web Asset Manager, but the rendering of the final page happens at a different stage, when the assets are loaded in the order defined in Joomla! Core. Style sheets added through the `HtmlHelper` method will be loaded after Web Asset Manager, so we can use this method to override our styles on the page, no matter when we load them in the template. We will explore template overrides in *Chapter 10*.

After adding our own styles to the page, we have finished our list view in the frontend. Now, we are going to create an item view to see the details of our projects.

Developing a frontend item view for our component

Adding a frontend item view to our component following the Joomla! MVC pattern is like adding an item view to the backend of our component. So, let's start by creating the `src/component/site/View/Project/HtmlView.php` file and defining the namespace and the class:

src/component/site/View/Project/HtmlView.php

```php
<?php
namespace Piedpiper\Component\Spm\Site\View\Project;
\defined('_JEXEC') or die;
use Joomla\CMS\MVC\View\HtmlView as BaseHtmlView;
use Joomla\CMS\MVC\View\GenericDataException;
class HtmlView extends BaseHtmlView
{
```

```
    public $item;
}
```

This file is like the one we created for the list of projects in the previous section. We can make some remarks here. As we are developing the project frontend area, our namespace now points to the `Site` folder that was created in the frontend **Projects** view.

We will add a couple of namespaces that we will use in our `display` method, which should have the following code:

```
public function display($tpl=null): void
{
    $this->item = $this->get('Item');
    if (count($errors = $this->get('Errors')))
    {
        throw new GenericDataException(implode("\n",
            $errors), 500);
    }
    parent::display($tpl);
}
```

In the detail view, we do not need to add filtering, pagination, or any other elements in the state, so in the `display` method, we will only call the `get('Item')` method to request from the model the data for our item.

We will also check for any errors in the model, using the `get('Errors')` method. If there are any, we will throw an exception showing them.

Now, we need to add the model class for our project detail view that retrieves the item.

Adding the model for the frontend item view

For our model, we need to extend the `BaseDatabaseModel` from the Joomla! libraries, which contains all the methods we need in this case. Let's create the class definition and fill the namespace for it. We will create the `src/component/site/src/Model/ProjectModel.php` file with the following content:

src/component/site/src/Model/ProjectModel.php

```
<?php
namespace Piedpiper\Component\Spm\Site\Model;
use Joomla\CMS\Factory;
use Joomla\CMS\MVC\Model\BaseDatabaseModel;
class ProjectModel extends BaseDatabaseModel
{
```

```
    protected $_item = null;
}
```

In Joomla! models, we usually start by setting up the state of the system, so we need to add the populateState method to our class:

```
protected function populateState()
{
    $app = Factory::getApplication();
    $params = $app->getParams();
    $id = $app->input->getInt('id');
    $this->setState('project.id', $id);
    $this->setState('project.params', $params);
}
```

The populateState method executes once on the model construction, and it extracts the ID of the project from the URL and adds it to the current state.

After populating the state, we can retrieve the item to show in the detail view, so we will add the getItem method using this code:

```
function getItem($pk = null)
{
    $id = (int) $pk ?: (int) $this->getState('project.id');
    if (!$id) {
        throw new \Exception('Missing project id', 404);
    }
    if ($this->_item !== null && $this->_item->id != $id) {
        return $this->_item;
    }
    $db = $this->getDatabase();
    $query = $db->getQuery(true);
    $query->select('*')
            ->from($db->quoteName('#__spm_projects', 'a'))
            ->where($db->quoteName('a.id') . ' = ' . (int)
            $id);
    $db->setQuery($query);

    $item = $db->loadObject();

    if (!empty($item)) {
        $this->_item = $item;
    }
```

```
        return $this->_item;
    }
```

In this method, we will pass the $pk optional argument. This $pk variable refers to the project ID that we want to show. If we call the method with no arguments, it tries to get the value from the state. As we previously added our populateState method, the state already contains the project ID, and we can use the getState method to retrieve it.

If there is no ID in our URL or the ID is 0, there is nothing we can retrieve, and we will throw an exception. This will abort the current execution cycle, and Joomla! will show an error page, similar to the one shown here:

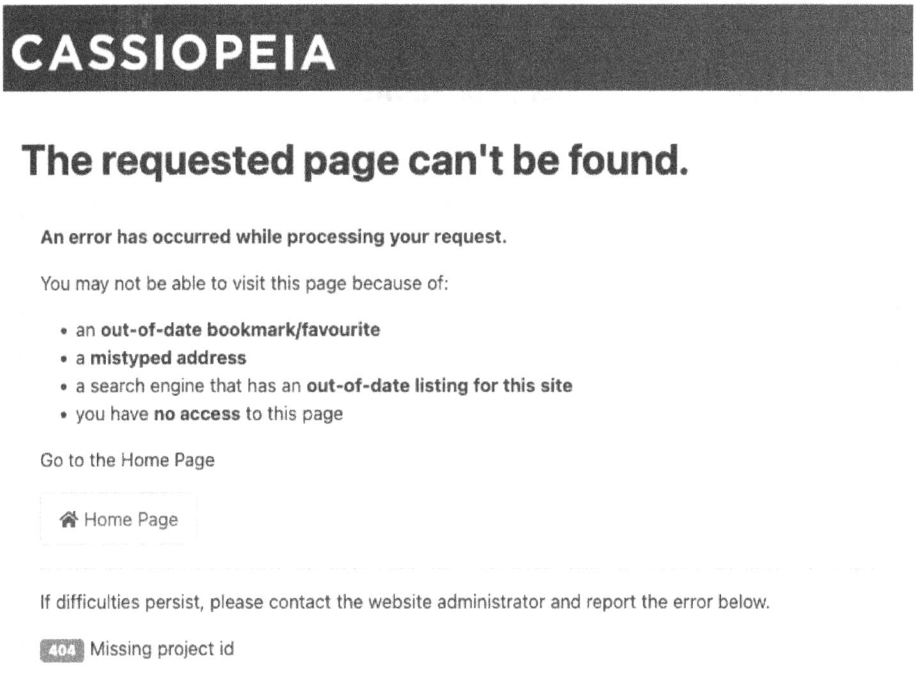

Figure 3.4 – An error page created from the Project not found exception

When calling the Extension class, we add a message and an exception code. Joomla! will show the message to the user and will add the exception code to the HTTP reply, and as a result, this error page will be shown.

Once we have checked that we have a project ID, the next block of code detects whether we have already retrieved the item for this ID to save querying the database.

If we have not requested this item in the current request, we have to retrieve the data from our database. So, we call the Joomla! DB Object to query our database and retrieve the data.

In this code, you may have noticed that we keep casting the ID variable to an `int` type. This is a security measure, as we are retrieving the ID from a public request (the URL added by the user), and it can have malicious code. This simple precaution will keep your components much safer.

Finally, we will return the item object directly to the view, and we are now ready to create a nice layout to show our data.

Adding the layout for the item detail

Now that we have everything we need to show the project to our users, we will add a nice layout, and then we are good to go. So, create the `src/component/site/tmpl/project/default.php` file with the following content:

---

src/component/site/tmpl/project/default.php

```php
<?php
defined('_JEXEC');
?>
<div class="project-item p-4">
    <h1><?php echo $this->item->name; ?></h1>
    <div id="created" class="date meta">
        <?php echo $this->item->created;?>
    </div>
    <p id="description" class="description">
        <?php echo $this->item->description; ?>
    </p>
    <div id="deadline" class="date">
        <?php echo $this->item->deadline; ?>
    </div>
</div>
```

This code shows each element of the project in a proper HTML markup.

If you happen to install the latest changes on your Joomla! site, you will notice that there is no way to access the project detail view. The only way right now is by using the direct URL. For instance, if you use `index.php?option=com_spm&view=project&id=1`, you will go to the detail view of your first project.

To allow proper navigation, we are going to link the projects in the projects view with their project detail view. So, replace the content of the `src/component/site/projects/default.php` file with the following code:

src/component/site/projects/default.php

```php
<?php
use Joomla\CMS\Router\Route;
?>
<a href="<?php echo Route::_('index.php?option=com
  _spm&view=project&id=' . $item->id);?>"><?php echo $item
    ->name; ?></a>
```

In this code, we now add a link to the project detail view. We will use the Route method, as it will help us to create a friendly URL in the following sections.

Once you are ready, you can zip your component folder and install it through Joomla! Extension Manager, observing the changes.

We have improved the usability of our component a lot by adding the link to the project detail view, but we still need to provide a simple way to check our projects list. In the following section, we will create a menu item for our list view that will make our component more useful.

Adding a menu item for our views

In Joomla!, we create our site structure using menus. In the menus, we add several menu items that link to the views of our components.

When we create a menu item, we get a nice link to our view in the navigation bar of our site. Creating a menu item for our component also allows us to have a nice and friendly URL for our view, instead of using the ugly index.php?option=com_spm&view=projects URL. This is very convenient for our users, so let's start registering our menu items!

First, we have to register a menu item type for our component. We can do so by adding an XML file to our tmpl folder for our view. So, let's start creating the src/component/site/tmpl/projects/default.xml file, and we will place inside it the following content:

src/component/site/tmpl/projects/default.xml

```xml
<?xml version="1.0" encoding="UTF-8"?>
<metadata>
    <layout title="COM_SPM_VIEW_PROJECTS_MENU_LABEL">
        <message>
            <![CDATA[COM_SPM_VIEW_PROJECTS_MENU_DESC]]>
        </message>
    </layout>
</metadata>
```

In this XML code, we will define the title we want to show for the menu item in the `title` attribute for the `<layout>` tag. We will also define the description that the site administrators will see when creating the menu item, using the `<message>` tag. We are not using descriptive text for the `title` attribute, nor the `<message>` tag; instead, we will use a descriptive label. In *Chapter 5, Harnessing the Power of Joomla! in Your Component*, we will add the language files we need to convert these labels into proper English (or whatever language we need) text.

In the following screenshot, you can see the result of adding this XML file:

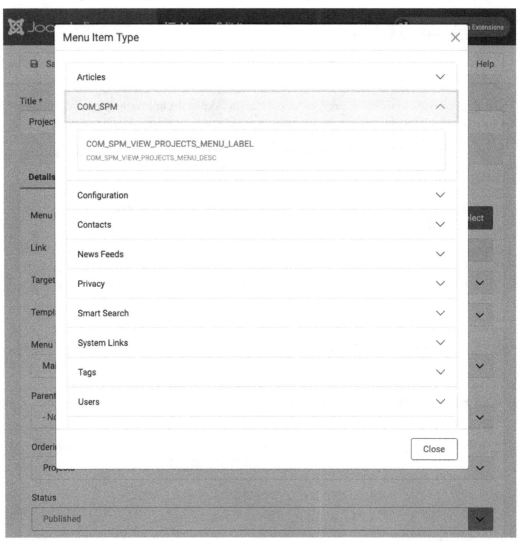

Figure 3.5 – The details of the menu item type selection for our component

In this screenshot, we see how there is an element for our **COM_SPM** component, with a child element showing the menu item type we created. In the child element, we can see the title and the description.

This works great for our list of projects, but how can we link specific projects in our menu? Well, we need to register a menu item type for our project detail view, and this is exactly what we will see in the following section.

Adding options to our menu items

Registering the menu item for the project detail view is exactly the same process as for the list view. Even so, in the detail view, we need to add a way for the site administrator to define which project to show from our list of projects.

Let's see how we can add options to our menu items. Create the `src/component/site/tmpl/project/default.xml` file and fill it with the following XML definition:

src/component/site/tmpl/project/default.xml

```
<?xml version="1.0" encoding="UTF-8"?>
<metadata>
    <layout title="COM_SPM_VIEW_PROJECT_MENU_LABEL">
        <message>
            <![CDATA[COM_SPM_VIEW_PROJECT_MENU_DESC]]>
        </message>
    </layout>
    <fields name="request">
        <fieldset name="options">
            <field
                name="id"
                type="text"
                label="COM_SPM_FIELD_ID_LABEL"
                required="true" />
        </fieldset>
    </fields>
</metadata>
```

This menu item definition is like the previous one, but the XML has a new `fields` section. Inside this section, we will add a `fieldset` section, with as many optional `field` items as we want to offer.

For the `fields` section, we will use the `name="request"` attribute to tell Joomla! that it needs to pass this value into the page request. This way, we do not need to change our model.

As usual, in XML definitions, we can add a `name` parameter that represents the field, and for the `fieldset` section, we will use the name `options`. This translates to a new tab in the menu item configuration, where all the fields included in this section will be.

If you choose another name, Joomla! will replace the name of the tab with the COM_MENUS_ YOURNAME_FIELDSET_LABEL construction. We will look at translations and language files in *Chapter 5, Harnessing the Power of Joomla! in Your Component*.

To make things simpler now, we are going to use a text field type that will appear as shown in the following screenshot:

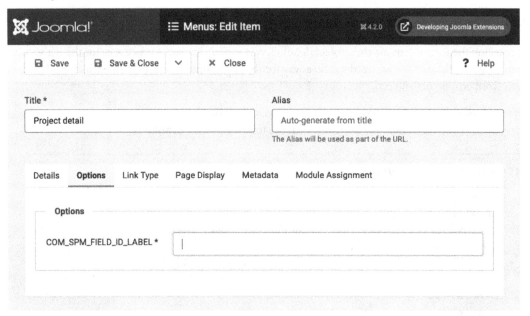

Figure 3.6 – The details of the new Options tab with the text field to include our project

This field allows us to type the ID of our projects and choose the one project we want to show.

We now can have different URLs for our projects in the menu. Also, every menu item in Joomla! has an associated friendly URL.

However, it's not practical to create a menu item for every project on our component, so we need a way to allow friendly URLs for our items. In the following section, we will start adding Joomla! services to our component for this.

Adding friendly URLs to our component

Friendly URLs in web development are a two-sided problem. On the one hand, when showing a URL to your users, you need to translate all your ugly links with parameters into words to make them more friendly. These words usually match the name of the page we are showing, and we call them *slugs* or *aliases*. For example, in the `https://YourDomain.com/joomla-4-extension-development` URL, the slug is `joomla-4-extension-development`.

The second problem starts when your users request a friendly URL, and you need to translate it into parameters for your Joomla! site to understand the request.

To handle these problems in Joomla!, we need to add a so-called router to our component. In Joomla!, we inject the router as a service.

To do this, edit the `src/component/admin/services/provider.php` file and add the following namespaces:

src/component/admin/services/provider.php

```
use Joomla\CMS\Extension\Service\Provider\RouterFactory;
use Joomla\CMS\Component\Router\RouterFactoryInterface;
```

After adding these new namespaces, we can register the `RouterFactory` class, so we will add it to the `register` method, as shown in the highlighted code:

```
return new class implements ServiceProviderInterface
{
    public function register(Container $container)
    {
        ...
        $container->registerServiceProvider(new
            RouterFactory('\\Piedpiper\\Component\\Spm'));
        ...
        );
    }
};
```

Finally, we will inject the `RouterFactory` class in the anonymous function of the container as shown in the highlighted code:

```
$container->set(
    ComponentInterface::class,
        function (Container $container)
        {
            ...
```

```
        $component->setRouterFactory($container->
            get(RouterFactoryInterface::class));
        …
        }
    );
};
```

With these new lines, we have registered the router service for our component, and we can now start coding the service.

The router of our component works in the frontend of our site, so we will create the `src/component/site/src/Service` folder and place therein a file called `Router.php`. We will start adding the namespaces and the class definition:

---

src/component/site/src/Service/Router.php

```php
<?php
namespace Piedpiper\Component\Spm\Site\Service;
use Joomla\CMS\Application\SiteApplication;
use Joomla\CMS\Component\Router\RouterView;
use Joomla\CMS\Component\Router\RouterViewConfiguration;
use Joomla\CMS\Component\Router\Rules\MenuRules;
use Joomla\CMS\Component\Router\Rules\NomenuRules;
use Joomla\CMS\Component\Router\Rules\StandardRules;
use Joomla\Database\DatabaseInterface;
use Joomla\CMS\Menu\AbstractMenu;
class Router extends RouterView
{
    private $db;
}
```

This is our `Router` class, and this code is where we tell Joomla! how to translate slugs into parameters, and vice versa.

In the constructor, we must set up which views of our component need an SEF URL and, we will also set up the rules to follow for every URL in our component.

For this class, we will set up a constructor that will set up our routing configuration. This is the code we need to add:

```php
public function __construct(SiteApplication $app, Abstract
    Menu $menu, $category, DatabaseInterface $db)
{
    $this->db = $db;
    $projects = new RouterViewConfiguration('projects');
```

```
        $this->registerView($projects);
}
```

To make things easy, we will register the $db property with our current database object. This object is passed to the object construction.

After that, we need to register the views in our component. We will use the RouterViewConfiguration class from Joomla's libraries. We must create one RouterViewConfiguration object per routable view in our component, and we will use the name of the view as the parameter for the constructor.

The first object we will create is for the projects view. Once created, we will register the object using the registerView method from the main class we are extending.

The projects view is a listing view, which means that it will contain other items that, presumably, will be further down in the URL hierarchy.

Then, we can register the view for individual projects, the project view. This view depends on the projects view, and we will reflect that in the SEF configuration. So, we will add this code immediately after registering the projects view:

```
$project = new RouterViewConfiguration('project');
$project->setKey('id')->setParent($projects);
$this->registerView($project);
```

In this code, we use the RouterViewConfiguration class, as we did for the $projects view, but with a couple of additions. As every project in our database is unique, our SEF URLs must be different for every one of them. So, for the project detail view, we need to set up a key to differentiate between projects. This key will be the ID of every project. This ID differentiates every project, so it is unique for every URL.

On the same line, we define the hierarchy. Our project detail view comes right after the projects general view, so we define the $projects object as its parent. We use the setParent method for this.

Once we have defined our views, we can call the parent __construct method, which initializes some variables needed in the routing process, and we will add some default rules to manage common scenarios. So, we will add the following code:

```
parent::__construct($app, $menu);
$this->attachRule(new MenuRules($this));
$this->attachRule(new StandardRules($this));
$this->attachRule(new NomenuRules($this));
```

In the final three statements, we will attach some extra rules that will take care of the routing part that is not directly related to our extension:

- The `MenuRules` class will take care of the language code for the SEF URL and inject the menu hierarchy into the URL

- The `StandardRules` class will make sure the component respects the generic URL routing of Joomla!

- The `NomenuRules` class will allow you to create SEF URLs for your component when it is not attached to any menu item

Translating parameters into a friendly URL

After setting up our router in the construct method, we need to instruct Joomla! how to translate our ugly URLs into friendly ones. To do this, we will define the `getViewNameSegment()` method. Every one of these methods represents a way in which Joomla! gets a slug or friendly URL for that view.

For our project view, you can add the following code to our `Router` class:

src/component/site/src/Service/Router.php

```
public function getProjectSegment($key, $urlQuery)
{
    $id = (int) $id;
    $query = $this->db->getQuery(true);
    $query->select($this->db->quoteName('alias'))
        ->from($this->db->quoteName('#__spm_projects'))
        ->where($this->db->quoteName('id') . ' = ' .
            (int) $key);
    $this->db->setQuery($query);
    $id = $this->db->loadResult();
    return [$id];
}
```

This method receives the value of the `$key` object we set in the view configuration, so in our case, it will have the ID of the project and the parameters passed to the URL.

For our projects, we only need the ID, so we will use it to get the alias from the database.

This covers the translation from an ID to a human-friendly word. Let's see in the next section how to instruct Joomla! to transform this alias into an ID to retrieve the proper project.

Translating SEF URLs into variables for our component

Once a SEF URL gets into our router, we need to translate it to the variables that define our project, routing the user to the correct view.

To do this, we will add the getProjectId method to our router code:

src/component/site/src/Service/Router.php

```
public function getProjectId($segment, $urlQuery)
{
    $query = $this->db->getQuery(true);
    $query->select($this->db->quoteName('id'))
        ->from($this->db->quoteName'#__spm_projects'))
        ->where($this->db->quoteName('alias') . ' = :
          alias')
        ->bind(':alias', $segment);
    $this->db->setQuery($query);
    return (int) $this->db->loadResult();
    }
}
```

This method receives from Joomla! the segment or alias and also the parameters that Joomla! has already discovered from other SEF rules, such as ItemId and similar.

In this method, we will use the alias to retrieve the unique key for our project (the unique ID) from the database. The alias is passed inside the $segment argument, and any other parameters are in the $urlQuery array.

If you pay attention to the database query we perform, you will notice that we use the bind() method to inject the alias into the query. We use this method to create **MySQL prepared statements** in Joomla!. In Joomla!, we should use prepared statements whenever possible, as they provide great protection against MySQL injection attacks. Prepared statements are more performant for repetitive queries, as the statements are cached in the database, which just replaces the variables of each respective query. In Joomla!, we use a variable name such as :alias in the query, and we bind the variable with its value, using the bind() method.

This completes the routing cycle and allows our component to translate its ugly URLs into nice SEF URLs, and vice versa.

We can now develop the frontend part of a Joomla! component, covering the most important parts of the development.

Summary

In this chapter, we developed the frontend part of our component. We created a list view to see the list of projects and a detail view to see more data for every project, and we added our own CSS to improve the user experience. Finally, we learned how to set up SEF URLs for these views. We can now develop the frontend part of a component and customize it with our own styles.

In the following chapter, we will see in detail how to use the `JForm` class to create forms for our extensions. This will allow us to add more interaction to our component with search and edit forms.

Further reading

- The *Pagination* object provides some interesting methods you can use to customize the pagination experience. You can find more details about the pagination object on its API documentation page: `https://api.joomla.org/cms-4/classes/Joomla-CMS-Pagination-Pagination.html`.

- You can get familiar with Bootstrap on its page: `https://getbootstrap.com/`.

- At W3Schools, there is a nice article about MySQL prepared statements: `https://www.w3schools.com/php/php_mysql_prepared_statements.asp`.

- There is a nice documentation page for Web Asset Manager at the Joomla! wiki: `https://docs.joomla.org/J4.x:Web_Assets#Overriding_an_asset`.

4

Creating Forms in Joomla!

HTML forms are an important part of web development as they allow you to ask for information from your users. In Joomla!, we can define our forms with a simple XML file; the Joomla! Framework™ takes care of almost all the work.

In this chapter, we will learn how to create HTML forms in Joomla!. We'll learn how to add the form fields that are already developed in Joomla! and how to create custom form fields. We'll also learn how to validate our users' input before they submit the form and how to check the data on the server side.

These are the main topics of this chapter:

- Defining forms in Joomla!
- Using standard Joomla! form fields
- Defining custom form field types
- Using the `subform` field
- Validating user input on the client side
- Validating user input on the server side

By the end of this chapter, you will be able to add different forms to your extensions and retrieve the data sent by them.

Technical requirements

In this chapter, we'll keep improving our Simple Project Manager extension, so you will require the following:

- Visual Studio Code (or a code editor of your preference)
- The Joomla! site we installed in the previous chapters

You can find the code files for this chapter on GitHub at `https://github.com/PacktPublishing/Developing-Extensions-for-Joomla-5/tree/chapter04`.

Defining forms in Joomla!

Joomla's `Form` class simplifies and standardizes the way you create HTML forms for your web projects. It was introduced in Joomla! 1.5, and it has improved since then.

Forms in Joomla! are defined in an XML file where you add all the fields your form needs and their basic properties. Joomla! then processes this information and generates a proper form and field definition.

This process saves you from dealing with HTML input field definition and standardizes the way you create your forms. It also allows you to use more elaborate interfaces in your extensions with very little effort. A nice example of this is the `accessiblemedia` field that was introduced in Joomla! 4, which not only allows the user to include an image, but it comes with some accessibility features out of the box.

But best of all, handling forms in Joomla! is like magic when using Joomla! MVC in our developments.

There are three main use cases we can consider for using Joomla! Forms in our component:

- Adding general options to our extensions
- Adding search and filter capabilities to our listings
- Editing or adding individual items

The form definition in all these cases will be the same: an XML file with the fields and all their properties. However, how we display the forms will be different in each scenario. We'll explore these cases in detail in the following sections.

Adding general options to our extensions

It's very common to have a set of general settings that apply to all our components. In our Simple Project Management extension, we can use these general settings to store our company data, such as **name**, **address**, and **ID number**.

To add these options to our component, we have to create the `src/component/admin/config.xml` file. This file contains the XML definition of our form:

```xml
<?xml version="1.0" encoding="utf-8"?>
<config>
    <fieldset name="company_data" label="COM_SPM_CONFIG_FIELDSET_
COMPANY_DATA_LABEL" description="COM_SPM_CONFIG_FIELDSET_COMPANY_DATA_
DESCRIPTION" >
        <field
            type="text"
```

```
                label="COM_SPM_CONFIG_COMPANY_NAME_LABEL"
                description="COM_SPM_CONFIG_COMPANY_NAME_DESCRIPTION"
            />
            <field
                type="text"
                label="COM_SPM_CONFIG_COMPANY_ADDRESS_LABEL"
                description="COM_SPM_CONFIG_COMPANY_ADDRESS_DESCRIPTION"
            />
            <field
                type="text"
                label="COM_SPM_CONFIG_COMPANY_ID_LABEL"
                description="COM_SPM_CONFIG_COMPANY_ID_DESCRIPTION"
            />
        </fieldset>
    </config>
```

This code starts with defining the format of the XML document, as in the manifest XML file we saw in *Chapter 2, Developing the Backend of a Basic Joomla! Component*, and the main content of the file is wrapped between `<config>` tags. This main content is our form definition and is where we can group our fields in different fieldsets.

We group the fields in different fieldsets in the XML as this will show each `fieldset` in a specific tab when rendering. Every `fieldset` might have `name`, `label`, and `description` properties.

`label` will be used as the name of the tab when rendering the form.

In this code, we have used text type fields. We will learn more about the types of fields we can use later in the *Using standard form field types* section.

After adding this new file, you need to include it in the component manifest for Joomla! to place it in the correct folder. So, edit your `src/component/spm.xml` file and include the `config.xml` file in the `<file>` tag for the administration section, as follows:

```
<files folder="admin">
    <folder>forms</folder>
    <folder>services</folder>
    <folder>src</folder>
    <folder>tmpl</folder>
    <file>access.xml</file>
    <file>config.xml</file>
</files>
```

We've included the file using the `<file>` tag in the XML.

Showing the options form in our component

The options form is generated automatically by Joomla!, and we do not need to worry about it. More specifically, it's the `com_config` component, which is responsible for showing the form.

To see our form in action, we just need to go to the backend of our Joomla! site and click on **System | Global Configuration**. On the left-hand side of the screen, we will see a list with all the installed components, and we click on **COM_SPM** to see our options.

Alternatively, you may go to `yoursite.com/administrator/index.php?option=com_config&view=component&component=com_spm`.

Adding search and filter capabilities to our listings

Joomla's `ListModel` class comes with a standard way to add filters to our listings. If you check the `ListModel` class definition in your Joomla! installation (at `libraries/MVC/Model/ListModel.php`), you may find the `getFilterForm` method.

This method checks for a file called `filter_ModelName.xml` and creates a Joomla! Form intended for filtering. Let's add a basic filter to our projects list. Create a file called `src/component/admin/forms/filter_projects.xml` that contains the following code:

```xml
<?xml version="1.0" encoding="UTF-8"?>
<form>
    <fields name="filter">
        <field
            name="search"
            type="text"
            label="COM_SPM_PROJECTS_FILTER_SEARCH"
            />
    </fields>
</form>
```

This form will be a text field where the administrator will type the name of the projects or any word in the project description. We need to wrap the field inside the `<fields>` tag to tell Joomla! it is a filter form.

After adding the form, we must instruct the view to retrieve the form from the model. So, we need to add the highlighted code to the `display` method of our view at `src/component/admin/src/View/HtmlView.php`:

```
public $filterForm;

public function display($tpl=null): void
{
```

```
...
    $this->filterForm    = $this->get('FilterForm');
    $this->activeFilters = $this->get('ActiveFilters');

    ...
}
```

In this code, we declare the `filterForm` property in which we will store the form data. When using `this->get('FilterForm')`, what we are doing is calling the `getFilterForm` method from the model. As we are extending the `ListModel` class for our project, Joomla! takes care of getting the filter form from the XML file.

We also set the `activeFilters` property to be aware of the filters that are being applied to our data.

Finally, we need to include the filter in our template file using the `filterForm` property. Next, we are going to look at the Joomla! way of showing this filter form.

Showing the filter form in the projects list

To show the filter in our list, we need to use the `filterForm` property to retrieve all the field information.

The `form` property contains an object of the `Form` class. This object contains all the fields defined in our XML file. These fields are stored in the `fields` property field of the object.

The Joomla! API provides an easy way to show this filter. Using Joomla! to show the filters will also offer a more consistent user experience to your users.

To show the filter form in our projects list, we must edit our layout and include the following highlighted code at the beginning of our form at `src/component/admin/tmpl/projects/default.php`, just below our `<form>` opening tag:

```
use Joomla\CMS\Layout\LayoutHelper;
<form action="<?php echo Route::_('index.php?option=com_
spm&view=projects'); ?>" method="post" name="adminForm"
id="adminForm">
...
<div class="row">
    <div class="col-md-12">
        <?php echo LayoutHelper::render('joomla.searchtools.default',
        ['view' => $this]); ?>
    </div>
</div>
```

In this code, we use Bootstrap 5 CSS classes to provide some styling to the view. Then, we use the `LayoutHelper` class to render the layout defined in the Joomla! site at `/layouts/joomla/`

`searchtools/default.php`. This will take care of showing all the fields in our form, including a submit button.

After submitting the form, we need to receive all the data in our model and process it to give the desired output to the user. In the next section, we will see how we can honor the user filter request.

Receiving fields info in the model

Not only do we need to define and show the forms to our users, but we also need to use this information in our model to filter the data according to our users' choices.

It makes sense to get this data in our model. This will help us optimize our data retrieval process as we will query our database with all our filter constraints.

We want these filters to be present in every request our users make. Imagine that a user is filtering our multipage listing by category and clicks on the second page. We want our model to remember the context and offer the next results for that category listing. Also, our filters need to be specific per session on the site, so it makes sense to add all the information for the filters in the `populateState()` method of the model.

If we check our current `populateState()` method, we can already see some filters being applied, such as all the pagination variables (`list.limit`, `list.start`, and so on). Let's add the request to get the search filter. Edit the `src/component/admin/src/Model/ProjectsModel` file and, above the call to the parent `populateState()` method, add the following highlighted lines:

```
protected function populateState($ordering = 'name', $direction =
'ASC')
{
    ...

    $search = $this->getUserStateFromRequest(
        $this->context
        . '.filter.search', 'filter_search'
    );
    $this->setState('filter.search', $search);
    Parent::populateState($ordering, $direction);
}
```

With this, we get the input in the search box from the request and we add it to our current state under the name of `filter.search`.

Once we have done this, we can retrieve the state in the `getListQuery()` method of our model and use it to modify our query. We add it before defining the `$orderCol` variable statement of the `getListQuery()` method using this code:

```
protected function getListQuery()
{
```

```
    ...
    $search = $this->getState('filter.search');

    if (!empty($search))
    {
        $search = $db->escape(trim($search), true);
        $search = str_replace(' ', '%', $search);
        $search = $db->quote('%' . $search . '%'));
        $query->where('(a.name LIKE ' . $search . ')');
    }
    $orderCol =
        $this->state->get('list.ordering', 'a.name');
    ...
}
```

Here, we request the `filter.search` variable from the state and check if it has any value.

Inside the `if` block, we must process the search value to provide the best results:

1. First, we must remove all the starting and ending whitespaces and pass the value through the `escape()` method from our `$db` class. This is necessary as it is an input provided by the user and we do not want to risk a SQL injection attack. We will learn more about security practices in *Chapter 13, Security Practices in Joomla!.*

2. Next, we must replace the whitespaces in our text query with the `%` symbol to perform a MySQL `LIKE` search. This is useful when the searched value is a multiword string as it will look for all the words in the text and not only the literal string.

3. The last transformation we perform on the `$search` value is adding database-friendly quotes for string search in the database. With that, we simply add the final `where` query to look for the text inside the name of the projects.

We can now add more fields to the filter form and provide a great search tool for our users. But there are many more things we can do with forms in Joomla!. In the next section, we will see how we can empower our extension edit pages using Joomla! forms.

Editing or adding individual items

In *Chapter 2, Developing the Backend of a Basic Joomla! Component*, we created our project edit form. There, we displayed every field directly in our layout using the `Form` object the model provided.

This gave us full control of the ordering of the fields; for instance, we may modify the HTML code around the fields, or we may omit some fields of our form, just not including them in our layout file. So, for instance, if we do not want to allow the deadline of the project to be edited, we can just remove the field from our TPL file.

But if you are as lazy as I am, there is a quicker way to show all the form fields in Joomla!: we can call the `form` render methods to display the form for us. In the `src/component/admin/tmpl/project/edit.php` file, replace the calls to `$this->form-renderField()` that we added in *Chapter 2, Developing the Backend of a Basic Joomla! Component*, with the following code:

```php
<?php foreach ($this->form->getFieldset() as $field) :?>
    <?php echo $field->renderField(); ?>
<?php endforeach;?>
```

This code will show all the fields of our form as per the XML definition in our form file: `src/component/admin/forms/project.xml`.

So far, we have added different forms to the component, but we are only using text fields for them. In the following section, we will explore other field types we can use to make our forms better.

Using standard Joomla! Form fields

Using only text input fields will work for all your projects as it is a universal way to get user input on the web. However, it will make a very bad user experience as the design will not be adapted to your data and your users will feel the pain.

In Joomla!, we can spice up our forms using several field types that provide different interfaces. This will make our forms easier to fill and our components more user-friendly.

You can find a link with all current Joomla! standard form fields and instructions in Joomla's official documentation: `https://docs.joomla.org/Standard_form_field_types`.

In this book, we are going to cover the more interesting field types.

In Joomla!, all field definitions share a common structure, so a generic field in Joomla! may have these properties:

- `name`: This will be the name we use internally to refer to the field. It should be unique for this form, and it must be defined.
- `type`: This will be one of the field types we can use for our field. It is mandatory. If Joomla! does not recognize the field type, it will show a text field type.
- `label`: This is the name of the field that will be shown to the user. You must define it and it supports Joomla's translation system (as we will see in the following chapters).
- `Description`: This is the tooltip or help text that will be added to the field definition. It also supports Joomla's translation system. You may omit it.
- `class`: This is the CSS class the field will have when it is shown. It is an optional attribute.
- `labelclass`: This is the CSS class we can add to the label of the field. It is not necessary to add it.

- `showon`: This optional attribute accepts the name of another field of the current form and a possible value. This way, a field with the `showon` attribute will only be shown if the referenced field contains the value specified. This is useful for hiding fields according to user options.

- `filter`: This property sets the filtering level for the text introduced by the user. We can use `safehtml` to allow only secure HTML tags or `raw` if we do not want any kind of filtering.

Now that we know a bit more about the generic attributes of our fields, let's dig into some of the standard fields and add them to our project.

Using the Editor form field type

When adding text to our extensions, we want to provide a rich editing experience for our users. Adding bold, italics, or more fancy stuff such as text coloring or typography selection will make for a better user experience.

In Joomla!, there are three standard text editors: TinyMCE, CodeMirror, and No Editor. Every one of these is a plugin of the **Editor** type and we can install many more editors if we need to.

To use an editor instead of a regular `<textarea>` field in our component, we can use the **editor** field. This field allows you to show one of the editors installed in your Joomla! site.

In our project, we will replace the `text` field we use for project descriptions and use the `editor` field. So, we'll edit the `src/component/administrator/com_spm/forms/project.xml` file and replace the `description` field with this code:

```
<field
    type="editor"
    name="description"
    buttons="image"
    hide="readmore, pagebreak"
    editor="tinymce|none"
    filter="safehtml"
    label="COM_SPM_PROJECT_DESCRIPTION"
    />
```

In the previous code, we have highlighted some properties that are exclusive to this field:

- `buttons`: This property indicates which of the Editors-Extended buttons we want to show to the user. You can find a link about these Editors-Extended buttons in the *Further reading* section.

- `hide`: This property indicates which of the Editors-Extended buttons we want to hide from the user.

- `editor`: Using this property, we can specify the editor we want to use for our field. The syntax is `desired editor|alternative editor`, meaning that in our case, it will look for the

TinyMCE editor that comes by default with Joomla!, and if it cannot find it, then it will use the none editor by default, which means it will show no editor. If none of the alternatives are found, Joomla! will use the global default editor that's configured in the global configuration settings.

Using the editor field is great for having more visual extensions, and users can use it to include images. However, if we want to use image fields, we need to go a bit further and use a specific image field type, as we will see in the next section.

Using the accessiblemedia field type

When adding images to our extension, we may want to integrate these images into our content. To meet accessibility standards, whenever an image is uploaded to our content, we need to provide a text description of this image. This usually means defining a file input to upload the image and a text field for the description.

In Joomla!, we can have both HTML fields in a meaningful way by using the `accessiblemedia` field type. This field type uses all the power of the new Joomla! `Media Manager` and creates a pop-up window where the editor can drag and drop the image or just pick it from already uploaded images. It also provides a text field where the editor can add an image description.

Using this field type is simple and we are going to add it to the project items in our component. We can do this by adding the following code to our `project.xml` file:

```
<field
    name="logo"
    type="accessiblemedia"
    directory="projects"
    label="COM_PROJECT_LOGO"
/>
```

In this field definition, we are using the `directory` attribute, which is exclusive to this field. This is the directory where our images will be stored. The path is relative to the `images` folder in Joomla!. Also, our users will be able to pick up images from this folder.

Now, we can offer our users a way to upload their images in an accessible way.

Creating select options from database tables

One of my favorite Joomla! standard form fields is the `sql` field type. This field allows you to show a dropdown where the options are created with data from your database. This is very useful when you have related entities. For instance, our tasks belong to a project and we want to group them by project. So, it will be great to be able to show a list of projects when editing a task that the user can choose.

In our task form at `src/component/admin/forms/task.xml`, we can add the following field:

```
<field
    name="id_project"
    type="sql"
    label="COM_SPM_TASK_PROJECT"
    sql_select="p.*"
    sql_from="#__spm_projects AS p"
    sql_group="name"
    sql_order="p.id ASC"
    key_field="id"
    value_field="name"
    />
```

This code will render an HTML select field in our form in which the option value for the HTML select will be the value of the field specified in `key_field` and the option to show will be the value specified for the `value_field` column of our `spm_projects` table.

Of course, to show this field in our form, we need to be sure that it has been added to the `src/component/admin/tmpl/task/edit.php` file. So, let's edit the file and add the field:

```
$this->form->field('id_project')->render();
```

When checking the documentation of the `sql` field type, you may find that there is a way to include your SQL directly using the `query` property. This is a legacy way of using this field and it's not recommended as it will inject the query directly into your database, which means you may lose compatibility with PostgreSQL or other databases supported by Joomla!.

The `sql` field is great for showing form fields specific to the current data from our database. But in some situations, we need to develop fields that fit our projects. In the next section, we are going to learn how to develop custom form fields.

Defining custom form field types

We have a lot of Joomla! Standard Form fields and they should be enough for most projects, but at some point, you might need to create your own form fields to extend some functionality of your form. In Joomla!, this is as easy as extending the `FormField` class.

To learn how to do this, we'll recreate our project selector from the previous section using a custom form field. This field will be a select dropdown where the user can choose a project from a list.

First, we need to extend the `FormField` class. This class is the one from which all Joomla! fields are created, and it provides all the required methods that allow Joomla! to show the fields defined in the XML forms.

So, let's start creating our new field. Create the `src/component/admin/src/Fields/ProjectField.php` field with the following content:

```php
<?php
namespace Piedpiper\Component\Spm\Administrator\Fields;
use Joomla\CMS\Form\Field\ListField;
class PiedpiperFormFieldProject extends ListField {
    protected $type = 'piedpiper.project';
}
```

In this code, we define the `$type` property, which will be the name of the type for our new field. We have prefixed the name of our field with our company name. This helps prevent clashes with other field types defined by other developers. This prefix should be added to the `type` property; it is also added to the class name for the field definition.

We extend the `ListField` class as the list field is like our field behavior, but we could extend any other field type of our choice.

To create the `select` box with our list of projects, we must create an override for the `getOptions()` method. This method only exists in the fields extended from the `ListField` class and we use it to retrieve a list of projects from the database:

```php
public function getOptions()
{
    $db = Factory::getContainer()->get('DatabaseDriver');

    $query = $db->getQuery(true);

    $query->select('ip.id, p.name')
        ->from('#__spm_projects')
        ->order('p.name', 'asc');

    $db->setQuery($query);

    $options = $db->loadAssocList('id', 'name');

    return $options;
}
```

In this code, we use the `loadAssocList()` method to get an indexed array with the `id` property of the projects as the index and name as the value.

This will show a standard HTML `select` with all our projects. We can customize this by overriding the `getInput` method from the `FormField` class. Let's replace `select` with a list of radio buttons with the following code in the `src/component/admin/src/Fields/ProjectField.php` file:

```
public function getInput()
{
}
```

Once we have defined our new field type, we can use it in our forms.

How to use the subform field type

Besides developing our own fields in Joomla!, we can also create complex fields by combining the standard form fields provided. This is a powerful feature we get from using the `subform` field in our forms. The `subform` field allows us to include forms as fields of another form.

In our case, we can use the `subform` field to add documents to our projects with a name and a description of our Simple Project Management extension.

Let's start by adding the `subform` definition to the `src/component/admin/forms/forms.xml` file by adding this code:

```
<field
    name="attachments"
    type="subform"
    label="COM_SPM_PROJECT_ATTACHMENTS"
    multiple="true"
    layout="joomla.form.field.subform.repeatable"
    >
    <form>
        <field
            name="attachment_file"
            type="file"
            label="COM_SPM_PROJECT_ATTACHMENTS_FILE"
            />
        <field
            name="attachment_name"
            type="text"
            label="COM_SPM_PROJECT_ATTACHMENTS_NAME"
            />
        <field
            name="attachment_description"
            type="textarea"
            label="COM_SPM_PROJECT_ATTACHMENTS_DESCRIPTION"
```

```
                    />
          </form>
      </field>
```

Here, we create a new field of the `subform` type and define the fields that are going to be inside this `subform` between the `<form>` tags. Also, as we want to allow multiple attachments for our projects (we could have an attachment with the proposal we send to the client, another document with the quote for the project, and another with some needed documentation…), we add the `multiple` attribute to the form field.

In the `subform` field, we also specify the layout to show the `subform` fields. Joomla! provides three layouts out of the box that we may use for this:

- `joomla.form.field.subform.default`: This is the simplest layout and it is not ready for repeatable fields, so avoid using it when the `multiple` attribute is set to `true`

- `joomla.form.field.subform.repeatable`: This layout is suitable for repeatable fields and it displays the different fields using `divs`

- `joomla.form.field.subform.repeatable-table`: This layout is also suitable for repeatable fields but it displays `subform` using an HTML table

We can make this a bit tidier by adding the form definition in a different file. This will also allow us to reuse the form in another subform field or as a form of its own if needed.

To do this, we need to create the `src/component/admin/forms/attachment.xml` file and place the following within our form definition:

```xml
<form>
    <field
        name="attachment_file"
        type="file"
        label="COM_SPM_PROJECT_ATTACHMENTS_FILE"
        />
    <field
        name="attachment_name"
        type="text"
        label="COM_SPM_PROJECT_ATTACHMENTS_NAME"
        />
    <field
        name="attachment_description"
        type="textarea"
        label="COM_SPM_PROJECT_ATTACHMENTS_DESCRIPTION"
        />
</form>
```

We must also replace the subform definition with the following code:

```
<field
    name="attachments"
    type="subform"
    label="COM_SPM_PROJECT_ATTACHMENTS"
    multiple="true"      formsource="administrator/components/com_spm/
forms/attachment.xml"
    layout="joomla.form.field.subform.repeatable"
/>
```

This makes our subform definition much easier to read. We have replaced the whole form definition with the `formsource` attribute, which indicates the relative path from Joomla's root folder to our subform XML file definition.

We can create any input form we need for our application and offer the most suitable interface for our users to provide the right data. But we also need to validate that the input is valid and can be used in our extension. In the next section, we'll learn how to detect invalid data and avoid human mistakes.

Validating user input on the client side

We need to be sure our users provide the right information when they're filling in a form. The sooner we communicate to the user an issue in the data, the better the user experience. That is why we want to check the errors even before the user sends the form to Joomla!. This is why we use client-side validation for our forms.

When using Joomla! standard form fields, there are some attributes we can use in our fields that will add validation to our forms out of the box. For instance, when we set the `required` attribute in the XML definition for our form field, the user will need to include data to send the form.

Let's add some validation to our **Client** edit form. So in the `src/component/admin/forms/client.xml` file, replace the `email` field definition with this code:

```
<field
    name="email"
    type="email"
    required="true"
    />
```

This will tell Joomla! that the user must fill in the field. Also, as we are using the `email` field type, the HTML input of the field will be of the `email` type. This will trigger browser validation for the field, so the user will not be able to fill in anything different than an email field. This also happens for the standard form fields for `url` and `tel` (used for phone numbers).

But for better client-side validation, we need to use JavaScript. In Joomla!, it's quite easy to do this using the validator core library. To add it to our form, we must edit the `.tmpl` file at `/src/component/admin/tmpl/client/edit.php` and add the following code below the last `use` declaration:

```
use Joomla\CMS\HTML\HTMLHelper;
HTMLHelper::_('behavior.formvalidator');
```

This code will load the JavaScript library that's necessary for validating the fields before submitting the form. This library uses JavaScript to look for the required attribute. It also looks for the following CSS classes in our fields:

- `validate-username`
- `validate-password`
- `validate-numeric`
- `validate-email`

Besides this validation, we can create our custom validation with some JavaScript code. To illustrate this, let's explore the edit view for our invoices element. Edit the `src/component/admin/forms/invoice.xml` file and change the `amount` field to this definition:

```
<field
    name="amount"
    type="text"
    inputmode="decimal"
    label="COM_SPM_INVOICES_FORM_AMOUNT"
    class="validate-notzero"
    required="true"
    pattern="[0-9]{1,}(\.[0-9]{1,2})?"
/>
```

This definition will add the following validations to the `amount` field:

- `required`: The `required` attribute will check if the field has any value before submitting it
- `pattern`: This attribute will trigger a validation that will check the data entered against the **RegEx** pattern we indicate here
- `validate-notzero`: Adding the `validate-notzero` class will enable us to look for the custom validation we need to inject into our JavaScript

After this, we just need to inject our JavaScript custom validation into the form. To do this, we must create the `validation-scripts.js` file with the following content:

```
window.addEventListener('DOMContentLoaded', function () {
    document.formvalidator.setHandler('notzero', function (value) {
```

```
        return value != 0;
    });
}
```

This JavaScript code will be called by Joomla's form validation before the form is sent and will check that the amount is greater than zero.

To include this file in our form, we must use the WebAssets Manager, as we saw in *Chapter 3, Developing the Frontend of a Basic Joomla! Component*. To do this, edit the `joomla.asset.json` file and declare the file with the following code:

```
...
{
    "name": "com_spm.validation",
    "type": "script",
    "uri": "com_spm/validation-scripts.js",
    "attributes": {
        "defer": true
    }
}
...
```

Finally, we must add the following code at the beginning of `src/component/admin/tmpl/invoice/edit.php`:

```
$document = Factory::getApplication()->getDocument();
$wam = $document->getWebAssetManager();
$wam->useScript('com_spm.validation');
```

With this code, we are calling the WebAssets Manager and using it to include our JavaScript file.

After completing this section, we can detect wrong input before the user submits forms using Joomla! API for validation. But in some scenarios, such as old browsers or users with no JavaScript capabilities, it's possible to skip this validation and submit the form to Joomla!. In the next section, we are going to see how we can check the data that's sent to Joomla! before it's saved.

Validating user input on the server side

Client validation usually detects and helps fix most user input errors in a web application. But for client validation to work, we fully rely on our user's browser. Client validation in Joomla! is accomplished using the new features in the HTML5 standard and some JavaScript libraries, and there is a chance that our users work with an old browser or have disabled JavaScript in their browser configuration. In any of these situations, the client validation will not work as expected and we need to set another validation method that does not depend on the user's browser.

In Joomla!, we can add server-side validation directly in our form definition, as we did for client-side validation.

Back to our edit client form, we can edit the `src/component/admin/forms/client.xml` file and replace the email field definition with the following code:

```
<field
    name="email"
    type="email"
    required="true"
    validate="email"
/>
```

In this code, we have added the `validate` attribute with a value of `email`. This code will trigger server-side validation in our model, and it will check two aspects:

- `required="true"` will check that the field has a value
- `validate="email"` will check that the field value is a valid email

In the *Further reading* section of this chapter, you will find a link that specifies all the validation rules we can use on the server side. In that list, there are interesting rules such as the **equals** rule, which checks that our field has the same value as another field of the form. But more generally, we want to include our own rules. In Joomla!, we can define our own custom rules for validation.

Let's create a custom server-side validation for our `amount` field so that it matches the client-side validation we added in the previous section.

First, we need to tell Joomla! where to look for our custom rules. So, we must add the `addrulepath` attribute to our form definition. Please edit the `src/component/admin/forms/invoice.xml` file and add the `addrulepath` attribute to the `fieldset` tag, as shown here:

```
<fieldset name="invoice" addrulepath="administrator/components/com_
spm/rules">
</fieldset>
```

The `addrulepath` attribute states the relative path from Joomla's main folder to our rules definition. Now, we need to create the `src/component/administrator/components/com_spm/rules/notzero.php` file with the following content:

```php
<?php
use Joomla\CMS\Form\FormRule;

class NotzeroRule extends FormRule
{
    protected $regex = '[0-9]{1,}(\.[0-9]{1,2})?';
}
```

Here, we are extending the FormRule class. In this simple case, we only define the regular expression our field value must meet to be valid, and we use the same pattern we used previously in the field definition.

If you do not want to deal with regex, or if you have a more complex scenario you need to check, instead of using the regex pattern, you can extend the test method, as shown in the following code:

```
public function test(SimpleXMLElement $element, $value, $group = null,
JRegistry $input = null, Form $form = null)
{
    if ($value > 0) {
        return true;
    }
    return false;
}
```

When we extend the test method, we need to return a Boolean value where true means that the value of the field is valid and false means otherwise. In this method, we can call other methods in our code or perform any operations we need to check the code.

Summary

Forms are a key aspect of the web. We need forms to request information from our users and we use that information to show them different data or to save this data in our web application. Joomla! offers a whole range of form fields, such as text, accessiblemedia, and subform, to create forms easily with different interfaces so that we can request this information in the easiest and most accessible way.

To trust our data, we need to be sure the information that's submitted is in a valid format and it's accurate. So, we must use validation to check the data that's been submitted in our forms. This validation should happen on the client side to provide quicker feedback to the user. With Joomla's client-side validation, we can add this validation by adding specific CSS classes or some JavaScript code. We also need to perform server-side validation to be fully sure the user is not bypassing our client validation. Joomla! helps us with this via the filter property and the rules definitions in our forms, which we can extend to cover all our needs.

At this point, you know how to add forms to our web application and how to validate the data before processing it.

So far, we have seen that using the Joomla! API to develop our extensions offers great advantages and minimizes the code we need to write, but we are still only scratching the surface. In the next chapter, we will dive deeper into how to use some Joomla! features to develop great web applications while taking advantage of the power of Joomla!.

Further reading

- You can learn more about all Joomla! standard form field types in the official documentation: `https://docs.joomla.org/Standard_form_field_types`

- The official Joomla! Extension Directory provides a whole section devoted to editors you may install on your site: `https://extensions.joomla.org/tags/editors/`

- You can learn more about the Editors-Extended group by reading the official documentation: `https://docs.joomla.org/Chunk4x:Extensions_Plugin_Manager_Edit_Button_Group/en`

- Joomla's official documentation provides a list of available rules for fields: `https://docs.joomla.org/J3.x:Server-side_form_validation#Validation_rules`

5

Harnessing the Power of Joomla! in Your Component

Joomla! is a feature-rich **content management system** (**CMS**) right out of the box. With a clean installation of Joomla!, you get a publishing tool with great features, including the following:

- Content creation

- Content categorization

- Extending your content architecture with custom fields

- Having a multilingual system out of the box

- And many more features

Joomla! provides an API to integrate some of its core features in your extensions. In this chapter, we will go through these features, and we'll learn how to use them to create more powerful extensions. Most of these features are related to publishing and editing web content, such as the possibility to organize our content into categories. But some of them, such as custom fields, can offer great flexibility to our extension.

We will cover the following topics in this chapter:

- Reviewing the Joomla! features you can use in your component

- Adding an ACL to our component

- Exploring the benefits and limitations of using Joomla! categories

- Using Joomla! categories in our component

- Introduction to Joomla! custom fields

- Using custom fields in our component

- Using Joomla! multilingual capabilities in our component

By the end of this chapter, you will be able to power your extension with Joomla! features, harnessing the power of Joomla! to create richly featured extensions with less effort.

Technical requirements

In this chapter, we will keep improving our Simple Project Manager extension, so you will require the following:

- Visual Studio Code (or a code editor of your preference)
- The Joomla! site we installed in the previous chapters

You can find the code files for this chapter on GitHub at `https://github.com/PacktPublishing/Developing-Extensions-for-Joomla-5/tree/chapter05`

Reviewing what Joomla! features you can use in your component

Joomla! comes packed with several generic features designed to support text article publishing. In a clean Joomla! installation, besides the article management tools, we also get, for instance, a category management functionality with which we can organize Joomla! articles. In your component, you can use this category management functionality to organize your content too.

Some of these features can be used in multiple use cases, so the Joomla! core developers decided to make them easy to integrate with other extensions. This will make our life as developers much easier. On one hand, less code needs to be added to add these complex behaviors to our extensions. On the other hand, we do not have to worry about integrating these features in our component with other parts of the Joomla! ecosystem. Many developers will embrace the given feature in their extensions and we can rest assured there will be no conflicts.

The following are the features we can use in our extension:

- **Joomla! Access Control List** (**ACL**): One of the best-designed and most robust features in Joomla! is the ACL permissions system. An ACL allows you to have several user groups on a Joomla! site, each with different permissions and capabilities. For our extensions, it's a great way to apply restrictions to certain actions based on the Joomla! user group in question.
- **Joomla! category management**: The Joomla! categories system is very powerful, and it is developed to be highly performant when sorting or searching data. Its design follows the popular nested-set model, which performs great in growing data environments.

- **Joomla! custom fields**: Joomla! administrators can add their own custom fields to articles. This makes possible some more flexible uses of Joomla!, including to develop directories, shops, and other kinds of great websites. You can benefit from that flexibility in your extension by allowing custom fields for some of your data types.

- **Multilingual capabilities**: One of the greatest features that come out of the box with Joomla! that no other CMS has beaten yet is the multilingual capabilities of a Joomla! site. Any web administrator can create a multilingual site out of the box or add different languages to an existing site with a couple of clicks. And of course, we can make our extensions multilingual by taking advantage of the Joomla! API.

- **Web Services API**: Joomla! includes a Web Services API so that we can create websites beyond the web browser. With the new Web Services API, we can manage most Joomla! features with any HTTP client. We can also extend the Joomla! Web Services to interact with our extensions, as we will see in the next chapter.

- **Command-Line Interface**: Joomla! offers a **Command-Line Interface (CLI)** for those tasks that are better done outside of the browser. With the CLI, we can execute heavy processing tasks or those jobs that need to be done automatically using a CRON job or a programmed task in our server. We will see how to create a CLI for our extension in *Chapter 9, Adding a CLI to Your Component*.

We will integrate all of these features using the Joomla! API, which will save us from building them from scratch. Let's start by adding permissions to our extension with a Joomla! ACL.

Adding an ACL to our component

As extension developers, we are aware of the situations faced by web administrators when configuring extensions. For instance, in our Simple Project Manager extension, we do not want the customer role to be able to edit invoices or organize our projects. Nor do we want not logged-in users to download our invoices.

We need to set up some permissions and stipulate the actions a user can do in our extension. So, let's start our example by creating some basic user groups in our Joomla! site to accommodate these permissions.

Setting up Joomla! user groups and viewing access levels

It's beyond the scope of this book to get into the details of the Joomla! user groups system and its configuration, but if you do need further details, please check the relevant link given in the *Further reading* section at the end of this chapter.

We are going to create the following user groups on our Joomla! site:

- Customer
- Project Manager
- Accountant

These user groups will depend on the regular **users** group. The purpose of each user group is as follows:

- **Customer**: The users in this group will only be able to see a very limited amount of data on the project, such as the tasks' progress, invoices, and a few more things.

- **Project Manager**: This group will only contain a few users, and they will be able to manage every aspect of the project.

- **Accountant**: This will also be a small group where the users will only be able to create and edit invoices.

To accomplish this behavior, we need to set up the **viewing access levels** for the groups. So, we go to the **Users: Viewing Access Levels** manager and add the following view levels for each group:

- **Customer**: Customer, Project Manager, Accountant, Administrator, Super User
- **Project Manager**: Project Manager, Administrator, Super User
- **Accountant**: Project Manager, Accountant, Administrator, Super User

This configuration gives us three different user groups with mixed access to our resources.

Once we have set up our user groups, we can add the permissions configuration to our component.

Adding the permissions configuration

By default in Joomla!, only components allow having permissions for specific actions. This allows us to create personalized actions alongside using the ones already present in Joomla!.

To provide the permission configuration for our component, we use the `/src/component/admin/access.xml` file we created in *Chapter 2*. For completeness, we add the following line to the `<section>` area:

```
<action name="core.edit.own" title="JACTION_EDIT_OWN"
  />
```

This line adds a new permission set called `EDIT_OWN`, which we will use to allow users to edit the content they have created.

After adding this line, we end up with the following file contents:

/src/component/admin/access.xml

```xml
<?xml version="1.0" encoding="utf-8"?>
<access component="com_spm">
    <section name="component">
        <action name="core.admin" title="JACTION_ADMIN" />
        <action name="core.options" title="JACTION_OPTIONS"
          />
        <action name="core.manage" title="JACTION_MANAGE"
          />
        <action name="core.create" title="JACTION_CREATE"
          />
        <action name="core.delete" title="JACTION_DELETE"
          />
        <action name="core.edit" title="JACTION_EDIT" />
        <action name="core.edit.own"
          title="JACTION_EDIT_OWN" />
    </section>
</access>
```

These actions are common to all Joomla! ecosystems. Let's review a short explanation of these actions:

- `core.admin`: This allows users to access the administration area of the extension

- `core.options`: This action specifies whether the user can see the component configuration page

- `core.manage`: With this action, we grant permission to manage the data of a component

- `core.create`: When permitted to perform this action, the user can create new items in the component

- `core.delete`: This allows users to remove data from the component

- `core.edit`: This allows users to edit any item in the component

- `core.edit.own`: This action allows a user to edit only the items created by that same user

When adding core actions to our extension, the component inherits the user group permission settings for that action. So, if the user belongs to the common **users** user group, it will not have permission to create or edit items unless the web administrator changes this setting in the permissions configuration.

After adding the `access.xml` file to your component, remember to also add it to the manifest file so that it is correctly installed. Go to the `src/component/spm.xml` file and add the following line to the `file` subsection under the `administration` section:

```
<file>access.xml</xml>
```

Once we have added the `access.xml` content to our component, we need to add the permissions to the configuration area for the component. So, we edit the `src/component/admin/config.xml` file, adding the following `fieldset` content to the `config` section just under the previous `company_data` fieldset that we created in a previous chapter:

```
<fieldset name="permissions" label=
  "JCONFIG_PERMISSIONS_LABEL">
    <field
        name="rules"
        type="rules"
        label="JCONFIG_PERMISSIONS_LABEL"
        filter="rules"
        validate="rules"
        component="com_spm"
        section="component"
    />
</fieldset>
```

With this new section, we tell Joomla! that we are using a permissions configuration in our component and Joomla! adds the interface on the component options page.

We can check the permissions configuration on the component options page, which you can find at this URL (covered in detail in the previous chapter): `http://yoursite.com/administrator/index.php?option=com_config&view=component&component=com_spm`.

Honoring the permissions in our extensions

After defining the permissions that we are going to use in our extension, we need to apply the restrictions in our code to make them happen. To do this, we need to check the user permissions before each action in our code. Joomla! provides some methods to help us with that, but if we define custom actions and permissions, we need to write some code to check every action specifically.

To see permissions in action, let's check whether the user is allowed to manage the extension content before showing the invoices list. To do this, edit the `src/component/admin/src/View/Invoices/HtmlView.php` file and add the following code to the display method:

```
$user = Factory::getApplication()->getIdentity();
if (!$user->authorise('core.manage', 'com_spm')){
```

```
        throw new GenericDataException('Not allowed', 403);
}
```

In this code, we get the user who is trying to access the listing and we use the `authorise()` method to check the specific permission. In this example, we check the permission for the `core.manage` action defined for the `com_spm` component. If the user is not allowed to manage the extension, Joomla! will throw an exception and will show a **Not allowed** message to the user.

The action name is exactly the same as defined in the `access.xml` file from the previous chapter, so we can add this permission check to any part of our extension we need.

This code will come prove itself handy for the custom actions we are going to define in the next section.

Defining custom actions for our component

In our extension, we have different areas that have conflicting permissions. For instance, the accountant user group should be able to create invoices, but this user group should not create tasks. We need to provide a way to differentiate these contexts; this is where custom actions come to the rescue.

Let's add a custom action to differentiate between these two contexts by adding the following code to our `src/component/admin/access.xml` file:

```
<action name="invoice.create"
  title="COM_SPM_ACTION_INVOICE_CREATE" />
<action name="invoice.edit"
  title="COM_SPM_ACTION_INVOICE_EDIT" />
<action name="task.create"
  title="COM_SPM_ACTION_TASK_CREATE" />
```

The custom actions in this code use the same syntax as the core actions. We only use different names, and of course, we give different titles to be shown to the user.

As these actions are not defined in Joomla!, we need to handle them in our extension.

Let's start by creating the code to restrict them in our extension. We face two different situations:

- Users who cannot create invoices should not be able to see the **New** button or access the URL to create the invoice.

- If the user somehow manages to send a valid request to create an invoice, Joomla! should reject the request.

In the list views of the SPM component, we added a nice toolbar to create new items. In the invoices listing, we also show this toolbar and we actually added the **New** button to create an invoice. So now we edit the `src/component/admin/src/View/Invoices/HtmlView.php` file, replacing the last line of the `addToolbar()` method with the following code:

```
$user = Factory::getApplication()->getIdentity();
if ($user->authorise('invoice.create', 'com_spm')){
    $toolbar->addNew('invoice.add');
}
```

This code checks that the user has sufficient permissions to create invoices, and if so, it adds the **New** button.

This covers the scenario for users that cannot create new invoices (Customers).

To address the second scenario, we need to go to `InvoiceController` and add the required check there. We edit the `src/component/admin/src/Controller/InvoiceController.php` file, adding the following code:

```
protected function allowAdd($data = [])
{
    $user = $this->app->getIdentity();
    return $user->authorise('core.create', $this->option)
      && $user->authorise('invoice.create', $this->
        option));
}
```

This overrides the `allowAdd()` method that is defined in the `FormController` instance we are extending to create our `InvoiceController`. In this method, we use the same `authorise()` method as in the previous paragraphs and we return the results as a true/false value.

This method is called by the controller before creating a new invoice, so we do not need to do anything else.

With this simple check, we can be sure that permissions will be respected in our extension and that our data will be kept secure.

Using Joomla! categories in our component

In *Chapter 1, Planning Your Component*, when we defined the database for our extension, we added an integer column called `category` to the **Projects** table. We did not create a database table to store our categories, because we want to integrate it with Joomla! categories.

We will now integrate our categories using the power of the Joomla! Framework™.

First, we edit the `src/component/admin/forms/project.xml` file to add the following field:

```
<field
    name="category"
    type="category"
    extension="com_spm"
    default=""
    label="COM_SPM_PROJECT_FORM_CATEGORY_LABEL"
    description="COM_SPM_PROJECT_FORM_CATEGORY_DESCRIPTION"
    required="true"
    >
    <option value="">JOPTION_SELECT_CATEGORY</option>
</field>
```

In this code, we are adding a new field of the `category` type. We use the `extension` attribute to state the name of our extension.

This will show a select box in our project edit form with all the categories used in the context of our extension. At this moment, there are none, but we can add one by pointing our browser to `yoursite.com/administrator/index.php?option=com_categories&extension=com_spm`.

This is the regular category manager interface, but adding the `extension?com_spm` parameter makes it consider only the categories in the `com_spm` component context.

To make this a bit more transparent to the users of the extension, we can add a menu in the backend to access this view. Let's go to our `src/component/spm.xml` file and add the following highlighted code to the `submenu` section of the main `administrator` section:

```
<menu link="option=com_spm&amp;view=projects" img="
  default">
        COM_SPM_PROJECTS
</menu>
<menu link="option=com_categories&amp;view=
  categories&amp;extension=com_spm" img="default">
        COM_SPM_PROJECT_CATEGORIES
</menu>
<menu link="option=com_spm&amp;view=tasks" img="default">
        COM_SPM_TASKS
</menu>
```

With this code, we provide direct access to the project categories list view to our users. On first access, they will see an empty list of categories and a **New** button with which they can add new categories. In the next section, we are going to see how we can offer some personalization options for our categories.

Customizing our component categories

Using Joomla! categories does not restrict our development to standard categories' data fields. We can add our custom properties to our project categories using Joomla! Forms. Let's add a color property to our project categories. That will help us visualize our projects more easily.

To add more properties, we create a `src/component/admin/forms/category.xml` file with the following content:

```
<?xml version="1.0" encoding="utf-8"?>
<form>
    <fields name="params">
        <fieldset name="com_spm" label="COM_
          SPM_CATEGORY_OPTIONS_FIELDSET" description="
            COM_SPM_CATEGORY_OPTIONS_FIELDSET_DESCRIPTION">
            <field name="color" type="color" default=""
             label="COM_SPM_CATEGORY_OPTIONS_FIELD_COLOR"/>
        </fieldset>
    </fields>
</form>
```

This code adds a new tab in the category edit view titled **COM_SPM_CATEGORY_OPTIONS_FIELDSET** with an info call-out box with the text **COM_SPM_CATEGORY_OPTIONS_FIELDSET_DESCRIPTION**, which contains a color select field.

You can add as many fields as you need to this `<fieldset>` group, along with as many fieldsets as you consider necessary for your extension.

Now we can use this new `color` option to create a more visual list of projects.

Exploring the benefits and limitations of using Joomla! categories

When building big sites, you need to pay attention to performance and make sure you offer the fastest and most reliable code possible. Joomla! is no exception to this, and every feature is coded to be the best possible solution for the most common or critical scenarios.

The Joomla! Category Manager is a good example of aiming to offer the best possible solution. When thinking about how to implement categories in your extension, you might be tempted to create your own solution. This solution is usually a single table with the name of your category. But then you notice you also want to have subcategories. And as your site grows, you notice that running searches in this structure is quite slow and you need another solution.

Joomla! categories, therefore, are developed to be performant on sites of all sizes, and best of all, you can integrate them into your extension.

The main benefits of using Joomla! categories instead of our own solutions are as follows:

- All internal logic is already coded and well tested
- You get the category listing with ordering, filtering, and edits already done
- It allows an unlimited number of categories and subcategories
- You can expand them with your own fields on parameters
- You can make use of the category item counters in the backend

The disadvantages of using Joomla! categories in your extension include the following:

- If you want to debug them, they are based on a complex algorithm (Nested set)
- Although you can personalize the categories to add some options, this is done by adding parameters, and might not be enough in some scenarios
- The categories listing in the backend will be a generic categories list with few options for changing the layout and styling

Of course, it is your job as the developer to determine whether the benefits exceed the limitations of your project. In our Simple Project Manager, we are going to use Joomla! categories to categorize our projects. In the next section, we will add the necessary code to integrate Joomla! categories into our component.

Using our categories' custom properties

So far, we have created a direct access to see our component's categories in the backend and we have added a field to associate our projects with a specific category in the database. But we need to inform our extension we are using Joomla! categories and inject the services related to them.

So, we need to add the proper services to our component boot method. To do this we edit the `src/component/admin/services/provider.php` file, adding the following highlighted code:

```
use Joomla\CMS\Categories\CategoryFactoryInterface;
use Joomla\CMS\Extension\Service\Provider\CategoryFactory;
return new class implements ServiceProviderInterface
{
  public function register(Container $container){
    $container->registerServiceProvider(new
      CategoryFactory('Piedpiper\Component\Spm'));
    $container->registerServiceProvider(new
      MVCFactory('\Piedpiper\Component\Spm'));
    $container->registerServiceProvider(new
      ComponentDispatcherFactory('\Piedpiper\
```

```
                Component\Spm'));
        $container->registerServiceProvider(new
          RouterFactory('\Piedpiper\Component\Spm'));
        $container->set(
            ComponentInterface::class,
            function (Container $container)
            {
                $component = new SpmComponent($container->
                  get(ComponentDispatcherFactoryInterface
                    ::class));

                $component->setMVCFactory($container->
                  get(MVCFactoryInterface::class));
                $component->setRouterFactory($container->
                  get(RouterFactoryInterface::class));
                $component->setCategoryFactory($container->
                  get(CategoryFactoryInterface::class));

                return $component;
            }
        );
    }
};
```

In the first highlighted line, we declare the namespace for our categories, and in the second one we add the `CategoryInterface` class offered by Joomla! to make category management easier. Then we inject the `CategoryFactory` capabilities.

We also need to edit the `src/component/admin/src/Extension/SpmComponent.php` file to implement the `CategoryServiceInterface` object, so this file now looks like this:

```
...

use Joomla\CMS\Categories\CategoryServiceTrait;
use Joomla\CMS\Categories\CategoryServiceInterface;


class SpmComponent extends MVCComponent implements
  CategoryServiceInterface, BootableExtensionInterface,
    RouterServiceInterface
{
    use RouterServiceTrait;
    use CategoryServiceTrait;
```

```
...

}
```

In the preceding code, we declare the service classes we are using and we implement the `CategoryServiceInterface` class to automatically call the category service on our component boot.

After this, there is one more thing we need to do. We need to create our **category service**, providing the details of the relationship between our data and the categories. This service is mainly intended for use in the frontend of our site, so Joomla! will look for it in the frontend part of our component. We add the `src/component/site/src/Service/Category.php` file with the following content:

```php
<?php
namespace Piedpiper\Component\Spm\Site\Service
defined('_JEXEC') or die;
use Joomla\CMS\Categories\Categories;
class Category extends Categories
{
  public function __construct($options)
  {
    $options = array_merge($options, [
      'extension'  => 'com_spm',
      'table'      => '#__projects',
      'field'      => 'category',
      'key'        => 'id',
      'statefield' => 'state',
      ]);
    parent::__construct($options);
  }
}
```

In this code, we only need to define this array with the following information on our extension:

- The name of our extension
- The table this category service should check
- The name of the field with the ID of the category in our table
- The field used as the primary key in the #__projects table
- The field in our table that represents the state

Now, the Joomla! categories functionality is completely integrated into our component. We can now use it to retrieve the category information in our data. Let's next add some colors to identify our projects in the project list.

We edit the `src/component/admin/src/Model/ProjectsModel.php` file, declaring the categories namespaces and adding the `getItems()` method:

```
use Joomla\CMS\Categories\Categories;
use Joomla\CMS\Categories\CategoryNode;

...

public function getItems()
{
    $items = parent::getItems();
    $categories = Categories::getInstance('spm');

    foreach ($items as &$item) {
        $item->category = $categories->get($item->
          category);
        $item->color = $item->category->getParams()->
          get('color');
    }

    return $items;
}
```

Joomla! calls the `getItems()` method to get the list of items from the database, so we add an override to go through the results and add the category data.

In the `category` property, we have the full information of our category, and we can get the `color` property from `params`. This code also replicates the `color` property from the category into the item to allow more direct access.

Finally, we need to go to the template layout for the list of items and use the color property. Edit the `src/component/admin/tmpl/projects/default.php` file, replacing the `td` field in code with the following code:

```
...
<?php foreach ($this->items as $item) : ?>
    <tr>
        <td  style="background-color: <?php echo $item->
          color;?>"><?php echo $item->id; ?></td>
        <td  style="background-color: <?php echo $item->
          color;?>"><?php echo $item->name; ?></td>
        <td  style="background-color: <?php echo $item->
          color;?>"><?php echo $item->deadline; ?></td>
    </tr>
```

```
<?php endforeach;?>
...
```

We have finally integrated Joomla! categories into our project. There is one remaining fundamental aspect that we need to cover to have full integration. In the next section, we will see how we can add ACL capabilities to these categories.

Adding ACL to our component categories

Adding ACL capabilities to our extension categories is easy using Joomla! ACL. We just need to add the following section to our `src/component/admin/access.xml` file:

```
<section name="category">
    <action name="core.create" title="JACTION_CREATE" />
    <action name="core.delete" title="JACTION_DELETE" />
    <action name="core.edit" title="JACTION_EDIT" />
    <action name="core.edit.state" title=
       "JACTION_EDITSTATE" />
    <action name="core.edit.own" title="JACTION_EDITOWN" />
</section>
```

These ACL rules will apply only to the categories within our extension context, so we could have a user group allowed to create content categories, but not authorized to add categories to our projects.

We have now full control over the categories in our extension and have even added some custom options to personalize the category experience. Let's see in the next section how we can offer further customization to our users by adding custom fields to our component.

Introduction to Joomla! custom fields

Joomla! custom fields were one of the most exciting features added to Joomla! 3.

This feature allows you to add more fields to any data entity in Joomla!. The most common use case here is to add more fields to a Joomla! article, but this feature is not limited to Joomla! articles. In fact, you can find custom fields for components such as `com_users` (responsible for managing Joomla! users) and `com_contact` (adding a contact directory to your site).

Using Joomla! custom fields, website administrators can adapt Joomla! without any coding knowledge required. Implementing custom fields in our extension will provide limitless possibilities to the users of our extension.

The first thing that came to mind when I started working with Joomla! custom fields was that I could use any of the Joomla! Standard Form Fields we saw in the previous chapter as custom fields. But to have a custom field type, you need to have a specific plugin for it. In any case, there are 16 different custom field types to choose from in Joomla!, which should be enough for almost any project.

Let's see how we add custom fields to our extension in the next section.

Using custom fields in our component

We can add custom field capabilities to any part of our component, so it is a good thing to decide in advance where in our extension it makes sense to use them.

In our Simple Project Manager extension, we had several entities: **Projects**, **Clients**, **Invoices**, and **Tasks**. Every business is different and has different needs. For our extension, I see great possibilities to implement custom fields for **Clients** and **Invoices**.

In Joomla!, we define custom fields by context. That means the fields created under the **Client** context will not be shown with or related to the ones created under the **Invoices** context.

Let's start the custom fields implementation in our component by defining the contexts we will add them to. To define the contexts for our custom fields, edit the src/component/admin/src/ Extension/SpmComponent.php file and add the following namespaces:

```
use Joomla\CMS\Fields\FieldsServiceInterface;
use Joomla\CMS\Factory;
use Joomla\CMS\Language\Text;
```

We also refactor the class definition into this:

```
class SpmComponent extends MVCComponent implements
  CategoryServiceInterface, BootableExtensionInterface,
    RouterServiceInterface, FieldsServiceInterface
```

In the preceding code, we introduced the FieldsServiceInterface to allow a custom fields definition.

Finally, we add the following methods:

```
public function getContexts(): array
{
    Factory::getLanguage()->load('com_spm',
      JPATH_ADMINISTRATOR);
    $contexts = array(
        'com_spm.project'    => Text::_
          ('COM_SPM_CONTEXT_PROJECTS'),
        'com_spm.client'     => Text::_
```

```
                ('COM_SPM_CONTEXT_CLIENTS')
      );
      return $contexts;
  }
  public function validateSection($section, $item = null)
  {
      if (($section === 'customer')) {
          $section = 'client';
      }
      if (($section === 'project')) {
          $section = 'project';
      }
      if ($section !== 'project' && $section !== 'client') {
          return null;
      }
      return $section;
  }
```

The getContexts() method will be called by the Joomla! custom fields manager to offer different contexts when adding custom fields to our extension. To see how it works, we need to go to the custom fields manager view for our projects. To do this, go to this URL in your demo Joomla! site: yoursite. com/administrator/index.php?option=com_fields&context=com_spm.project.

The validateSection() method is required by the interface implementation and returns the proper section according to the user context. This is useful when we use different names for our field contexts and views. In this case, we defined the clients field context but we are in the customers view, so we catch and fix the section on the validateSection() method.

And with that, you are done! You can now add custom fields to your projects from this view. Also on the right top of the component area, you will see a select box with which you can change to the **Client** context.

To make things easier for our users, we can add a link in the Joomla! components menu. To do this, add the following highlighted code to the manifest file at src/component/spm.xml:

```
<submenu>
    <menu link="option=com_spm&amp;view=projects"
      img="default">
            COM_SPM_PROJECTS
    </menu>
    <menu link="option=com_fields&amp;context=
      com_spm.project" img="default">
        JGLOBAL_FIELDS
    </menu>
    <menu link="option=com_fields&amp;view=groups&amp;
```

```
        context=com_spm.project" img="default">
        JGLOBAL_FIELD_GROUPS
    </menu>
</submenu>
```

In this code, we also add a link to the field group management for the project context. Custom field groups are a nice feature to help your users be more organized when working with custom fields.

Showing custom fields in our views

Your job here as a developer involves setting up the use of custom fields, but once done, you have no control over how your users will use the feature. So, to illustrate how to show custom fields in our forms and layouts, let's imagine a simple case of use for custom fields in our Simple Project Manager extension.

Let's pretend you (acting as your user) want to have a simple **Customer Relationship Manager** (**CRM**) functionality. To create that, you go to the custom field groups view for the Client context and create the **CRM** custom field group.

Then, you go to the custom field manager for the **Client** context and add the following fields:

- Birthday: a calendar field

- Married to: a Text field

- Children: an integer field

When we add or edit a client, we want to show the fields we defined in our XML form for the clients along with the custom fields we just created.

You may think that we now need to add something to our model to show these fields and their content. But as we are abiding by the Joomla! way, there is nothing we need to do for the model. The custom fields data is loaded magically by the custom fields system plugin. All we need to do is add the code to show the custom fields in the view. So, let's edit the `src/component/admin/tmpl/customer/edit.php` file and add the following code:

```
<fieldset name="custom_fields">
    <div class="row">
        <div class="col-md-9">
            <div class="row">
                <div class="col-md-6">
                    <?php foreach($this->form->
                    getFieldsets() as $name => $fieldset): ?>
                        <?php foreach($this->form->
                        getFieldSet($name) as $field
                        ) :?>
                            <?php echo $field->
```

```
                                        renderField(); ?>
                                <?php endforeach;?>
                        <?php endforeach; ?>
                    </div>
                </div>
            </div>
        </div>
    </fieldset>
```

With this, we are adding the markup for a new HTML `fieldset`, and we fill it with a `foreach` loop that gets the `fieldset` from the **Form** object (`$this->form`). Finally, we render the field using the `renderField()` provided by the **Field** object.

To show the custom fields in the frontend view, we also take advantage of the custom fields system plugin. To do this, we add the following code to the `src/component/site/src/ViewCustomer` file inside the `display()` method, before the call to the parent method:

```
$app = \Joomla\CMS\Factory::getApplication();
$app->triggerEvent('onContentPrepare', ['com_spm.customer',
  &$this->item]);
```

This line calls the proper method of the custom fields system plugin and provides the appropriate context to get all the custom fields attached to our item. Now, in our template layout, we can access all the custom fields inside the `jcfields` property of the `item` object.

To do this, we edit the `src/component/site/tmpl/customer/default.php` file to add the following block of code:

```
<div id="crm">
    <?php foreach ($this->item->jcfields as $field) :?>
        <dl>
            <dt>
                <?php echo $field->label; ?>
            </dt>
            <dd>
                <?php echo $field->value; ?>
            </dd>
        </dl>
    <?php endforeach; ?>
</div>
```

With this `foreach` loop, we go through all the different fields attached to our `item`. What is more interesting, the `$field` property contains all the properties of the field. That allows us to show the label from the field using the `$field->label` property. Also, if we are using a complex field that requires some preprocessing before showing the value, the `value` property will have the expected value. For instance, when using a select field, the `value` property will provide the text associated with the selected value. If you want to get the exact value as stored in your database, use the `rawvalue` property.

Adding an ACL to the custom fields

Joomla! custom fields come with ACL functionality already built in, and with the possibility of extensive customization. We can add this ACL to our extension's custom fields by adding the proper configuration to the `access.xml` file.

To add an ACL to our extension, we add the following fields to the `src/component/admin/access.xml` file:

```
<section name="fieldgroup">
    <action name="core.create" title="JACTION_CREATE"
      description="COM_FIELDS_GROUP_PERMISSION_CREATE_DESC" />
    <action name="core.delete" title="JACTION_DELETE"
      description="COM_FIELDS_GROUP_PERMISSION_DELETE_DESC" />
    <action name="core.edit" title="JACTION_EDIT"
      description="COM_FIELDS_GROUP_PERMISSION_EDIT_DESC" />
    <action name="core.edit.state" title=
      "JACTION_EDITSTATE" description="
        COM_FIELDS_GROUP_PERMISSION_EDITSTATE_DESC" />
    <action name="core.edit.own" title="JACTION_EDITOWN"
      description="COM_FIELDS_GROUP_PERMISSION_EDITOWN
        _DESC" />
    <action name="core.edit.value" title="
    JACTION_EDITVALUE" description="
      COM_FIELDS_GROUP_PERMISSION_EDITVALUE_DESC" />
</section>
<section name="field">
    <action name="core.delete" title="JACTION_DELETE"
      description="COM_FIELDS_FIELD_PERMISSION_DELETE_DESC"
        />
    <action name="core.edit" title="JACTION_EDIT"
      description="COM_FIELDS_FIELD_PERMISSION_EDIT_DESC"
        />
    <action name="core.edit.state" title=
      "JACTION_EDITSTATE" description="
```

```
            COM_FIELDS_FIELD_PERMISSION_EDITSTATE_DESC" />
        <action name="core.edit.value" title=
          "JACTION_EDITVALUE" description=
            "COM_FIELDS_FIELD_PERMISSION_EDITVALUE_DESC" />
  </section>
```

In the preceding XML, code we can see two main groups located in the `<fieldgroup>` and the `<field>` sections. The `<fieldgroup>` group of permissions sets the ACL for the group of fields feature. This allows the user to set what people can do with the fields that belong to the group. These are the settings available:

- `core.create`: Allows the creation of new fields inside the group
- `core.delete`: Allows the removal of the fields that belong to the group
- `core.edit`: Lets your users edit the fields belonging to this group
- `core.edit.state`: Allows the user to change the state of the fields inside the group
- `core.edit.own`: Allows the user to edit the fields that belong to the field group and were created by that same user
- `core.edit.value`: Sets which user groups can modify the value of a field in this field group

The `field` section sets the ACL for all the custom fields created in the context of our extension. This is of use to the website manager to set generic permissions for the fields, instead of using the field group permissions. These are the available settings:

- `core.edit`: Allows us to edit the custom field definition
- `core.edit.state`: Allows us to set the state of the custom field
- `core.edit.value`: Allows us to set which user groups can modify the value of a field in this field group

> **Note**
>
> The `state` permission also allows the user to move a field to the trash, so this permission could be considered a "remove items" option. Keep this in mind when using these permissions.

With custom fields, we offer the website managers using our extension a powerful and easily adaptable feature to extend our component that they will appreciate for sure. In the next section, we will explore how to add language translations to our component to expand our market.

Using Joomla's multilingual capabilities in our component

While developing our component, you may have noticed we never used natural language for our labels and texts. Instead, we used key strings with the syntax of COM_SPM_CONTEXT_DETAIL. This is to take advantage of the Joomla! translation system to allow us to provide our extension in multiple languages.

Joomla's translation system is very powerful, but it's also very simple. It is based on text files saved with the .ini extension. These .ini files contain a list of the key strings to translate followed by an equals sign and the translation surrounded by quotes. When loading the page, Joomla! reads these .ini files and uses them to translate all the words passed through the Text class. The simplicity of the system makes it possible to override translations easily and you may even override a core translation just by creating the same language key string. That is why we usually prefix our key strings with the name of the component: COM_SPM.

Let's add our first translation by creating a src/component/admin/language/en-GB/com_spm.ini file with the following content:

```
; General
COM_SMP_NAME="Simple Project Manager"
```

In the first line, we added a comment to state which section of our component the string relates to. This is not necessary and is only an instrument to help possible future translators discern the context of the language string.

In the translation part of the line, we can use spaces and any other character we need. There is only one caveat: we need to escape the double-quotes character if we use it in our translation. So, for example, we could remark the word Project using this:

```
; General
COM_SPM_NAME="Simple \"Project\" Manager"
```

One common scenario is the need to include HTML code in the language strings to enrich the text. There is no need for extra escaping or other considerations, as can be seen in the following example:

```
COM_SPM_DESCRIPTION="Simple Project manager is an example
component for the \"Developing Joomla Extensions\" book
published by <a href='https://packt.com'>Packt</a>"
```

This translation string includes a link. To make it easier to read, we use single quotes for the HTML attributes.

To detect and translate the key strings, Joomla! uses the \Joomla\CMS\Language\Text class. There's nothing else we have to change in the XML files such as our manifest file or the form's definition files. Joomla! passes all the possible key strings to the Text class and will show the result.

So, if we go back to the extension manifest located at `src/component/spm.xml`, we find the following entries:

```
...
<name>COM_SPM</name>
...
<description><![CDATA[COM_SPM_DESCRIPTION]]></description>
...
```

There are only a couple of key strings in this manifest file. One is the name of the extension (COM_ SPM_NAME) and the other is the description (COM_SPM_DESCRIPTION). After installing the extension, Joomla! shows these strings in the success message. But Joomla! only loads the `.ini` files relevant to the context. For example, when we install our extension, we are in the `com_installer` context and not in the `com_spm` context, which means Joomla! will not translate our key strings.

To fix this, we need to create a new language file in the same folder called `com_spm.sys.ini`. Joomla! always loads all the `.sys.ini` language files present in the system, no matter the context. We use this file to add translations for things that happen in other contexts such as installation and menus.

As Joomla! always loads this file, we should keep it to the smallest possible length. In our component, we use the following:

```
; General
COM_SMP_NAME="Simple Project Manager"
COM_SPM_DESCRIPTION="Simple Project manager is an example
  component for the \"Developing Joomla Extensions\" book
    published by <a href='https://packt.com'>Packt</a>"
```

There is no conflict when using the same translation keys on both files as the Joomla! language system loads all strings into memory, and the first match of the string key will be the translation shown.

Everything we have seen so far involved adding a translation map for the English language, the one used by default in Joomla!. If we want to include other languages, we need to create a different folder and create the relevant `.sys.ini` and `.ini` files. For instance, if we want to add support for the German language, we can duplicate the files into the `src/component/admin/language/ de-DE/` folder so that we have the following files:

- `src/component/admin/language/de-DE/com_spm.ini`
- `src/component/admin/language/de-DE/com_spm.sys.ini`

When working with PHP content, we keep using the `Text` class. If we see the `src/component/ admin/tmpl/projects/default.php` file, we will see the `Text` class declaration at the top of the file as follows:

```
use Joomla\CMS\Language\Text;
```

We also see the usage of the class with the following method:

```
Text::_('COM_SPM_PROJECTS_LIST')
```

This makes Joomla! look in the `com_spm.ini` file for the `COM_SPM_PROJECTS_LIST` key string and return the value declared on it.

Now that we understand how to add our translations, we can go a bit deeper and see a couple of features of the `Text` class to produce perfect translations.

Adding complex translations

Joomla! has more than 50 official language packs available so far, and more languages are on the way as users around the world discover its power. In all these languages we find interesting cases and ways to express a concept. Let's take the example of the following sentence:

20 items deleted.

This sentence informs us of the number of items removed. Should we create a different message for every possible number? Of course not! Joomla! allows us to use variables to handle these situations. These methods are the following:

- `Text::sprintf()`
- `Text::plural()`

The `Text::sprintf()` method takes the string with some placeholders that are replaced by the variables that follow the string. For instance, in our example, let's use the following key-value pair in the `com_spm.ini` file:

```
COM_SPM_REMOVED_ITEMS="%d items deleted"
```

And in our PHP code, we will use the following line:

```
echo Text::sprintf('COM_SPM_REMOVED_ITEMS', ["20"]);
```

One interesting thing about the `Text::sprintf()` method is that it works exactly as the PHP `sprintf()` function, so it accepts the same placeholders and behaves exactly the same as the former. However, note the following:

- You can set the type of data you expect (for instance, `%d` is for integer values).
- The ordering of the replacement respects the order of the variables in the array we provide after the string.
- You can choose to replace a specific variable using its position number in your placeholder. For example, if you add `%2$d`, the method will use the second variable passed in the array to replace that placeholder, no matter where the placeholder appears on the string.

The `Text::plural()` method is used to provide different translations for when the number of items changes. For instance, in English, the phrasing is not identical when we have one item versus multiple items. In our example, we can rewrite our code to the following:

```
echo Text::plural('COM_SPM_REMOVED_ITEMS', 20);
```

And then if we add the following string to our `com_spm.ini` file, when we have one item, the following value string will be used:

```
COM_SPM_REMOVED_ITEMS_1="Item successfully removed"
```

This is valid for any number. So whenever you find a language with different declination rules according to the number of items, Joomla! has you covered!

Now we are ready to translate our component and make it easier for our users to understand what we want to say, no matter the language they speak.

Summary

In this chapter, we discovered the most interesting features Joomla! offers out of the box for use in our extensions. In some cases, such as the ACL-related features, we only need to add some XML definition to our `access.xml` form. For other features such as **categories**, we needed to go a bit further and declare new services. We also saw that enriching our extension with custom fields is a piece of cake, as all we need to do is include the call to the custom fields API. Finally, we added translations to our extension, creating the necessary `.ini` files and using the `Text` class to process the translation keys.

The benefits of using these features are huge, and compared to the amount of work we would have to do to write them from scratch, this is a big win.

Now our component offers a common interface for the ACL and a more secure experience for our users. We also developed an easy-to-customize extension as our users can now add their own custom fields to the projects. We also offer a friendly interface in our users' chosen languages with great pluralization support.

We can now consider our first component finished! In the next chapter, we will begin with creating our first plugin to connect to it.

Further reading

- You can find a great tutorial about Joomla! ACLs in the official Joomla! documentation: `https://docs.joomla.org/J3.x:Access_Control_List_Tutorial`

- In the official Joomla! documentation, there is a detailed article with everything you need to know when translating your extension: `https://docs.joomla.org/International_Enhancements_for_Version_1.6#Pluralization_Support_for_Translation_Files`

- Joomla's `.ini` file format is described in the following official documentation: `https://docs.joomla.org/Creating_a_language_definition_file`

- The Joomla! Coding Standards page offers some directions for `.ini` files: `https://developer.joomla.org/coding-standards/ini.html`

6
Adding a Web Service API to Your Component

In this chapter, we are going to explore the recently added Joomla! Web Services API, which will allow us to integrate our Joomla! site with other websites and services. We will present a simple way to consume this Web Service API from our computer that will allow us to test our developments. We will also explore the authorization and permissions that affect the Joomla! Web Services, and finally, we will add a Web Service API for our component to read and add data to our site.

At the end of the chapter, you will be able to understand how Joomla! Web Services work and connect with any Joomla! site using it. You will also be able to create your own Web Services API for your Joomla! extension and set up the required permissions for it.

Using the Joomla! Web Services API allows us to exchange data with other websites and extend our sites beyond the web browser. One interesting area for a web developer is developing automation to integrate your sites with external systems for monitoring or importing content.

Developing a Web Service API for our component allows us to create further developments, such as a mobile or desktop application that uses our Joomla! website as the main server.

To cover all we need to know about developing a Web Services API, we will use these sections:

- What is a Web Service API?
- How can I use the Joomla! Web Service API?
- Authorization for a Web API
- Web Service API permissions
- Adding a Web Service API to your component
- Reading data from your Web Service – adding a GET endpoint to your component.
- Writing data from your Web Service – adding a POST endpoint to your component

In this chapter, we are going to learn how to query Joomla! Web Services and how Joomla! Web Services API authorization works. Finally, we will add a Web Services API to our Simple Project Manager extension.

Technical requirements

You will need the following for this chapter:

- The `curl` command-line tool or a PHP installation with `curl` support enabled
- Otherwise, you may use an online tool such as Postman or `HoppScotch.io` to test API calls

You can find the code files for this chapter on GitHub: `https://github.com/PacktPublishing/Developing-Extensions-for-Joomla-5/tree/chapter06`

What is a Web Service API?

Web Services are a means to allow machines to communicate. A good Web Service provides clear routes that we can integrate into external services. These routes are called *endpoints*. It also provides responses in a machine-readable way, which we can also integrate into these services.

There are different types of Web Service APIs such as **SOAP** or **REST**. Joomla implements a REST API, so all the concepts in this chapter relate to this kind of API.

To use a Web Service API, we submit an HTTP request to these endpoints, and we get a response with the data or some message related to our request. The main HTTP requests we can use in a Web Service are as follows:

- **GET**: You use this request when you want to retrieve data from the API. A good example of this is when you want to retrieve a list of articles from the site.
- **POST**: You use a `POST` request when you want to submit new data. For instance, when you want to create a new article in Joomla! using a Web Service API, you submit a `POST` request.
- **PATCH**: The `PATCH` request is useful to partially modify data on the site. For instance, to modify the title of an article on your Joomla! site, you would use a `PATCH` request.
- **DELETE**: This request is used to remove data from the site – for instance, to remove an article.

There are other types of requests such as `PUT` or `HEAD`, but they are not relevant for this chapter. You will find a link to the full list of them in the *Further reading* section at the end of this chapter.

Now that we know the basics of a Web Service API, let's learn how we can use them to retrieve and submit data.

How to consume any Web Service API

When we use any of the Web Service requests of an API, we say we are *consuming* it. So, in this section, we are going to see how we can consume this API and retrieve information or add data to an API.

The Swiss Army knife to call an API endpoint is **cURL**. This is a command-line program that is widely used for developers; no matter the API you want to check, you will find in the documentation recipes for the `curl` command.

> **Tip**
>
> If you use an online service such as Postman or Hoppscotch, both provide an import/export tool for cURL, so you can use the following examples with these services.

We are going to use **PHP cURL** in this book, which can easily be translated to a direct `curl` call, so you may use whatever system to perform the examples in this book.

Let's start by creating the PHP script to get data from the API, so create the `Scripts/api/` folder in your working directory and then create the `Scripts/api/get.php` file with the following content:

```php
<?php

if (extension_loaded('curl') == false) {
    throw new \Exception('curl not installed');
}


$url = 'https://jsonplaceholder.typicode.com/todos/1';

$connection = curl_init($url);

curl_setopt($connection, CURLOPT_RETURNTRANSFER, true);

$response = curl_exec($connection);
curl_close($connection);

print_r(json_decode($response));
```

In this code, we first check the `curl` PHP extension is installed in the server. This is a common feature that will most likely be installed, but in any case, we had better check to avoid uncatched errors. After that, we define the URL of the API, and we use it to start the cURL connection. This does not send the request immediately, so we edit the request using the `curl_setopt` function. By default, PHP cURL sends a GET request.

We use the `curl_setopt()` method to set the `CURLOPT_RETURNTRANSFER` parameter. It must be `true` to get the response in a string that we can store in a variable; otherwise, the server will show it.

The URL of the API we request in this example is `https://jsonplaceholder.typicode.com`. This is a demo API for testing purposes that you can use in your projects. At its main URL, it provides further instructions. In our case, as we have not introduced the Joomla! Web Service API, we use this API to check that our PHP script works.

When executing this script, we will see this message in our script:

```
stdClass Object
(
    [userId] => 1
    [id] => 1
    [title] => delectus aut autem
    [completed] =>
)
```

This is just the data for one of the items in the to-do list. You can replace the number 1 in the URL with a different number and you will get different data in the response. You can even omit the number and then you will get a list of the to-do items accessible via this API.

Now that we have covered the basics of Web Services, let's see how we can use the Joomla! Web Service API in the next section.

How can I use the Joomla! Web Service API?

In Joomla!, Web Services are enabled by default, so you can start using them out of the box. As a rule, there is an endpoint for all Joomla! data entities, so you can fully manage a Joomla! website from the Web Service API.

All Joomla! core components have an endpoint to retrieve and add data using the Web Service API. You will find a list of all endpoints in the Joomla! official documentation: `https://docs.joomla.org/J4.x:Joomla_Core_APIs`.

All these endpoints are handled by a Joomla! plugin of the `webservices` plugin type. This allows you to enable or disable Web Services in Joomla! from plugin management. So, if you go to your Joomla! backend and then to **System** -> **Manage Plugins**, you will be able to see all the available services filtering by the `webservices` type.

One good example of Joomla! Web Services is the `content` Web Service. With this Web Service, we can get the list of articles published on a Joomla! site using the following URL: `YourSite.com/api/index.php/v1/content/articles`.

That request will give you a response in JSON format similar to this:

```
{
  "links": {
    "self": "https://YourSite.com/api/index.php/v1/content/articles"
  },
  "data": [
    {
        "type": "articles",
        "id": "11",
        "attributes": {
        "id": 11,
        "asset_id": 148,
        "title": "Typography",
        "alias": "typograpy",
        ...
    },
    {
        "type": "articles",
        "id": "10",
        "attributes": {
        "id": 10,
        "asset_id": 147,
        "title": "New feature: Workflows",
        "alias": "new-feature-workflows",
        ...
    }
  ],
  "meta": {
    "total-pages": 1
  }
}
```

This is a JSON response that contains the requested list of articles of a demo Joomla! site. In this JSON response, there are three objects:

- links: This contains the links relevant to the reply. In this case, it contains the link we have requested. It might contain the link to the next page of results if any.

- data: This contains the data we have requested in an array. In this example, we can see an array of article objects with the article ID, title, alias, and other properties.

- meta: This is the meta information relevant to the response. In this case, it is the total number of pages that contains the list of articles.

In this section, we have omitted the authorization part. If you perform this query on your site, you will get a **403 forbidden** error message. In Joomla!, you need to be a user of the site with enough permissions to consume the Web Service API. Let's dive into how to include the authorization mechanism in our requests in the next section.

Authorization for the API

If you try using the URL of the previous section on your browser, you will get a *403 forbidden* response. Web Services in Joomla! are powerful as they allow you to fully manage and get information from your site. So, none of the Joomla! Web Services are public, and you need authorization to use them.

Joomla! comes with two different authorization methods:

- **Basic authorization**: This method is the most basic authorization and it's not recommended to use in live sites. It uses your username and password in the request.
- **Joomla! token authorization**: This method is more secure, and it uses a secure token linked to your user, which only the user can check.

Authorization for Joomla! Web Services is handled by the `api-authorization` plugin type so it's possible to add more authentication methods.

Let's see more details about these methods.

Basic authorization

The basic authorization method for Joomla! Web Services consists of adding your username and password to the request. This makes the use of this plugin insecure as an attacker would be able to retrieve your username and password and gain access to the full site.

This authorization method would allow, in any case, the use of the Joomla! Web Services API to any user with enough permissions. So, it may come in handy for some specific cases in which you need to provide quick access to the Web Services to your customers.

As this authorization method is not recommended, in the next section, let's see the Joomla! token authorization method, which is much more secure in all aspects.

Joomla! token authorization

This authorization method is the one enabled by default for the Web Service API. With this method, users can generate a random API token from their profile that is used to authenticate their request.

This method is more secure for the following reasons:

- It does not store the token directly in the database, but is the key to generate the random string that forms the token. This makes it very difficult for an attacker to guess the token in case of a data breach.

- The user password is not related to the token in any way, so an attacker cannot infer the user password from the token, and if you suspect any token has been compromised, you can easily create a different one and disable the compromised one.

- Only the owner of the token can see it in the profile. Super users or other users of the site cannot see other users' tokens.

In this method, by default, only users in the Super Users group can create an API token. To allow users in other user groups to create and use API tokens, you need to edit the configuration of the **User – Joomla API Token** plugin and choose the groups you want to allow. When users can create an API token, they can do so from their user profile where they can find a new tab with the token. You will find some examples of token authorization in the *Further reading* section.

These two methods of authorization are the ones that come with Joomla! and will be enough for most of your projects. In case you need other authorization methods, you can check the Joomla! Extensions Directory or even develop an authorization plugin yourself.

The authorization is one part of the security for the Joomla! API; it's basically to match the request with a user – we may think of it as when browsing a site and logging in. There is another part regarding security, which is the things you can do once logged in. In the next section, we will see how we handle Web Service API permissions.

Web Services API permissions

In Joomla!, the Web Services login by default is restricted to users in the Super Users group. The reason behind this is that, now, the API allows full management of a Joomla! site, so a broader permission range will pose a security risk for lots of sites.

We can change this in the **Permissions** tab in the **Global Configuration** of Joomla!. When you go there, you may notice a new permission called **Web Services Login**. This setting defines whether the user group can use the Web Services API.

When you extend the number of user groups who can use the Web Service API, there are some techniques you can use to limit the amount of data each user group can consume.

As each endpoint of the Web Service API is controlled by a plugin, we can limit the access to those endpoints simply by unpublishing these plugins. So, for instance, to avoid access to the contact endpoint with `https://YourSite.com//api/index.php/v1/contact`, we unpublish the **Web Services – Contact** plugin, and that will remove the endpoint from our Web Service API at that moment.

You may think that setting the access level permission of a Web Service plugin to `registered` or `special` restricts that endpoint to users with that level of permissions. Nevertheless, I'm afraid that will not work, as the endpoint check is performed before the authorization happens, so using a more restrictive **Access Control List (ACL)** will work as if we unpublish the item.

The good news is that the Web Service API respects the permissions and ACL of the component it relates to. So, we can control the ACL for the Web Service as if it is the standard ACL for the component. To prevent showing a contact in the Web Service API for people in the `registered` group, we just need to change the view level in that contact to a more restricted one (for instance, `special`).

Once we know how Joomla! Web Services work, we are ready to add an endpoint to access our Simple Project Manager data from the Web Service API.

Adding a Web Service API to your component

Developing a Web Service for our component is quite easy using the Joomla! Framework™. As we have used Joomla! classes and we have respected Joomla! MVC, Joomla! will take care of most of the stuff. To define our Web Service, we first need to define the entry points for the entities we want to expose and then connect our already created models with these entry points.

To define the entry points, we must create a Web Service plugin (we will see how to create plugins in more detail in *Chapter 8*, but this is a very basic one, so we can handle it right now).

Developing the Web Service plugin

The Web Service plugin defines all the endpoints of our Web Service API. It handles the routing of the endpoint inside the application, and it controls which endpoints need authorization.

Let's start by adding the manifest file, as we did for our component in *Chapter 2*. Create the `src/plugins/webservice/spm/spm.xml` file with the following content:

```xml
<?xml version="1.0" encoding="utf-8"?>
<extension type="plugin" group="webservices"
  method="upgrade">
    <name>plg_webservices_spm</name>
    <author>Carlos Cámara</author>
    <creationDate>January 2023</creationDate>
    <copyright>Copyright 2023 PiedPiper Inc.</copyright>
    <license>GNU General Public License version 2 or later;
      see LICENSE.txt</license>
    <authorEmail>carlos@hepta.es</authorEmail>
    <authorUrl>www.packt.com</authorUrl>
    <version>1.0.0</version>
    <description>PLG_WEBSERVICES_SPM_XML_DESCRIPTION
```

```
        </description>
    <files>
        <filename plugin="spm">spm.php</filename>
    </files>
</extension>
```

This content has the same structure as seen in *Chapter 2* in the *Creating a manifest file* section. You may notice, though, that in the <extension> section, we have replaced the type with the plugin keyword and we have also added the group property to set the plugin folder to which our plugin belongs.

In our <files> section, in this case, we only provide the main file of our plugin, spm.php. In the <filename> subsection, we need to define the plugin property with the name of our plugin. In our case, it is spm.

Once we have our manifest, we can create our plugin main file, which, as you may have guessed, will be at src/plugins/webservice/spm/spm.php and it will have the following content:

```php
<?php

use Joomla\CMS\Plugin\CMSPlugin;
use Joomla\Router\Route;

class PlgWebservicesSpm extends CMSPlugin
{
    public function onBeforeApiRoute(&$router)
    {
        $router->createCRUDRoutes(
            'v1/projects',
            'projects',
            ['component' > 'com_spm']
        );
    }
}
```

This PHP code creates the Plugin class for the Web Service and injects the API endpoints using the onBeforeApiRoute() method. Joomla! will call this method when receiving an API call to add the endpoint to the possible routes.

We need to use the createCRUDRoutes() method for every endpoint we want to add to our Web Service. This method simplifies the creation of endpoints as it handles the most common scenarios when creating an API route. Let's see it in detail in the next section.

Using createCRUDRoutes() to add our Web Service endpoints

The createCRUDRoutes() method registers the four basic types of possible HTTP requests to the system for the projects endpoint (GET, POST, PATCH, and DELETE).

In this method, we pass four different arguments:

- The endpoint we want to add to our API: v1/projects in the preceding code
- The name of the controller that will handle the request: projects
- The name of the component and other relevant options in the URL
- A true/false value indicating whether the endpoint requires authorization (this is true by default)

For the name of the component and other relevant options, we pass an array where the name of the option is the key, and the value of the element is the value of the array. In our example, this is ['component' => 'com_spm'].

A good example to demonstrate this parameter is when we want to create the endpoint for our project categories. In that case, we will add the following code to the onBeforeApiRouter() method:

```
$router->createCRUDRoutes(
    v1/projects/categories',
    'categories',
    ['component' => 'com_categories', 'extension' =>
      'com_spm'],
    true
);
```

In this code, you can see how we pass the 'extension' => 'com_spm' option to get only the categories from our component.

It is worth explaining a bit more about the last parameter of the createCRUDRoutes() method. We have seen in the previous sections how restrictive Joomla! is by default regarding the API authorization: only available to super users by default, and we need to allow permissions to the user groups. But when you are defining your own endpoints, you have the option to make them completely public just by using this last parameter. When this authorization parameter is set to false, the requests to your endpoint will be available to anyone consuming the endpoint.

This simplifies the creation of endpoints a lot, but what if we want to offer just the GET request for our endpoints? In this case, we need to add the request endpoints one by one using a different method. In the next section, we will see how to add a custom endpoint request to our Web Service.

Adding custom endpoint requests to our Web Service

The `createCRUDRoutes()` method is great because it handles most common scenarios when adding an API endpoint, but its downside is that it implements the four HTTP request verbs for the endpoint. So what happens when we only want to have a GET endpoint?

In that scenario, we need to implement every one of the endpoint requests using the `Joomla\CMS\Route` class.

For our invoices in the spm component, we will only allow checking them, and we will not allow editing or creating them from the API.

In that case, the `createCRUDRoutes()` does not fit our needs. So, we add this code to our `onBeforeApiRoute()` method:

```
$route = new Route(
            ['GET'],
            'v1/invoices',
            'invoices.displayItem',
            ['id' => '(\d+)'],
            ['component' => 'com_spm']
        );
$router->addRoute($route);
```

This code is a bit more complex than the previous `createCRUDRoutes()` method, but it gives us more control of the endpoint we are adding. Let's see the arguments we need for the Route class:

- `['GET']`: The first parameter is an array with all the methods our endpoint supports. In this case, we pass only the GET method to allow retrieving the data.
- `v1/invoices`: This is the endpoint for our API.
- `invoice.displayItem`: In this third parameter, we set the controller and the method that will handle this endpoint.
- `['id' '> '(\d+)']`: This parameter sets the rules to process the URL of our endpoint. This is usually a regular expression to detect variables in the URL. In this case, we indicate that there will be an `id` parameter that will match that specific regular expression (an integer).
- `['component' => 'com_spm']`: Finally, we add default variables for the route, such as the name of our component.

If we want to add another type of request, we just need to copy the preceding code and set the proper verb for the endpoint. In our component, we will allow the creation of invoices from the Web Service API. For that, we could use the same endpoint and just make the distinction in the type of request. Just under the previous code, add this block:

```
$route = new Route(
            ['POST'],
            'v1/invoices',
            'invoices.add',
            [],
            ['component' => 'com_spm']
        );
$router->addRoute($route);
```

This code is very similar to the previous one. We have just replaced the type of request with POST and adjusted the method that is handling our request, using the add method from the invoice controller. In this case, there is no need to set the rules for the request, so we leave the fourth parameter as an empty array.

Once we have defined our endpoints, we need to instruct Joomla! on how to handle the request received on these endpoints. Let's see how we can do that in the next section.

Handling the request in our component

When Joomla! receives the request on one of the endpoints, it passes the request to the Web Service API controller to handle it.

The Web Service uses its own architecture to handle the requests, so this API controller is not the same as the one we created for the backend of our component or the frontend of our component. We need to create a new context for our code. We are going to add this new context inside the src/component/api/components/com_spm/src/ folder in our code repository. Inside this folder, we replicate the code structure of the other contexts so we need to create the following folders:

- src/component/api/components/com_spm/src/Controller
- src/component/api/components/com_spm/src/View

This code structure looks very similar to the frontend and backend code structure and basically means that Joomla! keeps the MVC philosophy in the Web Service API.

We also need to reflect these changes in our component manifest file. So, edit the src/component/spm.xml file and add a new <api> section with the following content:

```
<api>
    <files folder="api/components/com_spm">
        <folder>src</folder>
```

```
    </files>
  </api>
```

Reading data from your Web Service – adding a GET endpoint to your component

Let's start creating `ProjectsController` to get the list of projects in our database. Please create the `src/component/api/components/com_spm/src/Controller/ProjectsController.php` file with the following content:

```php
<?php
namespace Piedpiper\Component\Spm\Api\Controller;
use Joomla\CMS\MVC\Controller\ApiController;
class ProjectsController extends ApiController
{
    protected $contentType = 'Projects';
    protected $default_view = 'Projects';
}
```

In this code, we indicate the namespace for our Web Service controller, and we create the class that handles its logic. We extend Joomla's `ApiController` class, which will save us lots of coding as this class already provides the basic methods such as `displayList()` and `add()`.

Inside the class, we need to define the `$contentType` and `$default_view` variables with the name of our data entity (`Projects`).

We are not adding any methods right now to the controller as the `ApiController` class takes care of all we need.

After this, we create the view for our projects. So, create the `src/component/api/components/com_spm/src/View/Projects/JsonapiView.php` file with the following content:

```php
<?php
  namespace Piedpiper\Component\Spm\Api\View\Projects;
  use Joomla\CMS\MVC\View\JsonApiView as BaseApiView;
  class JsonapiView extends BaseApiView
{
    protected $fieldsToRenderList = [
      'id',
      'title'
      ];
}
```

In this code, after setting up the namespace for the Web Service API view, we extend `JsonApiView` from Joomla! – again, to take advantage of the code reuse from the framework. The class for our view needs to be named `JsonapiView` as that is the class that Joomla is going to look for. So, to avoid confusion with the `JsonApiView` class we extend from Joomla! code, we use the alias `BaseApiView` when declaring the namespace usage.

Once in the class code, we only need to declare `$fieldsToRenderList` as an array containing the name of the fields from the `#__projects` table we want to include in our response.

And that's all!! With these simple files, you have added a `GET` endpoint to your Joomla! extension and you can get the list of projects from the list using the `get.php` script we coded at the beginning of the chapter. So just adjust the URL and your token to the script and execute it. You will see the list of projects on your site as a result.

We have not coded the model for the projects in the Web Service API. Joomla! Web Service implementation relies on the backend code structure of your extension. As in *Chapter 2*, we developed a model for the backend part of our component, and the Web Service relies on it to get the items from the database.

When using the `createCRUDRoutes()` method, Joomla! automatically creates the endpoints for the list and the individual items, so we can retrieve any project in our system using the `v1/projects/1` endpoint. This endpoint is routed through `ProjectsController` we have just created, and we only need to add a protected property to the `src/component/api/components/com_spm/src/View/Projects/JsonapiView.php` file we just created. So, please add this property:

```
protected $fieldsToRenderItem = [
    'id',
    'title',
    'description'
];
```

This property instructs Joomla! on the fields that should be shown from `ProjectsModel` when displaying a single item through the Web Service.

Writing data from your Web Service – adding a POST endpoint to your component

We have defined two endpoints so far: the `v1/invoices` and `v1/projects` endpoints. For both endpoints, we have enabled the `POST` request type so that users can create projects (implicit when using the `createCRUDRoutes()` method) and invoices (we explicitly added the `POST` route in our `WebServices` plugin).

In the previous section, we already added the controller to handle projects. The Joomla! Framework™ is really useful when we abide by its structure and you may just try to create a project using the POST request. We can test this by creating a post.php script as we did with the get.php script. So, create the Scripts/api/post.php file with the following content:

```php
<?php
if (extension_loaded('curl') == false) {
    throw new \Exception('curl not installed');
}
$url = 'https://YourSite.com/api/v1/projects/';
$data = array(
    'title' => 'Testing API',
    'alias' => 'testing-api',
    'description' => 'We are testing our API on this
      project.'
);
$connection = curl_init($url);
curl_setopt($connection, CURLOPT_RETURNTRANSFER, true);
curl_setopt($connection, CURLOPT_URL, $url);
curl_setopt($connection, CURLOPT_POST, true);
curl_setopt($connection, CURLOPT_POSTFIELDS,
  http_build_query($data));
$response = curl_exec($connection);
curl_close($connection);
if ($response === false) {
    echo 'Error: ' . curl_error($connection);
} else {
    echo 'Project created!';
}
```

In this PHP script, we are using the PHP curl library to send the POST request to our site. The main difference with the get.php script is that we now need to include the data we want to use to create our project.

We do not need to worry about the model as Joomla! will use the model we defined to manage projects in the administrator folder. For the view, Joomla! will use the view we created in the previous section to handle the response.

As for the invoices, we now just need to create the controller and the view as we did in the previous section, and we will have our Web Service API ready to add projects and invoices.

Summary

In this chapter, we have extended our component with a Web Service API. This will allow us to create further automations and integrations with other sites on the internet. We learned about the basics of any Web Service and how we can consume a Web Service API. We saw how easy it is to create a secure Web Service with Joomla! using the provided token authorization and we developed our first Joomla! plugin to create the endpoints for our Web Service. Finally, we connected these endpoints with our component logic to get the proper responses.

This chapter finished the first part of the book in which we learned all the basics of developing a modern Joomla! component. In the next part of the book, we will cover other types of extensions we can code for Joomla!. Specifically, in the next chapter, we will see how we can create a companion module for our component to show information to our customers.

Further reading

- Check the full list of HTTP request methods here: `https://developer.mozilla.org/en-US/docs/Web/HTTP/Methods`

- You can check the PHP cURL help page to learn more about how to use it: `https://www.php.net/manual/en/book.curl.php`

- At the Joomla! developers documentation site, there are some examples of the Web Services API: `https://manual.joomla.org/docs/general-concepts/webservices`

Part 2: Developing Modules and Plugins

Modules and plugins might seem like components' little siblings, but they are really powerful and can perform great tasks. Modules help you display information on your site using less code than components. Plugins offer you a way to hook into Joomla! and other extensions' lifecycles and inject your own code.

This part has the following chapters:

- *Chapter 7, Developing a Module*
- *Chapter 8, Developing a Joomla! Plugin*
- *Chapter 9, Adding a CLI to Your Extension*

7
Developing a Module

In previous chapters, we developed a fully featured component that allows us to add and retrieve information from our database with ease.

With our component, we can show information in a page view, and we can even consume this data using a Web Service. But, what if we need to show selected data along with other component views on our site? For this, we need to develop a companion module for our component.

Joomla! modules are a simple way to show data in any position on your site. As they can be added to any available positions in the template and can also be loaded using shortcodes in your content, they are the most versatile option to show information.

In this chapter, we will learn how to develop a companion module for our component that will show the list of projects we are working on, and you will have a better understanding of the new Joomla! Dependency Injection pattern we started to learn about in *Chapter 2*. When we address the module file structure, you will see that Joomla! module development is quite similar to component development and how the MVC pattern is now fully integrated into modules.

After finishing this chapter, you will be able to develop any kind of module you need to show any kind of information (related to your component or not) on your website.

We will follow this path to make it happen:

- Understanding the module file structure
- Using module configuration parameters
- Using module helpers

Technical requirements

In this chapter, we will keep improving our Simple Project Manager extension so you will require the following:

- Visual Studio Code (or the code editor of your preference)
- The Joomla! site we installed in the previous chapters

You'll find all the code used in this chapter on GitHub: `https://github.com/PacktPublishing/Developing-Extensions-for-Joomla-5/tree/chapter07`

Understanding the module file structure

Modules in Joomla! are inside the `modules` folder of our site. In any typical Joomla! installation, this folder is full of folders that belong to the modules. These folder names start with the prefix `mod_` to emphasize they are a module. This is not a rule when naming our modules, but Joomla! will add the prefix to the folder name if not present.

Since Joomla! 4, the module architecture has been the same as the component architecture.

So, when calling a module, Joomla! will look for the `provider.php` file inside the service modules. In the `provider.php` file, we will register the services we need in our module.

After registering our services, Joomla! looks for our module's `Dispatcher.php` file, which will be inside the `src/Dispatcher/` folder of our module. We will need a folder structure as follows:

- `services`: This folder contains the `provider.php` file. This file is like `src/component/admin/services/provider.php`, and it's used to register our module into Joomla!. It's actually the first file that Joomla! will look for when executing our module.
- `src`: This contains our module code, correctly organized in different folders. We may find here the `Dispatcher` folder or the `Helper` folder.
- `tmpl`: This contains different layout files for our module. It's common to have at least one `default.php` file with our layout.

These folders contain the new architecture of modules in Joomla!. Let's go through each of them to see how the modules work in Joomla!.

Creating the provider code

In Joomla! architecture, the provider's importance is paramount. As it happened with components, the `provider` file gets the **Dependency Injection Container** (**DIC**) and registers the different services to use in our module.

Add the following code to the `src/module/mod_projectslist/services/provider.php` file:

```php
<?php

use Joomla\CMS\Extension\Service\Provider\HelperFactory;
use Joomla\CMS\Extension\Service\Provider\Module;
use Joomla\CMS\Extension\Service\Provider\
  ModuleDispatcherFactory;
use Joomla\DI\Container;
use Joomla\DI\ServiceProviderInterface;

return new class () implements ServiceProviderInterface {
    public function register(Container $container)
    {
        $container->registerServiceProvider(new
          ModuleDispatcherFactory('\\Piedpiper\\Module
            \\ProjectsList'));
        $container->registerServiceProvider(new
          HelperFactory('\\Piedpiper\\Module\\ProjectsList
            \\Site\\Helper'));
        $container->registerServiceProvider(new Module());
    }
};
```

In this code, the provider returns an anonymous PHP class (exactly as it happens with components) in which we are registering the following services:

- `ModuleDispatcherFactory`: This registers our dispatcher namespace into the container

- `HelperFactory`: This registers the namespace where your helper classes live (we can omit it if we are not using helper classes)

- `Module`: This initializes the module provider in the container

These are the basic steps for Joomla! to start working with our module, but we still need to write the module code. We will do so in the dispatcher, so let's create the `src/module/mod_projectslist/src/Dispatcher/Dispatcher.php` file with the following code:

```php
<?php

namespace Piedpiper\Module\ProjectsList\Site\Dispatcher;
use Joomla\CMS\Dispatcher\AbstractModuleDispatcher;
use Joomla\CMS\Helper\HelperFactoryAwareInterface;
```

```
use Joomla\CMS\Helper\HelperFactoryAwareTrait;

class Dispatcher extends AbstractModuleDispatcher
  implements HelperFactoryAwareInterface
{
    use HelperFactoryAwareTrait;
    protected function getLayoutData()
    {
        $data = parent::getLayoutData();
        $data['projects'] = $this->getHelperFactory()->
          getHelper('ProjectsListHelper')->
            getProjects($data['params'], $this->
              getApplication());
        return $data;
    }
}
```

First, we define the namespace for our module dispatcher. This helps Joomla! find our module dispatcher. Then, we declare the namespaces we use in our code.

In our module, we are going to use helper classes to perform some operations and have a more modular code, so we need to declare the `HelperFactoryAware` namespaces.

The only method we need in our class is the `getLayoutData()` method, which will retrieve our project list and return it.

This method is where we can see the benefits of using Joomla! CMS™ classes and `HelperFactoryAware` classes, as it allows us to get the list of projects with one line of code.

In that line, we retrieve the helper class for our module, and we use the `getProjects()` method to get the data.

Since Joomla! 4, the use of helpers has been of great importance in our developments, and especially in modules, to have clean and easy-to-read code. Let's see how to work with helpers in our modules in the next section.

Using module helpers

Joomla! module architecture relies on the `getLayoutData()` method from the dispatcher to process the information that we will display in the module.

We could place all our logic inside this method and let it grow to whatever size we need, but that will make our code break lots of coding principles, such as **DRY** (short for **Don't Repeat Yourself**), single responsibility, and more.

As module helpers are a core part of Joomla! Module classes, we should take advantage of them and work with helper classes that lead to cleaner code.

Following the `Dispatcher.php` code from the previous section, there was a call to the module helper. Now, we need to create the code for our helper, so we create the `src/module/mod_projectslist/src/Helper/ProjectsListHelper.php` file with the following content:

```php
<?php
namespace Piedpiper\Module\ProjectsList\Site\Helper;

use Piedpiper\Component\Spm\Site\Model\ProjectsModel;
use Joomla\CMS\Application\SiteApplication;
use Joomla\CMS\Component\ComponentHelper;
use Joomla\CMS\Factory;
use Joomla\Registry\Registry;

class ProjectsListHelper
{
    public function getProjects(Registry $params,
      SiteApplication $app)
    {
        $model = $app->bootComponent('com_spm')->
          getMVCFactory()->createModel('Projects', 'Site',
            ['ignore_request' => true]);

        $model->setState('params', $app->getParams());

        $items = $model->getItems();

        return $items;
    }
}
```

In this code, we define the namespace for our helper. Then, we register all the rest of the namespaces we are going to use.

The first namespace we register is the namespace of `ProjectsModel`. This is because we are using our actual site component model to get the list of projects. This way, we do not need to rewrite the query to retrieve the projects and can use all the filters defined in our model.

In fact, we start the `getProjects()` method by instantiating the `ProjectsModel` class. In Joomla!, we use the `bootComponent()` method from the `Application` class to initialize our components. This allows us to get the model we need from the component.

Once we have the component, we add some context to it using the `setState()` method and, finally, we call the `getItems()` method to get the list of projects.

With this helper, we return the list of projects to the dispatcher, and we will see in the next section how to format our data using the Joomla! layouts system.

Adding the layout for the module

Once we have the data we want to display, we can display it. As we are extending `AbstractModuleDispatcher` to create the dispatcher for our module, we only need to create the default layout inside the `tmpl` folder. So we create the `src/module/mod_projectslist/tmpl/default.php` file and we initialize it with this simple code:

```
<ul class="mod-projects-list">
<?php foreach ($projects as $item) : ?>
    <li>
        <?php echo $item->name; ?>
    </li>
<?php endforeach; ?>
</ul>
```

This code will show an unordered HTML list where each item of the list will be the name of one of our projects.

It's interesting to note that we retrieve our projects from the `$projects` variable. This is the name of the key we used to store our list of projects in the preceding dispatcher (`$data['projects']`).

Writing the manifest for our module

To install our module and use it in Joomla!, we need to create a manifest file. This file is like the one we already wrote for our component in *Chapter 2*, with some differences that we are going to address in this section.

The manifest file for our module is an XML file, and it contains all the data Joomla! needs to install and configure the module.

Let's create the `src/module/mod_projectslist/mod_projectslist.xml` file with the following content:

```
<?xml version="1.0" encoding="UTF-8"?>
<extension type="module" client="site" method="upgrade">
    <name>MOD_SPM_PROJECTSLIST</name>
    <author><![CDATA[Carlos Cámara]]></author>
    <authorEmail>carlos@hepta.es</authorEmail>
    <authorUrl>extensions.hepta.es</authorUrl>
```

```
<creationDate>2022-07-21</creationDate>
<copyright>(C) 2022 Piedpiper Inc.</copyright>
<license>GNU General Public License version 2 or later;
   see LICENSE.txt</license>
<version>0.1.0</version>
<description><![CDATA[MOD_SPM_PROJECTSLIST
   _DESCRIPTION]]></description>
<namespace path="src">Piedpiper\Module\ProjectsList
   </namespace>
<files>
    <folder module="mod_projectslist">services</folder>
    <folder>src</folder>
    <folder>tmpl</folder>
</files>
<languages>
    <language tag="en-GB">language/en-GB/
       mod_projectslist.ini</language>
    <language tag="en-GB">language/en-GB/
       mod_projectslist.sys.ini</language>
</languages>
</extension>
```

In this XML code, we cover all the metadata related to our module using XML tags, such as <name>, <author>, or <license>.

We use capital letters for the language labels to show that they are translatable. We will use them as keys for the module name and description in our translation.

With the tag, we tell Joomla! the namespace for our module and Joomla! will now know where to find our Module classes.

In this section, we define the folders of our module and we explicitly tell Joomla! to relate our services folder with the module, adding the module property to its tag.

Finally, we add our language files to the manifest. In this case, we are adding the English translation, so we also need to create these files.

So, create the src/module/mod_projectslist/language/en-GB/ folder and add the mod_projectslist.ini and mod_projectslist.sys.ini language files, and we then add the translation for the language strings we have already added to the module:

```
MOD_SPM_PROJECTSLIST="Projects List"
MOD_SPM_PROJECTSLIST_DESCRIPTION="A simple projects list
   module to show projects of the Simple Project List
   component"
```

The language translation system is the same as seen in *Chapter 5*.

Once we have created the manifest file, we can package our code in a ZIP file and install it into Joomla!. As it is right now, our module only serves one purpose – to show the list of projects in a specific order – so let's add some configuration parameters to make it more flexible in the next section.

Using module configuration parameters

When you start using the module, you may notice it can serve several purposes. You could, for instance, use the module to display all the projects that you are working on, on a home page. Or you may use it to show the projects related to a specific customer.

Sometimes you would like to show only three projects, and other times you may want to change the ordering of the list. Developing the same module and changing the database query is not practical, and we will not respect the DRY principle as we will have the same code but a different limit for the list query.

So, let's give our module some parameters that our users can change to make the module fit their needs. To add parameters to our module configuration, we need to create a new section in the XML manifest file following the form definition we saw in *Chapter 4*.

Following the first paragraph of this section, let's create the following parameters:

- **Customers**: This will be a multi-select dropdown where we can choose from a list of customers

- **Maximum projects to show**: This will be a textbox to input an integer

- **Ordering**: This will be a drop-down selection where we will have three options: newest, oldest, and random

We can start adding the following `<config>` section to the manifest file located in `src/module/ mod_projectslist/mod_projectslist.xml`, just before closing our tag:

```xml
<config>
    <fields name="params">
        <fieldset name="basic">
            <field name="customer"
                type="sql"
                label="MOD_SPM_PROJECTSLIST_CONFIG_CUSTOMER_LABEL"
                description="MOD_SPM_PROJECTSLIST_CONFIG
                _CUSTOMER_DESCRIPTION"
                header="MOD_SPM_PROJECTSLIST_CONFIG_CUSTOMER_ALL"
                multiple="multiple"
                sql_select="id, CONCAT(firstname, ' ',
                    lastname) AS name"
                sql_from="#__spm_customers"
```

```
                    key_field="id"
                    value_field="name"
                    sql_order="lastname ASC"
                />
            </fieldset>
        </fields>
    </config>
```

In this code, we have defined the `<config>` section of the manifest file. Inside this section, we see a `<fields>` section where we will define the tabs of the `Configuration` area. The first tab will be a `<fieldset>` subsection of this called `basic`. Finally, we define our first field. This is an SQL field to get our customers' data and show it in the selection. We have defined this field as `multiple` to allow showing projects of different customers. Also, to make it easier for the module users, we show the customers ordered by their last name.

For the `total` field, we include the following code in our `fieldset` subsection:

```
<field name="total"
                type="number"
                label="MOD_SPM_PROJECTSLIST_CONFIG
                    _TOTAL_LABEL"
                description="MOD_SPM_PROJECTSLIST_CONFIG_
                    TOTAL_DESCRIPTION"
                default="5"
                filter="integer"
                min="1" max="5"
                validate="number"
            />
```

We are only allowing 5 projects per listing and that will be the default too, so we set the `max` field to be sure our users respect this limit.

Finally, the `ordering` field is a simple list field with `newest` as the default value to show the latest projects. So, we add it to the fieldset:

```
<field name="ordering" type="list"
    label="MOD_SPM_PROJECTSLIST_CONFIG_ORDERING_LABEL"
    description="MOD_SPM_PROJECTSLIST_CONFIG_ORDERING_DESC"
    default="newest"
>
    <option value="newest">
        MOD_SPM_PROJECTSLIST_CONFIG_ORDERING_OPTION_NEWEST
    </option>
    <option value="oldest">
        MOD_SPM_PROJECTSLIST_CONFIG_ORDERING_OPTION_OLDEST
```

```
        </option>
        <option value="random">
            MOD_SPM_PROJECTSLIST_CONFIG_ORDERING_OPTION_RANDOM
        </option>
    </field>
```

We include three options for the list, and `newest` will be the option by default.

There are lots of strings in this `Configuration` section, so let's add the translations to our `src/module/language/en-GB/mod_projectslist.ini` file:

```
; Configuration
MOD_SPM_PROJECTSLIST_CONFIG_CUSTOMER_LABEL="Customer's
  Project"
MOD_SPM_PROJECTSLIST_CONFIG_CUSTOMER_DESCRIPTION="Show
  projects of the selected customers"
MOD_SPM_PROJECTSLIST_CONFIG_CUSTOMER_ALL="All"
MOD_SPM_PROJECTSLIST_CONFIG_TOTAL_LABEL="Max projects"
MOD_SPM_PROJECTSLIST_CONFIG_TOTAL_DESCRIPTION="This will
  limit the maximum number of projects to show. A maximum
    of 5 projects is allowed."
MOD_SPM_PROJECTSLIST_CONFIG_ORDERING_LABEL="List ordering"
MOD_SPM_PROJECTSLIST_CONFIG_ORDERING_DESC="Choose how do
  you want to order the projects on the list"
MOD_SPM_PROJECTSLIST_CONFIG_ORDERING_OPTION_NEWEST="Newest
  projects first"
MOD_SPM_PROJECTSLIST_CONFIG_ORDERING_OPTION_OLDEST="Oldest
  projects first"
MOD_SPM_PROJECTSLIST_CONFIG_ORDERING_OPTION_RANDOM="Show
  projects in random order"
```

After adding the translations to the language file, we can access the module configuration and we will see our parameters to configure the module. You may notice the `Configuration` area with our parameters is located in the first tab of our module and there is no **Advanced** tab as in the rest of the modules of Joomla! core.

The **Advanced** tab is not needed when developing a Joomla! module, but it's present in all core Joomla! modules and most developers use it in their modules, so it's a nice-to-have feature for our users. Let's see how we can add it in the next section.

Adding an Advanced tab to our module configuration

As the main purpose of a module is to display content, we can expect it to have a direct relation with the template of our Joomla! site. In the end, Joomla! will get all the module layout content and plug it into the specific position of the template.

To provide further flexibility, all Joomla! core modules offer an **Advanced** tab at the module configuration where you can configure some specifics on how you want to display your module.

These settings are usually related to how the template shows the information, so you might expect it to not be present in all scenarios. But as a matter of fact, most Joomla! developers have adapted these settings as a de facto standard and it's a good idea to offer them in our module configuration.

To add these parameters to our current configuration, we need to include a new subsection inside our section, so let's add this code to the `src/module/mod_projectslist/mod_projectslist.xml` file before the closing tag:

```
<fieldset name="advanced">
    <field
        name="layout"
        type="modulelayout"
        label="JFIELD_ALT_LAYOUT_LABEL"
        class="form-select"
        validate="moduleLayout"
    />
    <field
        name="moduleclass_sfx"
        type="textarea"
        label="COM_MODULES_FIELD_MODULECLASS_SFX_LABEL"
        rows="3"
        validate="CssIdentifier"
    />
    <field
        name="cache"
        type="list"
        label="COM_MODULES_FIELD_CACHING_LABEL"
        default="1"
        filter="integer"
        validate="options"
        >
        <option value="1">JGLOBAL_USE_GLOBAL</option>
        <option value="0">COM_MODULES_FIELD_VALUE_NOCACHING
            </option>
    </field>
    <field
```

```
            name="cache_time"
            type="number"
            label="COM_MODULES_FIELD_CACHE_TIME_LABEL"
            default="900"
            filter="integer"
        />
    </fieldset>
```

This addition adds the following parameters to the **Advanced** tab of our module configuration:

- **Layout**: Users may specify here a different layout file for our module in case we offer more than the default layout or they create an override.

- **Module class suffix**: When modules are displayed in the template, they are wrapped inside an HTML element with a specific class determined by the template. The parameter also may include a CSS class to allow better module styling. This parameter allows us to add a suffix to the default class.

- **Cache**: This parameter sets whether Joomla should use the configured cached system when displaying this module. It's definitely a nice option to offer to our users.

- **Cache time**: This parameter sets how often the module should refresh its cache.

- **Cache mode**: This last parameter is actually hidden for the user, but we need to specify it to set the type of caching for the module. We will see a bit more about caching in the next section.

For these parameters, we do not need to add any translation to our language files as we are using generic key strings already present in Joomla!.

Caching Joomla! modules

The last three parameters we have added to our advanced configuration are related to the Joomla! cache. For modules, when using this Joomla! module architecture, you do not need to worry about calling any caching methods from Joomla! CMS classes.

Just by adding these parameters, Joomla! will take care of all the needed steps to provide cached content for the modules.

For modules, we have four cache modes that we can use in Joomla!:

- `static`: This mode caches all the modules of the same type by their parameters, so different module instances of the same module with the same parameters will share their cache. It also allows you to have the same module type several times on the same URL without sharing their cache information, so in case of doubt, it's a safe default mode to use for modules.

- `id`: This mode caches the modules by their unique internal ID. That means that two different instances of the same module are not going to share a cache.

- `itemid`: This cache mode allows different caches per menu item (`itemid`). That means the same module instance in different pages will create its own cache file.

- `safeuri`: This mode creates a different cache file per combination of some parameters of the URL and it's usually used to show modules whose content changes according to the item we are browsing.

We have created a very flexible module according to our configuration, but so far, these parameters do not change our module behavior by themselves. Now, we need to instruct the module to retrieve and honor them in the code.

Using saved parameters in your code

Adding the `Configuration` area for our module has been easy using Joomla! CMS capabilities. Now, we need to read the module configuration in our code to reflect the changes in the resulting projects list.

The module configuration settings are available in the `Dispatcher.php` module as the `params` property of `$this->module`. This property returns the module settings as a `Registry` object encoded as a JSON string. As we are using the `Registry` class, we need to add the proper namespace to the dispatcher, so please add this line to your namespaces declaration in the `src/modules/mod_projectslist/src/Dispatcher/Dispatcher.php` file:

```
Use Joomla\Registry\Registry;
```

Then, you may plug this code in the `getLayoutData()` method of the dispatcher file:

```
$settings = new Registry($this->module->params);
dump($settings);
```

This code will retrieve the module configuration, create a `Registry` object, and show it in a nicely formatted dump message.

But actually, we do not need to do that because, inside `getLayoutData()`, we call the parent class with `$data = parent::getLayoutData()` at the beginning and this call initializes the `$data` array with the following parameters:

```
[
    'module'   => $this->module,
    'app'      => $this->app,
    'input'    => $this->input,
    'params'   => new Registry($this->module->params),
    'template' => $this->app->getTemplate(),
];
```

These are all the parameters that are relevant to our module, so we can use just the $data array from now on.

If we carefully check the call to our helper in getLayoutData(), we notice we are passing $data['params'] to our module helper to get the list of projects:

```
$data['projects'] = $this->getHelperFactory()->
    getHelper('ProjectsListHelper')->
    getProjects($data['params'], $this->getApplication());
```

Most of our settings affect only the way we get the projects list, so let's go to where we get the list of projects and let's use the parameters there. Let's start setting the total number of projects to show. For this, we edit the src/module/src/Helper/Helper.php file, and before getting the items, we add the following line:

```
$model->setState('list.limit', (int) $params->get('total',
    5));
```

This line will save the number of items in the running state and as we are using our Site Projects Model, it will be set in the database query at the getListQuery() method from src/component/site/src/Model/ProjectsModel.php.

To add the ordering setting, we need to add some more code. First of all, we are going to use the database classes to get the database random setting. In Joomla!, we can get the database object in our classes by implementing DatabaseAwareInterface, so we need to modify a bit our class definition and we also need to use a couple of extra namespaces. So, let's replace the line with our class definition with these lines:

```
use Joomla\Database\DatabaseAwareInterface;
use Joomla\Database\DatabaseAwareTrait;

class ProjectsListHelper implements DatabaseAwareInterface
```

Now, in our getProjects() method, we can add the following code just after setting the list. limit state from the previous paragraph:

```
switch ($params->get('ordering', '')) {
    case 'random':
        $db = $this->getDatabase();
        $ordering = $db->getQuery(true)->rand();
        break;
    case 'oldest':
        $ordering = 'a.created ASC';
        break;
    case 'newest':
```

```
      default:
          $ordering = 'a.created DESC';
  }
  $model->setState('list.ordering', $ordering);
  $model->setState('list.direction', '');
```

We cannot use the values of the `ordering` parameters directly in our database (remember, they were `newest`, `oldest`, and `random`) as they make no sense, so in this code, we populate the `$ordering` variable with the proper database code to get our projects in the right order. For the random case, we use the `getDatabase()` method to get the `Database` object, which provides a means to get the `rand()` method to create our random ordering.

We use the `newest` case as the default case, and we have added it to the code for clarity, but you may remove the case line and just leave the default line.

Once we have the `$ordering` variable properly set, we just inject its value into the model state.

You may wonder why we need to set the `'list.direction'` parameter. Well, as we are using our component site model, that parameter gets populated with `'ASC'`, so we need to clear it as we are already including direction in the `'list.ordering'` parameter.

Finally, we restrict the projects list by customer. So, we need to add the following code after the previous one:

```
$model->setState('filter.customer', (int) $params->
   get('customers', 0));
```

At this point, it is worth checking that our `getListQuery()` method checks for all these state variables. For this, we can go to the `src/component/site/src/Model/ProjectsModel.php` file and check that the following code exists:

```
$orderCol  = $this->state->get('list.ordering', 'a.name
   ASC');
```

This code gets the `ordering` state from the model and sets it into the query, so if it's not present, the state means nothing.

We also need this code:

```
$id_customer = $this->state->get('filter.customer', 0);
if ($id_customer) {
    $query->where(
            $db->quoteName('a.id_customer')
            . ' = ' . (int) $id_customer
    );
}
```

This code gets the value of the `customer` state variable and if it's a positive number, it restricts the query to these customers.

Summary

In this chapter, we have developed our first module using the Joomla! architecture. We looked at how Joomla! uses this new architecture to dispatch the module. We have learned how to create the manifest file for the module and how to add configuration parameters to the manifest file. We have created the English language files for the module and we have set them in the manifest. We have learned about standard module settings that are present in most of Joomla! core modules and how to add them to our module. Finally, we have learned how to use the configuration settings in our module code to have a more flexible display.

In *Chapter 8, Developing a Joomla! Plugin*, we will see again the Joomla! architecture in action and the differences in the manifest file for plugins. You will learn about the Joomla! plugin system and see how to use Joomla! events and how to add your events to the component. I will guide you in the process of developing a Joomla! plugin that will take your project to the next level.

Further reading

There is a nice article in *Joomla! Community Magazine* describing module configuration options here: `https://magazine.joomla.org/all-issues/december-2021/explore-the-core-a-look-into-the-advanced-parameters-from-modules`

8

Developing a Joomla! Plugin

Joomla! plugins are a powerful tool to modify the webpage of any site. Indeed, even the basic Joomla! installation comes packed with several plugins that extend a site's capabilities.

In this chapter, we will learn these plugins are such powerful tools for our development work. We will see how Joomla! plugins are grouped into different families and types for better organization. We will learn what plugin events are and how we can add them to our component. We will also understand the basic file structure for any plugin and will create the manifest file to register our plugins into Joomla! and add some configuration parameters. Finally, we will create a content plugin for our extension to show our project's information inside an article.

By the end of this chapter, you will understand how plugins work in Joomla! and you will be able to create your own Joomla! plugins to extend Joomla's capabilities or to add more features to your own developed components.

Plugins allow you to create premium features for your components or interact with other parts of a Joomla! site without modifying any existing code. Often, Joomla! plugins do not need a layout or any visual representation, but they can completely change the Joomla! output. For instance, you could use them to obfuscate email addresses shown on your site to prevent bots from using them; change the color of specific words; or even completely replace the text to be shown. It's a good idea therefore to use plugins as your first option for a project as they give you more effective ways of finding solutions.

These are the main topics we will cover in this chapter:

- What is a plugin in Joomla!?

- What families of plugins are there in Joomla!?

- Understanding Joomla's plugin file structure

- Creating the manifest file for our plugins

- Creating a content plugin

Technical requirements

In this chapter, we will work on improving our Simple Project Manager extension, so you will require the following:

- Visual Studio Code (or the code editor of your preference)

- The Joomla! site we installed in the previous chapters

You'll find all the code used in this chapter on GitHub: `https://github.com/PacktPublishing/Developing-Extensions-for-Joomla-5/tree/chapter08`

What is a plugin in Joomla!?

Joomla! plugins are the smallest type of extension you can write, but they are also the most powerful. Joomla! plugins are executed in response to certain events in Joomla!. For instance, some plugins are executed upon the creation of a new user. There are lots of events throughout the Joomla! life cycle and we can hook our plugins into each of these events.

Plugins integrate into Joomla's ACL system and you can set different permissions per Joomla's view level. This creates a flexible system that provides website administrators with lots of possibilities.

Joomla! plugins are organized into different groups according to the contexts in which they are used. This categorization allows triggering plugins in specific contexts. We can create more types if we need and we can group our plugins as we think they fit best.

The plugin groups we can find in a Joomla! installation are as follows:

- API Authentication

- Authentication

- Behavior

- Captcha

- Content

- Editors

- Editors-xtd

- Extensions

- Fields

- Filesystem

- Finder

- Installer

- Media Action

- Privacy

- Quick Icons

- Sampledata

- System

- User

- Web Services

- Workflow

In *Chapter 6*, we created a plugin that belongs to the **Web Services** type to create the endpoint router for our API. In the following sections, we are going to develop a **Content** plugin and a **Finder** plugin.

Plugins also have a configuration page out of the box in Joomla!, just like modules. We will also create this page in the manifest file of the plugin, just as we did with the modules.

Before we start developing our plugin, let's see in the next section how we can trigger plugin execution from a component.

Calling Joomla! plugins from our component

Plugins in Joomla! execute when the event they are hooked to is triggered. In our component, we can call these events and thus use plugins to enhance our results.

Actually, as we are following Joomla's MVC pattern in our development, there are some events being triggered that we had not even noticed! In *Chapter 2*, we developed our models by extending Joomla's `Table` class. If we check this class, we can find the following code inside the `store()` method:

```
$this->getDispatcher()->dispatch('onTableBeforeStore',
    $event);
```

This code delegates triggering the event to the current dispatcher. The `event` we call in this code is the `onTableBeforeStore` event that allows us to perform changes on the table row data before saving it to the database.

This is the code you need to dispatch a plugin event in your code. The `dispatch()` method takes two arguments:

- The name of the event we want to trigger

- An `Event` object with the data for your event

The Event object contains all the information the plugin needs to handle the event. This object can easily be created using the following code, where we add all the arguments for our event in the second variable as keys of the array:

```
$event = AbstractEvent::create('NAME OF THE EVENT',
  ['argument1' => 'Value']
```

Calling Joomla! plugins from our component is a nice trick we can use to allow further customization of our components. To see this in action, let's call the onContentPrepare event in our component to allow the user to customize the project descriptions with plugins.

We start editing by the src/component/site/src/View/Project/HtmlView.php file, first adding the AbstractEvent namespace. The namespace declaration looks as follows:

```
<?php
namespace Piedpiper\Component\Spm\Site\View\Project;

use Joomla\CMS\MVC\View\HtmlView as BaseHtmlView;
use Joomla\CMS\MVC\View\GenericDataException;
use Joomla\CMS\Factory;
use Joomla\CMS\Event\AbstractEvent;
use Joomla\CMS\Plugin\PluginHelper;

class HtmlView extends BaseHtmlView
{
...
}
```

The highlighted lines in the preceding code block are the new ones.

After this, we can include our trigger for onContentPrepare in the display() method by adding the following highlighted code:

```
public function display($tpl=null): void
{
    $this->item = $this->get('Item');
    $article       = new \stdClass();
    $article->text = $this->item->description;

    $event = AbstractEvent::create(
        'onContentPrepare',
        [
            'context' => 'com_spm.project',
            'article' => $article
        ];
```

```
    );

    PluginHelper::getPlugin('content', 'projectlink')

    Factory::getApplication()->getDispatcher()->
        dispatch('onContentPrepare', $event);

    $this->item->description = $article->text;

    if (count($errors = $this->get('Errors')))
    {
        throw new GenericDataException(implode("\n",
            $errors), 500);
    }
    parent::display($tpl);
}
```

In this particular example, as the onContentPrepare event is meant to be used for Joomla! articles, we need to adapt our variables to match what content plugins will expect for this method. So in our call, when we define the array with the variables we can use, we pass the $article object with the text property containing the text we want to check for the content.

We call the PluginHelper::getPlugin() method to subscribe our content plugin to Joomla! events. This will allow our content plugin to be called two lines later with the onContentPrepare event.

An easier way of triggering onContentPrepare

Triggering the onContentPrepare event is quite common, and Joomla! offers some helpers to reduce the amount of code in your extensions. So, to trigger this event, we could use the Joomla\CMS\HTML\Helpers\Content::prepare(this->item->description) method instead, which saves us from creating the $article object.

Finally, the content plugins will return the modified text inside the text property of our $article object, so we get it and update our $this->item->description property.

So, when triggering plugins in your code, you just need to import the plugin type, ask the Application to trigger the event you need, and pass all the parameters in the array.

This will be the case for all plugin events that you want to trigger from your component, even the ones you create from scratch for your own projects. Let's see in the next section how we can create different plugin group types and events to add more features to our developments.

Understanding Joomla's plugin file structure

Since Joomla! 4, plugins follow the same architecture as modules and components. The immediate result of this is that Joomla! 4 loads much faster than previous versions of Joomla!. The disadvantage is that we move from a single file structure to the file-and-folder structure we saw in *Chapter 2*, when starting our component, and in *Chapter 7*, when writing our modules.

Our plugins will have the following folder structure:

- `services`: This file contains the `provider.php` file. This registers the plugin copy of the dependency injection container. This means any service injected with our plugin will not be available automatically to other extensions (unless they inject it). This serves the purpose of isolating the plugin from other parts of the Joomla! execution cycle and making sure it does not affect other parts of the framework.

- `src`: This folder contains the classes we use in our plugin, organized in different folders. It can contain as many folders as our namespaces require, but it must at least contain the `Extension` folder with the main plugin file.

- `src/Extension`: This subfolder contains the main file of our plugin along with the different methods to handle the events. The main file will use the same casing as defined in the namespace when they are triggered.

- `tmpl`: When our plugin outputs some HTML code, we use this `tmpl` folder to store the layout of that code. This way, the user will be able to override the design easily.

On top of this, we have a `manifest.xml` file with our plugin definition and settings, as we will see in the next section.

Creating the manifest file for our plugins

Every extension we want to install in Joomla! needs to have a proper manifest file declaring its properties. We already created a manifest file for our component in *Chapter 2* and we created another one for our module in *Chapter 7*. The manifest file for plugins in Joomla! is very similar to the one we created for modules, in the sense that it includes not only the technical details for the extension, but also the configuration parameters (if any) for the plugin.

A basic manifest file looks as follows:

```xml
<?xml version="1.0" encoding="UTF-8"?>
<extension type="plugin" group="PluginType"
    method="upgrade">
    <name>plg_PluginType_PluginName</name>
    <author>Carlos Cámara</author>
    <creationDate>2023-05</creationDate>
    <copyright>(C) 2023 Piedpiper, Inc.</copyright>
```

```xml
        <license>GNU General Public License version 2 or later;
            see LICENSE.txt</license>
        <authorEmail>carlos@hepta.es</authorEmail>
        <authorUrl>https://extensions.hepta.es</authorUrl>
        <version>1.0.0</version>
        <description>PLG_PLUGINTYPE_PLUGINNAME_XML_DESCRIPTION
            </description>
        <namespace path="src">Piedpiper\Plugin\PluginType
            \PluginName</namespace>
        <files>
            <folder plugin="PluginName">services</folder>
            <folder>src</folder>
            <folder>tmpl</folder>
        </files>
        <languages>
            <language tag="en-GB">language/en-GB/
                plg_PluginType_PluginName.ini</language>
            <language tag="en-GB">language/en-GB/
                plg_PluginType_PluginName.sys.ini</language>
        </languages>
        <config>
            <fields name="params">
                <fieldset name="basic">
                </fieldset>
            </fields>
        </config>
    </extension>
```

In the preceding code, we need to replace the value of the `group` attribute with the group of our plugin (Content, Finder, etc.). Actually, in this code, we need to replace it whenever `PluginType` appears, and also replace `PluginName` with the name of our plugin.

This manifest allows us to easily create our own plugin groups. If we use a plugin type that does not exist in our current Joomla! installation, Joomla! will create the specific folder for the group and will install your plugin there.

In the `<files>` section, just as we did with our component and module, we define the different files and folders that are part of our plugin. But in this case, you may notice the `<folder>` tag declaring the `services` folder has the `plugin` property and the value of the property is the name of our plugin. This is how we tell Joomla! where our plugin provider file is, which is the first file Joomla! will check when looking for our plugin.

In this manifest, we define the namespace of our plugin. Namespaces use the syntax of `\Company name\Plugin\Type of plugin\PluginName`, so to create a content plugin, we would use a namespace such as the following:

```
\Piedpiper\Plugin\Content\ProjectLink
```

With the preceding code, we declare the namespace for a content plugin called `ProjectLink`, which we will develop in the next section.

Creating a content plugin

An interesting use case of content plugins is using them to include content from other components inside Joomla! articles or even in modules. This gives the administrator of a Joomla! site lots of flexibility and is easy to implement from a developer's point of view. So, we are going to develop a content plugin that allows the website manager to include these projects in their content.

It's customary that this kind of plugin uses a **shortcode** to indicate the project we want to include, so our plugin will use the shortcode `{projectlink 42}` to embed a link to the project with ID 42 in a Joomla! article:

1. Let's write our manifest file for this plugin:

```xml
<?xml version="1.0" encoding="UTF-8"?>
<extension type="plugin" group="content"
  method="upgrade">
    <name>plg_content_projectlink</name>
    <author>Carlos Cámara</author>
    <creationDate>2023-05</creationDate>
    <copyright>(C) 2023 Piedpiper, Inc.</copyright>
    <license>GNU General Public License version 2 or
      later; see LICENSE.txt</license>
    <authorEmail>carlos@hepta.es</authorEmail>
    <authorUrl>https://extensions.hepta.es</authorUrl>
    <version>1.0.0</version>
    <description>PLG_CONTENT_PROJECTLINK_XML
      _DESCRIPTION</description>
    <namespace path="src">Piedpiper\Plugin\Content\
      ProjectLink</namespace>
    <files>
        <folder plugin="projectlink">services</folder>
        <folder>src</folder>
        <folder>tmpl</folder>
    </files>
    <languages>
```

```
            <language tag="en-GB">language/en-GB/
                plg_content_projectlink.ini</language>
            <language tag="en-GB">language/en-GB/
                plg_content_projectlink.sys.ini</language>
        </languages>
        <config>
            <fields name="params">
                <fieldset name="basic">
                </fieldset>
            </fields>
        </config>
    </extension>
```

In this code, we define our plugin as a content plugin with the name ProjectLink. For the value of the plugin, we use the plg_content_projectlink string. This string will be translated on installation with our language strings when we create the .ini files.

We also include the name of our plugin, but now we use projectlink as it is the real name for our plugin.

2. Now let's create our language folder with our language strings. Create the src/plugins/content/projectlink/language/en-GB/plg_content_projectlink.sys.ini file with the following content:

```
PLG_CONTENT_PROJECTLINK="Project Link"
PLG_CONTENT_PROJECTLINK_XML_DESCRIPTION="Content
plugin to include project details in your content. To
include the link to a project in your articles you
need to add the shortcode: {projectlink ID} Where ID
is the id of the project."
```

This provides the translation for the strings we have added to the XML file. At this point, we can copy this file into src/plugins/content/projectlink/language/en-GB/plg_content_projectlink.ini.

3. Next, create a src/plugins/content/projectlink/services/provider.php file with the following content:

```php
<?php

use Joomla\CMS\Extension\PluginInterface;
use Joomla\CMS\Plugin\PluginHelper;
use Joomla\CMS\Factory;
use Joomla\DI\Container;
use Joomla\DI\ServiceProviderInterface;
use Joomla\Event\DispatcherInterface;
```

```
use Piedpiper\Plugin\Content\ProjectLink\
  Extension\ProjectLink;


return new class implements ServiceProviderInterface
{
    public function register(Container $container)
    {
        $container->set(
            PluginInterface::class,
            function (Container $container) {
                $dispatcher = $container->get
                  (DispatcherInterface::class);
                $plugin     = new ProjectLink(
                    $dispatcher,
                    (array) PluginHelper::getPlugin
                        ('content', 'projectlink')
                );

                $plugin->setApplication
                  (Factory::getApplication());

                return $plugin;
            }
        );
    }
};
```

This code is the smallest provider you can have for a plugin. It gives you a copy of Joomla's dependency injection container and initializes your plugin class with `$dispatcher`.

4. Now we have to create the main class for our plugin. To do this, create the `src/plugins/content/projectlink/src/Extension/ProjectLink.php` file and add the following code:

```
<?php

namespace Piedpiper\Plugin\Content\
  ProjectLink\Extension;

use Joomla\Event\SubscriberInterface;
use Joomla\CMS\Plugin\CMSPlugin;
use Joomla\Event\Event;
```

```
class ProjectLink extends CMSPlugin implements
  SubscriberInterface
{
    protected $autoloadLanguage = true;

    public static function getSubscribedEvents():
      array
    {
        return [
            'onContentPrepare' => 'getProjectLink'
        ];
    }

    public function getProjectLink(Event $event)
    {
        $context = $event->getArgument('context');

        if ($context != 'com_content.article') {
            return;
        }
    }
}
```

In the Plugin class, we extend the CMSPlugin class. Using this class takes care of all required setup for a plugin, such as registering the events; it provides the database in the $db property and other bootstrapping stuff.

Our plugin class also implements SubscriberInterface, which means we are taking advantage of the modern and fastest method to load plugins in Joomla!. Using the SubscriberInterface, our plugins can stop event execution if needed and all the parameters will be encapsulated inside the $event object, which makes it easier to handle than the legacy technique for handling events in Joomla!, which was no more than a simple PHP callback.

In our plugin class, we define the $autoloadLanguage property. This property, when set to true, will make Joomla! inject the language files on plugin class creation. Use it only when you have language strings that need to be shown when your plugin executes.

As our plugin implements SubscriberInterface, we need to tell it what events to listen to. We do that using the getSubscribedEvents() method, where we return an array with the event we are listening to as the key of the array and with the method handling it as the associated value.

5. Finally, we define the getProjectLink() method that handles the onContentPrepare event. This method only receives the $event object passed by Joomla! and we get everything we need to know from this object.

    Right now, we are not doing that much work to handle the event. We just check the context and then exit if we are not in the proper context.

    We can replace our getProjectLink() method with the following code to add functionality:

```php
public function getProjectLink(Event $event)
{
    $context = $event->getArgument('0');

    if (strpos($context, 'com_content.article') ===
      false) {
        return;
    }

    $pattern = '/{projectlink\s([1-9[0-9]*)}/i';

    $article = $event->getArgument('1');

    if (str_contains($article->text, '{projectlink ')) {
        preg_match_all($pattern, $article->text,
          $matches, PREG_SET_ORDER);
        if ($matches) {
            foreach ($matches as $projectId) {
                $id = trim($projectId[1]);
                $projectLink = LinkHelper
                  ::formatProjectLink($id);
                $shortcodeStart = strpos($article->
                  text, $projectId[0]);

                $article->text = substr_replace
                  ($article->text, $projectLink,
                  $shortcodeStart, strlen
                    ($projectId[0]));
            }
        }

        $event->stopPropagation();
    }
}
```

When the onContentPrepare is triggered, we have defined in the getSubscribedEvents() method that it will be handled by the getProjectLink() method. So, in the preceding code, we receive the event from Joomla! and we first check the context. We only want to include the project link inside our article view, so we limit the allowed contexts to 'com_content. article'. If you also want to allow this feature in other contexts of your Joomla! installation, you can modify this logic accordingly.

When in the right context, we define the pattern to detect our shortcode and we receive the article from the event object. To speed up the search, we do a quick check for our shortcode in the article and if not present, we just skip the logic.

Finally, we do a regular expression search to get the project ID from our shortcode. Once we know the ID of the project we have to look for, we need to replace it with a link to our project.

To replace the link, we are going to create a helper class that will do the work. So before adding the $projectLink = LinkHelper::formatProjectLink($id); line, we need to do a couple of extra steps. First of all, we create the src/plugins/content/projectlink/ src/Helper/LinkHelper.php file with the following minimum content:

```php
<?php

namespace Piedpiper\Plugin\Content\ProjectLink\Helper;
class LinkHelper
{
}
```

This is where we define our helper class and set the proper namespace for it. As we have created the namespace, we can add its declaration at the top of the src/plugins/content/ projectlink/src/Extension/ProjectLink.php file:

```php
use Piedpiper\Plugin\Content\ProjectLink\Helper
  \LinkHelper;
```

After this, we can go back to our LinkHelper class and start coding its functions.

6. We now add the formatProjectLink() method to the class:

```php
public static function formatProjectLink($id)
{
    $link = Text::_('PLG_CONTENT_PROJECTLINK_
      PROJECT_NOT_FOUND');

    $app = Factory::getApplication();

    $model = $app
        ->bootComponent('com_spm')
        ->getMVCFactory()
        ->createModel(
```

```
            'Project',
            'Site',
            ['ignore_request' => true]
        );

    $item = $model->getItem($id);

    if ($item) {
        $item->url = Route::_(
            'index.php?option=com_spm&view=
              project&id=' . $item->id
        );
        $link = '<a href="' . $item->url . '">' .
          $item->name .'</a>';
    }

    return $link;
}
```

This method is where we do most of the replacing tasks. First, we define a generic message for situations where the project cannot be found on our system. To do this, we use the language capabilities of Joomla! we explored in *Chapter 5*. As we are using Joomla's Text class, we will need to declare the use of its namespace on top of our file. We are also using the Route class, so we also need to declare its namespace. Alongside these, we are using the Factory class to the instance of Joomla! web app, so above our class definition, we add the following:

```
use Joomla\CMS\Language\Text;
use Joomla\CMS\Router\Route;
use Joomla\CMS\Factory;
```

To take advantage of ProjectModel we created in *Chapter 2*, we load the component model. We use the bootComponent() method to start our component properly and we get a copy of the model object to use in our plugin. From this model, we can get the project using the getItem() method. This method initializes the component (in this case, our own SPM component) as if we were accessing any of its views. This way, we can take advantage of all its power in any part of Joomla!. In this case, we use it to get the project's model and our specific project title and link.

Once we have our project in the $item variable, we get its URL using the Route class, create the code for the link, and return it.

7. To finish our plugin, we need to add the language key translation to our main language file, `src/plugins/content/projectlink/language/en-GB/plg_content_projectlink.ini`:

```
PLG_CONTENT_PROJECTLINK_PROJECT_NOT_FOUND="Project Not
found"
```

And with that, we have a functional content plugin for our project manager. But what happens if our customers want to customize the link? This would be impossible without editing our plugin code.

8. To allow easy customization of our plugin's display, we have to use a plugin layout. To do so, we have to create the `src/plugins/content/projectlink/tmpl/link.php` file with the following content:

```
<div id="spm-project-<?php echo $item->id;?>"
  class="spm-project">
    <a href="<?php echo $item->url; ?>">
        <?php echo $item->name; ?>
    </a>
</div>
```

This HTML code is a bit more elaborate than the simple link we had at the end of *step 6*. In the preceding code, we create a unique element ID for each link's `<div>` container and we even add a CSS class.

To make use of this `link.php` layout file, we need to replace the `if` structure of the helper file above with this code:

```
if ($item) {
    $item->url = Route::_(
        'index.php?option=com_spm&view=project&id=' .
          $item->id
    );
    $layoutFile = PluginHelper::getLayoutPath(
        'content',
        'projectlink',
        'link'
    );
    ob_start();
    include $layoutFile;
    $link = ob_get_clean();
}
```

Here, we use the `PluginHelper::getLayoutPath` method to get our layout. We pass the type of our plugin (`content`), its name (`projectlink`), and the name of our layout file (`link`). That gives the path to the layout file and also checks for overrides of this file in the current template. In Joomla!, we do not have a native function to show plugin layouts, so we use the `ob_start()` and `ob_get_clean()` PHP functions to capture the output of the code between these two methods. We use the PHP `include` statement to generate the HTML code to be displayed to the user and we capture the output in the `$link` variable with the `ob_get_clean()` method.

As we are using Joomla's `PluginHelper` class, we also need to include it at the top of our namespaces for the helper, so we include the following statement just below the other namespace declarations:

```
use Joomla\CMS\Plugin\PluginHelper;
```

And with that, we have completed our plugin code. Now we have a functional content plugin that uses the component model to retrieve a specific project and replaces a shortcode with the correct URL.

Adding plugins to our component

In the previous sections, we covered how to call Joomla! plugins from our component. We also created our own content plugin that looks at our component and displays it where needed using just a shortcode. If we put these two things together, we can deduce another benefit of using plugins in our projects: the ability to extend our features without changing our code.

In our Simple Project Manager component, we can add as many plugin events as we need for this. For instance, we could add an event that is called before a new customer is added to our system. In this event, we could fix the casing of our customer email before saving it into the database.

The first thing we have to do is create the trigger for our event. This step will be exactly as we saw in the previous *Calling Joomla! plugins from our component* section.

So, to proceed, we edit the, `/src/component/admin/src/Model/CustomerModel.php` file, adding the `save()` method to include our plugin trigger:

```
public function save($data)
{
    PluginHelper::importPlugin('spm');

    $event = new GenericEvent(
        'onSpmCustomerBeforeSave',
        [
            'data' => $data
        ]
    );
```

```
$this->getDispatcher()->dispatch
    ('onSpmCustomerBeforeSave', $event);

$data = $event->getArgument('data');

return parent::save($data);
}
```

This function is an override of the `save()` method of the `AdminModel` class, so we only need to include our plugin trigger and then call the parent class method.

First, we use the `PluginHelper::getPlugin()` method to subscribe our plugin to the `onSpmCustomerBeforeSave` event. This will tell Joomla! to look for the `onSpmCustomerBeforeSave` event in all plugins of the spm type.

After that, we can trigger our `onSpmCustomerBeforeSave` event. We trigger the event using the Joomla! dispatcher and to pass the information to our event, we use a `GenericEvent` object we have instantiated before calling the dispatcher.

To instantiate the `GenericEvent` object, we need two arguments, the name of the event and an indexed array with the arguments we want to pass. In this array, the keys represent the name of the arguments that we will use to retrieve them. In this example, we only pass the data we receive in the model.

Dispatching the event hooks all the plugins of the spm type into the `onSpmCustomerBeforeSave` event, gets the data, and performs some operations with it. Some of these plugins might modify the data we pass (indeed, the plugin we are about to write to illustrate this example will do this) with all the modifications stored in the `$event` object.

To retrieve the modified data, we need to call the `getArgument()` method by passing the name of the argument we want to retrieve.

After getting the changes, we can save our data, and as we do not intend to make any more changes, we call the parent `save()` method.

Finally, as we are using the `GenericEvent` class provided by Joomla!, we need to specify its namespace, so at the top of the file, we add its declaration:

```
use Joomla\CMS\Event\GenericEvent;
```

This modification allows us to hook plugins into our customer saving process, but we do not have any plugin that can use this feature yet, so in the next section we will develop a plugin that fixes the casing of all customer email addresses.

Creating our customer's plugin

Once our component is ready to trigger events, we can develop plugins that use these events. In the previous section, we restricted our event to all plugins only in the spm plugin type. This is not a default plugin type – it is a new type we are creating as an example for our project.

This means the plugins of this new spm type will be stored in their own folder when installed on the site. Indeed, creating this new type in Joomla! is as simple as installing the first plugin of this type. As seen at the beginning of this chapter, the plugin type is defined in the plugin manifest file, so let's start by creating the file, called src/plugins/spm/customers/customers.xml, containing the following content:

```xml
<?xml version="1.0" encoding="UTF-8"?>
<extension type="plugin" group="spm" method="upgrade">
    <name>plg_spm_customers</name>
    <author>Carlos Cámara</author>
    <creationDate>2023-05</creationDate>
    <copyright>(C) 2023 Piedpiper, Inc.</copyright>
    <license>GNU General Public License version 2 or later;
        see LICENSE.txt</license>
    <authorEmail>carlos@hepta.es</authorEmail>
    <authorUrl>https://extensions.hepta.es</authorUrl>
    <version>1.0.0</version>
    <description>PLG_SPM_CUSTOMERS_XML_DESCRIPTION
        </description>
    <namespace path="src">Piedpiper\Plugin\Spm\Customers
        </namespace>
    <files>
        <folder plugin="customers">services</folder>
        <folder>src</folder>
        <folder>services</folder>
    </files>
    <languages>
        <language tag="en-GB">language/en-GB/
            plg_spm_customers.ini</language>
        <language tag="en-GB">language/en-GB/
            plg_spm_customers.sys.ini</language>
    </languages>
    <config>
        <fields name="params">
            <fieldset name="basic">
            </fieldset>
        </fields>
```

```
    </config>
</extension>
```

This is a simple manifest file. You can see how, just by defining the plugin type in the `group` attribute of the tag, the plugin will belong to this type.

Of course, in the namespace, we also reflect the type of the plugin in the route, and as is customary, we use the name of the group in the name of the language files.

This plugin will not display any data to the user, so we do not add a `tmpl` folder.

We can continue building the rest of the plugin file structure by creating the `src/plugins/spm/customers/services/provider.php` file with the following content:

```php
<?php

use Joomla\CMS\Factory;
use Joomla\CMS\Extension\PluginInterface;
use Joomla\CMS\Plugin\PluginHelper;
use Joomla\DI\Container;
use Joomla\DI\ServiceProviderInterface;
use Joomla\Event\DispatcherInterface;
use Piedpiper\Plugin\Spm\Customers\Extension\Customers;

\defined('_JEXEC') or die;

return new class implements ServiceProviderInterface
{
    public function register(Container $container)
    {
        $container->set(
            PluginInterface::class,
            function (Container $container) {
                $dispatcher = $container->get
                  (DispatcherInterface::class);
                $plugin     = new Customers(
                    $dispatcher,
                    (array) PluginHelper::getPlugin('spm',
                        'customers')
                );

                $plugin->setApplication
                  (Factory::getApplication());

                return $plugin;
```

```
            }
        );
    }
};
```

This `provider.php` file works using the same principles as explained in the previous sections. Just note that we instantiate the `Customers` class from our `Extension` folder, so let's create the class in the `src/plugins/spm/customers/src/Extension/Customers.php` file with the following code:

```php
<?php

namespace Piedpiper\Plugin\Spm\Customers\Extension;

use Joomla\Event\SubscriberInterface;
use Joomla\CMS\Plugin\CMSPlugin;
use Joomla\Event\Event;

\defined('_JEXEC') or die;

class Customers extends CMSPlugin implements
  SubscriberInterface
{
    protected $autoloadLanguage = true;

    public static function getSubscribedEvents(): array
    {
        return [
            'onSpmCustomerBeforeSave' => 'fixCasing'
        ];
    }

    public function fixCasing(Event $event)
    {
        $data = $event->getArgument('data');

        $data['email'] = strtolower($data['email']);

        $event->setArgument('data', $data);
        return;
    }
}
```

This class is where all the magic happens. First, we need to declare the events we hook to using the `getSubscribedEvents()` method. In this method, we return an array in which the keys are the name of the event we want to subscribe to our plugin, and the value is the name of the method that will handle the event; in this case, the `fixCasing` method is used to handle the `onSpmCustomerBeforeSave` event.

The `fixCasing()` method receives the `$event` object we previously passed as an argument when dispatching the event in the model. So we get the argument by name and process it as per our needs.

Once we have finished processing the received data, we update the event data using the `setArgument()` method provided by the `Event` class.

Finally, to complete our plugin, we only need to add the language files. So we create the `src/plugins/spm/customers/language/en-GB/plg_spm_customers.ini` and `src/plugins/spm/customers/language/en-GB/plg_spm_customers.sys.ini` files with the following content (the same for both files):

```
PLG_SPM_CUSTOMERS="SPM Customers plugin"
PLG_SPM_CUSTOMERS_XML_DESCRIPTION="This plugin fixes
   customer's email casing before saving it"
```

After installing and enabling our plugin in Joomla!, every time we save a customer, the customer email will be converted to lowercase.

Summary

In this chapter, we covered everything related to plugin development in Joomla!. We explored the Joomla! plugin architecture and how it follows the same pattern as other extensions such as modules and components. We also learned how plugins can be triggered into action after certain events in Joomla!. We developed our own content plugin to include the appropriate project links from our Simple Project Manager component in our articles. We also discovered how to subscribe our plugin to these events and even how we can trigger our own events. Finally, we created our own plugin group to easily include our own events in Joomla!.

In *Chapter 9*, we will explore the **Command-Line Interface** (**CLI**) in Joomla! and how we can use it to execute tasks outside our web browser, as well as automate processes in Joomla!.

Further reading

The official Joomla! documentation has an interesting article on plugins:

- Description of plugin events by group: `https://docs.joomla.org/Special:MyLanguage/Plugin/Events`

9

Adding a CLI to Your Extension

Command-Line Interfaces (**CLIs**) are a popular tool for developers to automate certain tasks. CLI applications are intended to be used through a terminal emulator, such as xterm on Linux systems, Windows Command Prompt on Windows systems, or the Terminal app on macOS.

The most common reason people use a CLI web application is to automate certain tasks. This can be accomplished with Cron Jobs or by including the CLI commands in a development automated pipeline (for example, a continuous integration pipeline).

Many PHP CMS and frameworks implement a CLI application with different naming, so for instance, you can find Laravel Artisan, the Symfony Console, WP-CLI for WordPress, or even the PrestaShop CLI. Some of these systems actually share code and packages to create their CLIs. Joomla! CLI is based on the Symfony Console component.

In this chapter, we are going to explore Joomla! CLI and see the options it offers. We will learn how to create a CLI application that detects tasks close to the deadline, sending us a reminder email using a Cron Job.

By the end of this chapter, you will understand how to interact with Joomla! CLI and how to create your own Joomla! CLI applications.

These are the specific topics we are going to explore:

- What is a CLI?
- How to use Joomla! CLI
- Adding a Joomla! CLI command to Joomla!
- Adding parameters to your CLI command

Technical requirements

- A terminal emulator to connect to your Joomla! site

- SSH access or direct terminal access to the server of your Joomla! site

- A way to program Cron Jobs on your site

- The site we previously created

You can find the code used in this chapter on GitHub: `https://github.com/PacktPublishing/Developing-Extensions-for-Joomla-5/tree/chapter09`

What is a CLI?

A CLI is a text-based interface to interact with your website, using text commands typed on your keyboard. In a CLI, you cannot use your mouse to perform any action, as it actually does not even have a graphical interface.

CLI applications have some advantages over regular web applications:

- They are more performant than web pages, as they do not have to show graphic elements, and as they are triggered through the server command line, they are great for creating automation. In fact, you cannot access a CLI application through your web browser.

- Using a CLI application, you can avoid some server limitations such as a maximum execution time limit. So, running time-consuming scripts from the server terminal will not result in a timeout error.

- CLI applications are more secure than Webhooks, as they can only be triggered through your server internals. This prevents attackers from trying to reach them to cause harm to your site.

To interact with a CLI, we need to use a terminal emulator or a command prompt, such as xterm on Linux, Terminal on macOS, or Windows Command Prompt on Windows systems.

When using the CLI on a website in a remote server, we usually connect through SSH to the server to interact with the CLI.

In some scenarios, we will not be able to connect through SSH to the server for security reasons – for instance, shared web servers do not allow SSH access. On these systems, we can still use a CLI application through their Cron Job feature.

What is a Cron Job?

A **Cron Job** is a time-based task scheduling system present in Linux-based systems.

Cron Jobs are very popular in web management to automate repetitive or unattended tasks. Hence, most servers implement them or a similar tool.

To configure a Cron Job, you need to define a specific time frame and the command you want to execute. The expression to define our Cron Job consists of five fields that define the timing of the task – minute, hour, day of the month, month, and day of the week. After that, we add the command to execute.

For instance, a common Cron Job configuration could be the following:

```
05 3 * * * php cli/joomla.php update:extensions:check
```

This Cron Job expression will check for extension updates on our Joomla! website every day at 3:05. Sometimes, you need to add the full path to your PHP version, and you also may need to include some extra folders to reach Joomla's `cli` directory.

In any case, you may find them in your server management tools as **scheduled tasks**, **Cron tasks**, or a similar name. If you are working on your own computer, you can access the tasks using the `Cron Tab` command in your terminal. Check the *Further reading* section at the end of this chapter to find out more about Cron Jobs.

Now that you know what a CLI application is and how you can use it with your task scheduling system, let's dive into the specifics of Joomla! CLI.

How to use Joomla! CLI

Joomla! CLI is based on the Symfony Console, and you can access it by calling the `cli/joomla.php` file of your website. As stated previously, you cannot access it from your web browser. To access Joomla! CLI, you need to use a terminal and type the commands.

In this book, we will assume that you have SSH or direct access to your Joomla! installation. So, start your terminal and set it on your Joomla! `root` folder.

First, we will check the PHP version in use in the terminal. It's possible that your server uses a specific PHP version for your Joomla! website and a different one for the PHP CLI. To check our PHP version, we will type the following:

```
php -v
```

If it's the same as the one running your website, you are good to go. If it's not the same version, you need to check that it's at least the lowest PHP version you can run Joomla! on.

Once we are happy with our PHP-CLI version, we can start working with Joomla! CLI. To invoke the CLI application, we need to call the `joomla.php` file inside the `cli` folder, so we type in our terminal the following:

```
php cli/joomla.php
```

This will list a help message, with the usage options of Joomla! CLI. In this message, we can see the available commands or applications for our Joomla! installation and the generic options we can use.

The syntax of Joomla! CLI is as follows:

```
php cli/joomla.php COMMAND OPTIONS ARGUMENTS
```

Let's see in detail how to work with these commands.

Introducing Joomla! CLI commands

Joomla! CLI commands are the actions we can perform on our Joomla! site. We can add more commands to the ones that come out of the box. Commands are grouped in namespaces. In this context, namespaces represent different areas of your site. In a basic Joomla! installation, you may find namespaces such as **Database**, which groups all commands related to database actions, or **Extension**, which covers all commands related to managing your extensions. You can find all the available commands and namespaces using the list command:

```
php cli/joomla.php list
```

After executing this command in your terminal, you will see a brief usage message, followed by all the commands grouped by namespace. In a basic Joomla! installation, we have 11 namespaces with at least one command per namespace. All the commands are formed with the name of their namespace and the action they performed. For instance, for the extension namespace, we have the following commands:

- extension:discover: This command will make Joomla! discover uninstalled extensions in the folder structure

- extension:discover:install: This command will perform a discovery and then it will install the extensions discovered

- extension:discover:list: This will just list the discovered extensions

- extension:list: This command lists all the extensions installed on the site

- extension:remove: This command must be followed by the extension ID that we want to remove, and it will remove that extension from the site

Some of the commands require arguments to perform their actions, but in any case, all commands accept some generic options to modify their output. In the following section, we will go deeper into these options.

Introducing generic options for Joomla! CLI

CLI commands might accept options to modify their output and adapt it to our needs. Each command might have several options, which will appear when you check their help (which you can reach by adding the -h option to the command), but there are also generic options you can use. These are the generic options available at the time of writing:

- –live-site[=LIVE-SITE]: Where LIVE-SITE is the actual URL of your site. The CLI application does not know the URL of the site, so adding this parameter will state the URL of the website. It's useful when a CLI application should return URLs of the site, such as activation links. If it's not present, the CLI will try to use the $live_site parameter from Joomla's configuration.php file.

- -h, –help: This option will show a help message for the command you want to use. If you specify no command, it will show a short help message.

- -n, –no-interaction: This option will avoid asking questions to the user.

- -q, –quiet: This option will silence the output of the command. It will also set the no-interaction option.

- -V, –version: Adding this option will display your Joomla! version.

- –ansi: This option forces the output to be colorful as long as the terminal supports ANSI.

- –no-ansi: This option disables ANSI output.

- -v|vv|vvv, –verbose: With this option, you can choose the amount of information in the output.

The regular way of using an option is to precede it with two dashes, - -, but some commands have a short form that is preceded by just one dash – for instance, -h is the same as - -help.

This provides great flexibility, as we probably want to use different options according to our scenario. For instance, for continuous integration tasks, the -n option seems an interesting choice, and for Cron Job operations, the -q option will save us from getting lots of emails.

Now that we are familiar with Joomla! CLI, let's create our own CLI application for the Simple Project Manager project.

Adding a Joomla! CLI command to Joomla!

In Joomla!, we can add our own commands to the CLI, creating a plugin for every command we want to add. These plugins belong to the **console** plugin group. Out-of-the-box commands do not have a plugin associated, but they are included in Joomla! libraries, so you will not see the console plugin group in a basic Joomla! installation.

After *Chapter 8*, we know how to code Joomla! plugins, so we can start creating our basic plugin structure and adding the manifest. Let's create the file, `src/plugins/console/spm/spm.xml`, with the following content:

```
<?xml version="1.0" encoding="UTF-8"?>
<extension type="plugin" group="console" method="upgrade">
    <name>plg_console_spm</name>
    <author>Carlos Cámara</author>
    <creationDate>2023-05</creationDate>
    <copyright>(C) 2023 Piedpiper, Inc.</copyright>
    <license>GNU General Public License version 2 or later;
      see LICENSE.txt</license>
    <authorEmail>carlos@hepta.es</authorEmail>
    <authorUrl>https://extensions.hepta.es</authorUrl>
    <version>1.0.0</version>
    <description>PLG_CONSOLE_SPM_XML_DESCRIPTION</description>
    <namespace path="src">Piedpiper\Plugin\Console\Spm
      </namespace>
    <files>
        <folder plugin="spm">services</folder>
        <folder>src</folder>
    </files>
</extension>
```

This may be familiar to you, as it's the same basic manifest we used in the previous chapter. The only difference is that we can see the plugin group in this manifest is set to `console`, and also, we do not have a `tmpl` folder to store our layout templates, as in `console`, it makes no sense.

We will create a plugin for our CLI command to inject it at the beginning of the Joomla! CLI execution cycle. So, let's create a plugin class to register our plugin to the **Before Execute** event. We will create the `src/plugins/console/spm/src/Extension/SpmConsolePlugin.php` file with the following content:

```php
<?php

namespace Piedpiper\Plugin\Console\Spm\Extension;

use Joomla\Event\SubscriberInterface;
use Joomla\CMS\Plugin\CMSPlugin;
use Joomla\Application\ApplicationEvents;
use Piedpiper\Plugin\Console\Spm\CliCommand\
  SpmTaskDeadlineCommand;

class SpmConsolePlugin extends CMSPlugin implements
```

```php
    SubscriberInterface
{

    public static function getSubscribedEvents(): array
    {
        return [
                ApplicationEvents::BEFORE_EXECUTE =>
                    'registerCLICommands'
        ];
    }

    public function registerCLICommands(ApplicationEvent
        $event): void
    {

        $app = $event->getApplication();

        $app->addCommand(new SpmTaskDeadlineCommand());
    }
}
```

In this code, we are going to use the `registerCLICommands` method to register our commands. We will register just one command, and we need to create its code first. So, we will create the `src/plugins/console/spm/src/CliCommand/SpmTaskDeadlineCommand.php` file with the following content:

```php
<?php

namespace Piedpiper\Plugin\Console\Spm\CliCommand;

use Symfony\Component\Console\Command\Command;
use Symfony\Component\Console\Input\InputInterface;
use Symfony\Component\Console\Output\OutputInterface;
use Symfony\Component\Console\Style\SymfonyStyle;
use Joomla\Console\Command\AbstractCommand;

class SpmTaskDeadlineCommand extends AbstractCommand
{
    protected static $defaultName = 'spm:task:deadline';

    protected function configure(): void
    {
        $this->setDescription('List upcoming task
            deadlines');
        $this->setHelp('The <info>$command.name%</info>
            command lists all the tasks with upcoming
```

```
                        deadlines. <info>php
%command.full_name%</info>');
    }

    protected function getDeadlines() : array
    {
        $deadlines = [];

        $days = 7;

        $db = $this->getDatabase();
        $query = $db->getQuery(true);
        $query->select('*')
            ->from('#__spm_tasks');

        $query->where('deadline BETWEEN NOW() AND
          DATE_ADD(NOW(), INTERVAL ' . $days .' DAY)');

        $query->setQuery($query);

        $deadlines = $db->loadAssocList('id');

        return $deadlines;
    }

    protected function doExecute(InputInterface $input,
      OutputInterface $output):   int
    {
        $outputStyle = new SymfonyStyle($input, $output);
        $outputStyle->title('Simple Project Manager
          Upcoming Deadlines');

        $deadlines = $this->getDeadlines();

        if (empty($deadlines)) {
            $this->outputStyle->note('There is no upcoming
              deadlines');
        } else {
            $this->outputStyle->table(['Deadline',
              'Project', 'Task'], $deadlines);
        }
```

```
        return Command::SUCCESS;
    }
}
```

This class is contained in our namespace, `Piedpiper`, and it's where all the magic happens. First, we can see how it relies heavily on the Symfony Console, as most of the namespaces we use are from its namespace, but we can also see how we use the `AbstractCommand` class from the Joomla! Framework Console namespace. This class is the one we will extend, as it provides a solution for CLI commands' common tasks.

In the `$defaultName` variable, we will define the command to use in the CLI. We will set the exact command to be used, and ideally, we will split the different parts, such as the command namespace with the `:` character. In this scenario, our CLI namespace is `spm`. We also add the `task` context and, finally, the `deadline`-specific command. So, our command will be `spm:task:deadline`.

In the `configure()` method, we set up all other information of the command, such as the description and the help message. For this, we will use the `setDescription()` and `setHelp()` methods of `AbstractClass`. For the message in the `setHelp()` method, we have included the tag. This tag will print the text in a different color in the terminal. In the *What Symfony console output tags can we use?* section, we will provide a list of the tags you can use.

Finally, in the `doExecute()` method, we will add the code that creates the output of the command. To provide styling and take advantage of the benefits of the Symfony console, we will use the `SymfonyStyle` class. This class takes care of styling the output according to our suggestions.

So, we will define the title using the `title()` method, and immediately after that, we will get the deadlines we want to show with our internal `getDeadlines()` method. This method returns an array with the upcoming deadlines for the next seven days. If no deadline is found, it returns an empty array.

In this case, we will show an informative message using the `note()` method from the `SymfonyStyle` class. Otherwise, we would create a table showing all the tasks with upcoming deadlines, using the `table()` method.

We will end our console application by returning the `SUCCESS` constant from the `Symfony Console` class.

This is our first Joomla! CLI application. Installing and enabling this plugin in a Joomla! box will add our `spm:task:deadline` CLI application to the CLI. However, we can improve this command, so let's dive a bit deeper and see how we can create a more informative CLI application.

In the following section, we will dive into the `SymfonyStyle` output methods to provide better styling for our messages.

Exploring SymfonyStyle methods

For most commands, a basic output will provide enough information. For instance, when we want to indicate there are no upcoming deadlines, a simple text message is enough. However, what happens when we need to indicate several task deadlines? We need some kind of styling to make the information easier to read for our users.

We can use the following methods to provide some nice output:

- `title($title)`: This helps define a title. You are supposed to use it just once to set the main title of your output.
- `section($title)`: This formats text as the title of a new section.
- `text($message)`: This method is used to show regular text-like messages or instructions.
- `listing($list)`: This method accepts an array of strings, and it displays each element of the array in an unordered list.
- `table($header, $body)`: This method displays a table. It accepts two arrays as an argument. The first one is the header of the table, and the second array is used as the body of the table.
- `horizontalTable($header, $body)`: This method displays a horizontal table and accepts the same arguments as the previous one.
- `definitionList([$term => $definition])`: This accepts an indexed array and shows its content as a definition list, where the keys of the array are used as the definition term and the values are used as the definition text.
- `newLine($lines)`: This method adds a new line to the text. It accepts an integer argument, indicating the number of blank lines you want to include.
- `note($message)`: This shows the text provided highlighted to reflect it is important information.
- `caution($message)`: This method is similar to the `note()` method, but it displays the message more prominently.

What Symfony console output tags can we use?

With CLI applications, we cannot use the same styling that we have on our website. However, there are some tags that we can use to style our output:

- `<info>`: This prints the enclosed text in green.
- `<comment>`: This prints the enclosed text in yellow.
- `<question>`: This prints the enclosed text with a blue background.
- `<error>`: This prints the enclosed text with a red background.

- `<bg=COLOR>`: This tag sets the background color of the enclosed text. `COLOR` might be any hexadecimal color value (e.g., `#00FF00` for green) or its natural name in English. When the terminal does not support it, it shows the closest color. You need to use the same tag for the closing tag – `</bg=COLOR>`.

- `<fg=>`: This tag sets the foreground color of the enclosed text. The same restrictions as for `<bg=>` apply.

As with HTML, we also have to close these tags using the same syntax – for instance, `<info>INFORMATION</info>`.

We also have some shortcodes available to make it easier to maintain our messages:

- `%command.name%`: This returns the name of the command.

- `%command.full_name%`: This returns the script path followed by the name of the command. In Joomla!, when executed from the main Joomla! folder, the script path is always `cli/joomla.php`.

Using these tags, our messages will look nicer. Another step to make them better is adding the capability to show the messages in the user's language. Let's see in the next section how we can translate the messages into different languages.

How to internationalize CLI messages

Finally, we can use the Joomla! language system to translate our CLI messages. We can even use the Symfony tags we learned in the previous message in our language strings.

Even when using only a single language in our CLI app, using the translation system will improve our code, making it simpler. As an example, think of the `setHelp()` call we have in the `SpmTaskDeadlineCommand.php` file. In that file, we added this code:

```
$this->setHelp('The <info>$command.name%</info> command
   lists all the tasks with upcoming deadlines. <info>php
%command.full_name%</info>');
```

Using the Joomla! translation system, we can replace it with the following:

```
$this->setHelp(Text::_('PLG_CONSOLE_SPM_
   TASK_DEADLINE_HELP'));
```

This makes our code simpler to read.

To make our CLI app translatable, we need to make some changes to our current code. First of all, we will set the protected `$autoloadLanguage` property to `true` in the `SpmConsolePlugin` class. We need to do this because Joomla! will not load any language file for these plugins, especially since we are not in a web environment. So, we will edit the `src/plugins/console/spm/src/Extension/SpmConsolePlugin.php` file and add the property above our first method:

```php
<?php

...

class SpmConsolePlugin extends CMSPlugin implements
    SubscriberInterface
{
    protected $autoloadLanguage = true;

    public static function getSubscribedEvents(): array

    ...
}
```

Now, we will create our language files, so we will add the following files:

`src/plugins/console/spm/language/en-GB/plg_console_spm.sys.ini`

```ini
PLG_CONSOLE_SPM="SPM CLI"
PLG_CONSOLE_SPM_XML_DESCRIPTION="Simple Project Manager
    Command Line Interface Commands"
```

The `.sys.ini` file contains only the strings that we need to manage Joomla!. Also, we will create the `src/plugins/console/spm/language/en-GB/plg_console_spm.ini` file:

```ini
PLG_CONSOLE_SPM_TASK_DEADLINE_DESCRIPTION="List upcoming
    deadlines"
PLG_CONSOLE_SPM_TASK_DEADLINE_HELP="The <info>
    %command.name%</info> command lists all the tasks with
    <bg=#00FF00>upcoming deadlines</bg=#00FF00>. <info>php
    %command.full_name%</info>"
PLG_CONSOLE_SPM_TASK_DEADLINE_DEADLINE_HEADER="Deadline"
PLG_CONSOLE_SPM_TASK_DEADLINE_NO_DEADLINE="There is no
    upcoming deadlines"
PLG_CONSOLE_SPM_TASK_DEADLINE_TITLE="Simple Project Manager
    Deadlines"
```

This file contains all the strings related to the command. As you can see, we can accommodate the styling tags in the strings with no issues.

Once we have our key and translated strings, we will replace all the strings in our SpmTaskDeadlineCommand class with the Text::_() method, and we end up with this code:

```php
<?php

namespace Piedpiper\Plugin\Console\Spm\CliCommand;

use Symfony\Component\Console\Command\Command;
use Symfony\Component\Console\Input\InputInterface;
use Symfony\Component\Console\Output\OutputInterface;
use Symfony\Component\Console\Style\SymfonyStyle;
use Joomla\Console\Command\AbstractCommand;
use Joomla\CMS\Language\Text;

class SpmTaskDeadlineCommand extends AbstractCommand
{
    protected static $defaultName = 'spm:task:deadline';

    protected function configure(): void
    {
        $this->setDescription(Text::_('PLG_CONSOLE
          _SPM_TASK_DEADLINE_DESCRIPTION'));
        $this->setHelp(Text::_('PLG_CONSOLE_SPM
          _TASK_DEADLINE_HELP'));
    }

    protected function getDeadlines() : array
    {
        $deadlines = [];

        $days = 7;

        $db = $this->getDatabase();
        $query = $db->getQuery(true);
        $query->select('*')
            ->from('#__spm_tasks');

        $query->where('deadline BETWEEN NOW() AND
          DATE_ADD(NOW(), INTERVAL ' . $days .' DAY)');

        $query->setQuery($query);

        $deadlines = $db->loadAssocList('id');
```

```
        return $deadlines;
    }


    protected function doExecute(InputInterface $input,
      OutputInterface $output): int
    {
        $outputStyle = new SymfonyStyle($input, $output);
        $outputStyle->title(Text::_('PLG_CONSOLE_
          SPM_TASK_DEADLINE_TITLE'));

        $deadlines = $this->getDeadlines();

        if (empty($deadlines)) {
            $outputStyle->note(Text::_('PLG_CONSOLE_SPM_
              TASK_DEADLINE_NO_DEADLINE'));
        } else {
            $outputStyle->table([Text::_('PLG_CONSOLE_
              SPM_TASK_DEADLINE_DEADLINE_HEADER'),
                'Project', 'Task'], $deadlines);
        }


        return Command::SUCCESS;
    }
}
```

Note that we have also added the `Joomla\CMS\Language\Text` namespace to the class to use the translation system.

Finally, we will add the section to our XML manifest file, just below the section:

```
    ...

    </files>
    <languages>
        <language tag="en-GB">language/en-GB/
          plg_console_spm.ini</language>
        <language tag="en-GB">language/en-GB/
          plg_console_spm.sys.ini</language>
    </languages>
```

This will install the language files in the proper folders on `package install`.

Now, our CLI application speaks your language, and the code is not mixed up with your help messages. However, wouldn't it be great if we could take it a bit further and add different options for a user? In the next section, we are going to add arguments to allow for a more powerful CLI application.

Adding parameters to your CLI command

Our CLI application is very useful to get a quick view of the upcoming deadlines within a week, but what about the upcoming deadlines for the month? We could just change the time parameter in our SQL query, but that would not be very practical, so let's add arguments to our CLI command to allow for better flexibility.

We'll add an option to our command to pass the number of days we want to consider for the deadline.

As we saw in the previous section, *Introducing generic options for Joomla! CLI*, we added two dashes before the name of the option. We are calling our option days, so our command will look like this:

```
php joomla.cli spm:task:deadline --days 7
```

Here, we can replace 7 with any number of days when executing our command.

Joomla! provides several interesting methods to make it easier to define these CLI options. Let's start editing the src/plugins/console/spm/src/CliCommand/SpmTaskDeadlineCommand. php file, replacing our configure() method with this code:

```
    protected function configure(): void
    {
        $this->setDescription(Text::_('PLG_CONSOLE
          _SPM_TASK_DEADLINE_DESCRIPTION'));
        $this->setHelp(Text::_('PLG_CONSOLE_SPM
          _TASK_DEADLINE_HELP'));

        $this->addOptions();
    }

    protected function addOptions()
    {
        $description = Text::_('PLG_CONSOLE_SPM_TASK
          _DEADLINE_OPTION_DAYS_DESCRIPTION');
        $this->addOption('days', 'd', InputOption::
          VALUE_OPTIONAL, $description, 7);

        return;
    }
```

In this code, we call a new `addOptions()` method to add the options for our class. Inside this method, first, we get our translated description. Then, we use the `addOption()` method from the extended `AbstractCommand` class to configure the option. The `addOption()` method takes five arguments:

- `-days`: This is the name of the option.
- `-d`: This is the abbreviated form for the option. You need to be careful not to use the same abbreviation for two different options with this command.
- `InputOption::VALUE_OPTIONAL`: This is a constant defined in the `InputOption` Symfony class.
- `$description`: This is the help message a user will see when using the `-h` option.
- `7`: The last argument is the default value for the option.

We need to clarify some extra things regarding the `InputOption::VALUE_OPTIONAL`. First of all, to use this constant, we need to declare the namespace to use. So, add its declaration at the top of your class, just after the rest of the namespaces:

```
use Symfony\Component\Console\Input\InputOption;
```

Then, we can use the following constants:

- `VALUE_NONE`: When the option accepts no value. When using this, the default value for the `addOption()` method should be `null`.
- `VALUE_REQUIRED`: When a user must specify a value for the option.
- `VALUE_OPTIONAL`: When a user can omit the value and use the default value we provide as the last argument in the `addOption()` method.
- `VALUE_IS_ARRAY`: When the user can add different values to the option – for instance, –days=7 -days=8*.
- `VALUE_NEGATABLE`: When a user can have a positive or a negative value – for instance, –ansi or –no-ansi.

After defining our options, the next step is retrieving and using them in the `doExecute()` method. So, let's replace that method with the following code:

```
protected function getOptions() : array
{
    $options = [];

    $options = $this->cliInput->getOptions();

    return $options;
```

```
    }

    protected function doExecute(InputInterface $input,
      OutputInterface $output):  int
    {
        $this->cliInput = $input;

        $outputStyle = new SymfonyStyle($input, $output);
        $outputStyle->title(Text::_('PLG_CONSOLE_SPM_TASK
          _DEADLINE_TITLE'));

        $options = $this->getOptions();

        $deadlines = $this->getDeadlines($options);

        $outputStyle->block('this is a block of text');

        if (empty($deadlines)) {
            $outputStyle->note(Text::_
            ('PLG_CONSOLE_SPM_TASK_DEADLINE_NO_DEADLINE'));
        } else {
            $outputStyle->table([Text::_('PLG_CONSOLE_SPM_
              TASK_DEADLINE_DEADLINE_HEADER'), 'Project',
                'Task'], $deadlines);
        }


        return Command::SUCCESS;
    }
```

With this change, we retrieve the options using the new getOptions() method. That method uses the InputInterface class to retrieve all the options passed through the command line or their default values in an array. Once we have that array, we pass it to our getDeadlines() method for use in our query.

So, to implement the option passed, we need to modify our getDeadlines() option to accept the $options variable and take care of the days option. Using this code will make it happen:

```
    protected function getDeadlines($options) : array
    {
        $deadlines = [];

        $days = (int)$options['days'];

        if ($days <= 0) {
            $days = 7;
```

```
        }

        $db = $this->getDatabase();
        $query = $db->getQuery(true);
        $query->select('*')
            ->from('#__spm_tasks');

        $query->where('deadline BETWEEN NOW() AND
          DATE_ADD(NOW(), INTERVAL ' . $days . ' DAY)');

        $query->setQuery($query);

        $deadlines = $db->loadAssocList('id');

        return $deadlines;
    }
```

The InputInterface classes do not handle the type of arguments passed to the CLI, so we cast the option to an int type to ensure we are dealing with a positive INT value. Otherwise, we use the default 7 days. In the where clause, we use the BETWEEN operator and the NOW() and DATE_ADD(() MySQL methods to form our query.

Finally, we need to include the last translation in the src/plugins/console/spm/language/ en-GB/plg_console_spm.ini file, adding this line to the end of the file:

```
PLG_CONSOLE_SPM_TASK_DEADLINE_OPTION_DAYS_DESCRIPTION="
Number of days in the future to check the deadlines"
```

Summary

In this chapter, we learned about Joomla! CLI applications and how we can use Joomla! CLI on a Joomla! site. We have also learned about integrating CLI applications in Cron Jobs to automate some tasks in our systems. Then, we discovered how to check CLI applications installed in a Joomla! site and how to add options to these commands, adapting the results to our needs.

Once we were familiar with Joomla! CLI applications, we started developing a plugin to add our own CLI application to Joomla!. In this path, we learned more about the Symfony Console, how to style our messages, and how to use Joomla's language system to make our CLI application available in more languages. Finally, we learned how to provide options for our commands, allowing for a more flexible CLI application.

In the next chapter, we will explore how to use template overrides in Joomla! to adapt their views to our designs.

Further reading

- In the *Joomla Magazine*, there is a detailed article about how to use Joomla! CLI called *Joomla 4: A Powerful CLI Application*: `https://magazine.joomla.org/all-issues/june-2022/joomla-4-a-powerful-cli-application`

- The Symfony Console component has great documentation: `https://symfony.com/doc/current/components/console.html`

- You can see how to style your console output using Symfony output in this article: `https://symfony.com/doc/current/console/coloring.html#using-color-styles`

- You can read more about Cron Jobs on Wikipedia: `https://en.wikipedia.org/wiki/Cron`

Part 3: Extending Templates

Templates allow us to change the style and design of our site without affecting the site functionality. Joomla! comes with one great frontend template, which we can use in our projects, but we can also install third-party templates. In any case, to adjust the design of your templates and make them look even better, you can use template overrides or child templates. Also, extending what you learn in this part a bit further will lead you to develop your own templates.

This part has the following chapters:

- *Chapter 10, Creating Unique Web Applications with Template Overrides*
- *Chapter 11, Creating a Child Template in Joomla!*

10

Creating Unique Web Applications with Template Overrides

Every successful web application must be visually appealing to your users and simple to use. No matter how good your software is, if it's not attractive to your users, you will see less success.

In Joomla!, templates are a powerful tool to match any design specification we need. In fact, templates are a great way to split functionality from design, as they only affect the look and feel of a Joomla! site.

When we work on a full-featured project, not only do we have to create extensions to fulfill the project requirements, but we also need to adapt the site design to fit visually.

In this chapter, we are going to learn about template overrides in Joomla!. Template overrides allow us to adapt any Joomla! component or module to match our required designs.

These are the specific sections we will cover in this chapter:

- What is a Joomla! template?
- What are template overrides?
- Creating a template override for Joomla! views
- Creating alternative layouts
- Overriding CSS and JS

Technical requirements

In this chapter, we will not work on our code base; instead, we are going to work directly on our demo site, so we will need the following:

- The Joomla! site we installed in the previous chapters should be enough, as Joomla's template manager tools are basic but powerful
- It will be nice to have FTP access to the files on our Joomla! site
- If you have FTP access, using Visual Studio Code (or the code editor of your preference) to edit the files will be fine

You can find the code files for this chapter on GitHub: `https://github.com/PacktPublishing/Developing-Extensions-for-Joomla-5/tree/chapter10`

What is a Joomla! template?

Joomla! templates are a special type of extension on a Joomla! website. They control the design of your website, and you can think of them as a real-world extension of the Model-View-Controller pattern. Templates should only affect the design of your website.

In Joomla!, we use templates for the backend and frontend to change the design of both parts of a site. With Joomla!, besides the default backend template, some other backend templates appear, but it's not very common to use a different backend template. In any case, the principles under which templates operate are the same for both the backend and frontend.

Backend templates are inside the `/administrator/templates` of your Joomla! site. When you check inside that folder, you will see the `atum` folder, which contains all the files and folders for the default Joomla! backend template.

Frontend templates live in the `/templates` folder of your site, and in a clean Joomla! installation, you will see the `cassiopeia` folder inside.

Developing a template for Joomla! might be as simple as creating an `index.php` file and its corresponding `install.xml` file inside a folder in your `/templates` folder.

However, a typical Joomla! template will consist of these files:

- `templateDetails.xml`: This is the manifest file of the template. It's like the manifest files we wrote for our component, module, and plugins, although it has some specific tags for templates.
- `index.php`: This is the entry point of the template. Joomla! will go through this file to display the site. This file might contain intermixed PHP and HTML code.
- `error.php`: This file handles creating the layout of your error pages. Besides loading the CSS and JS files needed to match your design, it shows the error message to users.

- `component.php`: This file generates the simplest page possible to match your design, showing only the view for your component. It's typically used to load modal windows from different views.

- `offline.php`: This file creates the look and feel of a page when the **Offline** setting is on.

- `joomla.asset.json`: This file defines the web assets we can use in our template, and it works exactly as we saw in *Chapter 3, Developing the Frontend of a Basic Joomla! Component.*

- `media` files: These are the web assets of the template, such as CSS, JS, fonts, and icons. They are not located inside the template folder. Instead, they are placed in their own folder, inside the `/media/templates/site/` folder of your Joomla! site.

- The `html` folder: This folder contains all the template overrides we need to force Joomla! extensions to match our own look and feel.

One of the most powerful features of templates resides in the `html` folder, as it makes it possible to override the design of other extensions. In the next section, we will explore what template overrides are and how we can create our first override.

What are template overrides?

A template override in Joomla! is a way to change how our components look when we access any of their views. What we do when creating a template override is replace a `tmpl` file of our component view with our own `tmpl` file, without affecting the original `tmpl` file. This is usually done by creating a different version of the `tmpl` file inside a specific path within our template folder.

When creating a template override in Joomla!, we do not modify the original file, which is a key part of the overrides. This allows a user to modify the design of an extension with an override and ensure that it's not going to be lost with the next update. This results in users and developers quickly updating their extensions, leading to a more secure platform.

In a template override, we have complete freedom to create whatever output we need to match our design. However, we need to remember that all our changes will only affect how we show the output of that extension, and we will not be able to inject different server behavior just with our override. Also, template overrides are specific for the template in use, so any changes in your template will not affect how other templates on your site look.

Some use cases for template overrides I find interesting are as follows:

- Creating different versions of an output to adapt your extension to different Joomla! versions.

- Replacing links and form actions to redirect a user to other extensions of our site – for instance, redirect the "remember my password" link to a contact form page.

- Fixing non-accessible designs with a better HTML structure

- Showing the same content with different designs – for instance, **A/B testing**

- Template overrides are great, but they have a downside – they might break with disruptive changes in the extension you override. However, these changes are not that common, and they only happen between major versions of extensions.

Let's create our first template override in the next section to see how easy it is.

Creating a template override for Joomla! views

In Joomla!, we can create template overrides for our component views, module layouts, plugin output, and Joomla! generic layouts. We can create template overrides for any Joomla! extension that respects Joomla! coding guidelines and provides a layout file.

To create a template override, we first need to locate the files of the view we want to override. For instance, for Joomla! components, these files will be inside the `tmpl` folder of our component. Once we have the files, we must copy them to their proper subfolder in the **HTML** folder of our template. Once everything is in place, Joomla! will use the new files instead of the ones inside the component.

The process is very manual, but to make it even simpler, you can use **the create override** feature that comes with Joomla! to create your overrides.

This tool is part of the Template Manager in Joomla!, so to access it, you must log in to the administrator of your Joomla! site and go to **System | Templates**. Then, click on **Cassiopeia Details and Files** (or the analog link of the template you want to create the overrides for). Finally, choose the **Create Overrides** tab. You will now see four visual groups, one for each origin of the override – **Modules**, **Components**, **Plugins**, and **Layouts**.

Every one of these groups contains the elements you can override. If you have followed all the chapters of this book precisely, you may see our component name, `com_spm`, in the **Components** listing. You will also see the `spm` plugin group inside the **Plugins** listing.

Clicking on any of these items expands the elements, which you can override with a **Copy** icon on the left. When clicking on any of these items, Joomla! will create the override in the appropriate folder.

Let's start creating overrides for our project in the following section.

Creating a template override for a component view

To show how template overrides work, we will change our projects view for the SPM component. We will replace our current card view with an accordion view.

The first thing is to create an override of the view. When creating the override manually, we need access to the files in our Joomla! site, so on our Joomla! site, we will copy the `/components/com_spm/tmpl/projects/default.php` file into the `/templates/cassiopeia/html/com_spm/projects/` folder. Henceforth, Joomla! will use this file instead of the one in the component folder.

When creating an override using the overrides manager, you need to look for the `com_spm` element in the **Components** section, click on it to expand it, and then click on **projects** to create the override.

One interesting feature of the overrides manager is that it does not replace an existing override. When an override for your view is already in place, instead of overwriting it, it saves the new file with a timestamp in the name. This way, you cannot lose your work by mistake.

Now, replace the recently created file with the following code:

```php
<?php

use Joomla\CMS\Router\Route;
use Joomla\CMS\HTML\HTMLHelper;
use Joomla\CMS\Factory;
?>

<form>
<div class="items-limit-box">
    <?php echo $this->pagination->getLimitBox(); ?>
</div>
<div class="projects">
<?php foreach ($this->items as $item) : ?>
    <details>
        <summary>
            <?php echo $item->name; ?>
        </summary>
      <div class="details">
        <div class="project-id meta">
            <?php echo $item->id; ?>
        </div>
        <div class="project-deadline meta">
            <?php echo $item->deadline; ?>
        </div>
        <div class="project-link">
          <a href="<?php echo Route::_('index.php?
            option=com_spm&view=project&id=' . $item->
              id);?>">Go to project</a>
        </div>
      </div>

    </details>
<?php endforeach;?>
</div>
<p><?php echo $this->pagination->getResultsCounter(); ?></p>
<?php echo $this->pagination->getListFooter(); ?>
    <input type="hidden" name="task" value="projects">
    <?php echo HTMLHelper::_('form.token'); ?>
</form>
```

This code replaces the `<div class="card">` items with `<details>` items, which provide a native way to create an accordion in HTML5. Also, to make it clearer and separate the actions, we have removed the link from the project name and added it as a dedicated link to the details.

Creating an override for a module follows the same logic; let's see how we can add a deadline to our `ProjectsList` module in the next section.

Creating a template override for a module

Creating an override for modules replicates the actions we followed for components. For modules, we have no views, but we do have layouts to override inside the `tmpl` folder of the module. To illustrate this, we will create an override of our `ProjectsList` module, making it add a deadline for each of the projects shown.

We will start by copying `/modules/mod_projectslist/tmpl/default.php` into `/templates/cassiopeia/html/mod_projectslist`. Exactly as it happened with components, henceforth, Joomla! will use this file instead of the one provided in the module.

When creating the override using the overrides manager, you need to look for `mod_projectslist` in the **Modules** section. In this instance, when you click on the item, Joomla! will create the override immediately.

Now, we will replace the code in the `default.php` file with this code:

```
<ul>
<ul class="mod-projects-list">
<?php foreach ($projects as $item) : ?>
    <li>
        <?php echo $item->name; ?>
        <?php echo $item->deadline; ?>
    </li>
<?php endforeach; ?>
</ul>
```

In this file, we will add the deadline property to the output, so now, when you check the module in the frontend, you will see the name of the project and the associated deadline.

Now that we know how to create an override for components and modules, let's look at when we can create an override for a plugin.

Creating a template override for a plugin

So far, we have created overrides for components and modules, and you will find very few of these that cannot be overridden. However, when it comes to plugins, it's a different scenario, as some plugins are not meant to provide an output but, instead, to change the behavior of Joomla!.

A quick way to know whether a plugin can have a template override is to look for the `tmpl` folder inside its base folder. When the folder is present and has a PHP layout file inside, the plugin can have a template override.

In *Chapter 8, Developing a Joomla! Plugin*, we created a couple of plugins, one for the **content** group and the other for our own **spm** group. We are going to override our **content** Type with the **projectlink** plugin to show how to create a template override.

By checking the code for that plugin, we will discover that our layout file inside the `tmpl` folder is `link.php`. That's fine – layouts can have different filenames, and we just need to be careful and copy the files correctly.

So, we will copy the file from our Joomla! site, `/plugins/content/projectlink/tmpl/link.php`, into `/templates/cassiopeia/html/plg_content_projectlink/link.php`, and we will edit this file to open the links in a new window:

```
<div id="spm-project-<?php echo $item->id;?>" class="
   spm-project">
     <a href="<?php echo $item->url; ?>" target="_blank">
         <?php echo $item->name; ?>
     </a>
</div>
```

By adding `target="_blank"` to the tag in the HTML, our project links on this site, using this template, will open in a new tab.

Like the previous sections, we can also create an override using the overrides manager. For this, we need to find the **content** element in the **plugins** section and click on it. Once clicked, content plugins available for a template override will appear. We will click on the **projectlink** element, and our override file will appear in the appropriate subfolder in the `html` folder of our template.

Creating alternative layouts

Overriding views is a great way to adapt our views for every project in Joomla!. Having the capability to replace the whole markup of our view is very powerful and provides great flexibility to Joomla! site integrators. However, template overrides affect the whole site. What happens if we want to offer our projects card view and accordion view on different areas of the same site? This is when adding different item views makes sense.

Adding an alternative menu item for a component view

In Joomla!, we can define different layouts for our views in the `overrides` folder. To see this, let's move our template override to a new item type for the component.

First, create the /templates/cassiopeia/html/com_spm/projects/alternative. xml file inside Joomla! with the following content:

```
<?xml version="1.0" encoding="UTF-8"?>
<metadata>
    <layout title="COM_SPM_VIEW_PROJECTS_ALTERNATIVE
      _MENU_LABEL">
        <message>
            <![CDATA[COM_SPM_VIEW_PROJECTS_ALTERNATIVE_MENU_DESC]]>
        </message>
    </layout>
</metadata>
```

In this file, we define the elements for the menu item configuration. Check out *Chapter 3, Developing the Frontend of a Basic Joomla! Component*, for further reference. This XML file is the same one we added to the view subfolder inside the tmpl folder of the component.

Now, rename the override file from /templates/cassiopeia/html/com_spm/default. php to /templates/cassiopeia/html/com_spm/alternative.php.

And that's it! We have created a new menu item type for our component that is exclusive to this website and template, using all the logic of the project's model and view.

Now, when you create a new menu item for the SPM component, you will see a new menu item type corresponding to this new **alternative** view.

This technique is only suitable for components, but we can use a similar technique for modules. Let's see how to do it in the next section.

Adding an alternative layout for a module

In Joomla!, we may have the same module displayed in several areas of our website. So, it makes even more sense to have alternative layouts instead of modifying the default module layout.

With modules, we do not have XML item type definitions, so creating alternative layouts is easier. We just need to rename our template override for the module layout, and we will be able to choose between the default layout and the new alternative one.

To see this in action, rename the override you have created for the module, /templates/ cassiopeia/html/mod_projectslist/default.php, to /templates/cassiopeia/ html/mod_projectslist/deadlines.php.

After doing this, the module will revert to using the default layout packed with the component. However, when you edit the module configuration now, on the **Advanced** tab, you will see there is a new option in the **Layout** field. So, you can choose from the following:

- **From Module : default**

- **From cassiopeia Template: deadlines**

And just like that, you have empowered the display of your modules, offering more options to a user of the site.

For plugins, we do not have any of these mechanisms for alternative layouts.

Overriding views and adding new layouts help a lot to improve our markup and adapt our designs, but this might not be enough, and we may need to replace CSS and JS. If so, the next section shows how we can override style sheets and JS in Joomla!.

Overriding CSS and JS

In Joomla!, all the style sheets and JS files should be managed through the Web Assets Manager. We introduced Joomla's Web Assets Manager in *Chapter 3, Developing the Frontend of a Basic Joomla! Component*. This offers great flexibility, as we can use Web Assets Manager methods to enable, disable, or override our CSS and JS.

Overriding assets with the Web Assets Manager

When creating a template override, we modify the look and feel of a specific page, and we may need to use a different version of a JS library or replace a CSS file completely.

In those cases, the Web Assets Manager is of great help, as it allows us to replace assets in our template overrides easily. Let's see an example, replacing the jQuery library that Joomla! uses with a different version.

Add the following lines to the `/templates/cassiopeia/html/com_spm/alternative.php` override, just after declaring your namespaces:

```
$wam = Factory::getApplication()->getDocument()->
  getWebAssetManager();
$wam->registerScript('jquery', 'https://code.jquery.com/
  jquery-3.7.0.min.js');
```

In these lines, we first instantiate the Web Assets Manager object and use the `registerScript()` method to register the new **jQuery** version. The key part of this call is that we use the same asset name that the current jQuery library uses, so the Web Assets Manager, when looking for the asset, uses our latest registered version.

It's interesting to note that overriding assets work with our `joomla.asset.json` extension too, so if you need to always use a specific version of a common asset, you can use this feature by registering the asset in your extension.

Adding new assets to our overrides

When you want to add some changes, overriding existing assets might not be the easiest option. For those situations, you can add new assets using the Web Assets Manager.

To do this, create a CSS file in your template at `templates/cassiopeia/css/alternative.css` with the following content:

```
* {
    color: red;
}
```

This simple CSS makes all the text red, and you will easily detect the change.

Now, in the `/templates/cassiopeia/html/com_spm/alternative.php` file, after registering the **jQuery** library, add the following line:

```
$wam->registerAndUseStyle('alternative',
    'templates/cassiopeia/css/alternative.css');
```

This line uses the Web Assets Manager object we instantiated in the previous section and registers and loads the new `.css` file in our template. When we check now, all the text for our new alternative view should be red.

Disabling assets in our overrides

Besides replacing assets or adding new asset files, we can use the Web Assets Manager to disable those elements that we do not want to show in our override.

In our override, we do not need to load the `com_spm.projects` asset, as we are not using the cards interface and only the expanded view. To save a bit of loading time, we can disable adding this line of code, just below the line where we declare the $wam variable:

```
$wam->disableStyle('com_spm.projects');
```

This call to the `disableStyle()` method only needs the name of the style asset you want to disable.

Disabling JavaScript assets is analog, but it uses the `disableScript()` method.

Summary

In this chapter, we went deeper into customizing Joomla's look and feel. We first learned about templates in Joomla! and their basic structure. Then, we looked into template overrides, a powerful technique to adapt any Joomla! extension to our designs. We also learned how to create new menu item types for our components. Finally, we explored Web Assets Manager's great features to override, disable, and add new assets to our overrides.

In *Chapter 11*, *Developing a Child Template for Joomla!*, we will investigate more visual changes for our site by creating our first child template.

Further reading

- There is a nice article introducing **JLayouts** on the Joomla! official documentation site: `https://docs.joomla.org/J3.x:Sharing_layouts_across_views_or_extensions_with_JLayout`

- There is an extensive article about customizing Cassiopeia on the official Joomla! documentation site: `https://docs.joomla.org/J4.x:Cassiopeia_Template_Customisation`

- If you want to know more about the Overrides Manager in Joomla! 4, check out this article in *Joomla Magazine*: `https://magazine.joomla.org/all-issues/july-2022/joomla-override-management`

- Joomla! documentation on Web Assets Manager is a great resource to learn more about it: `https://docs.joomla.org/J4.x:Web_Assets`

11

Creating a Child Template in Joomla!

Child templates are one of the greatest features introduced in Joomla! 4.1, and they address a long-standing request from Joomla! users to have a more flexible platform.

Before child templates appeared, you could clone a site template and edit it to fix your needs, but managing updates was cumbersome, as you must create an update package for your clone, taking into account your changes. Child templates address this issue, replacing the need to duplicate all the files of a template.

In this chapter, we are going to create our own child template from Joomla's Cassiopeia template. That will allow us total flexibility when developing our custom web apps. We can modify child templates as much as we need and modify their module positions, or even replace assets. We will see how to identify templates that allow child templates, how to manage template overrides in child templates, and finally, how we can reuse our child templates on other sites.

To learn all about child templates in Joomla!, we are going to follow this road map:

- Why do we need child templates?
- Creating a child template
- Adding a new module position to the template
- Reusing child templates on different sites

Technical requirements

In this chapter, we are going to work back into our coding structure, so you will need the following:

- Visual Studio Code (or the code editor of your preference)
- The Joomla! site we installed in the previous chapters

- You can find the code files for this chapter on GitHub at `https://github.com/PacktPublishing/Developing-Extensions-for-Joomla-5/tree/chapter11`

Why do we need child templates?

In *Chapter 10, Creating Unique Web Applications with Template Overrides*, we saw the power of Joomla! to create custom-designed web applications with template overrides. We can use template overrides to change the design of our component area for a website, we can add new styles or JavaScript-loading new assets, or we can even create new view types for our menus. This might seem enough, but there are some additional points:

- With template overrides, we cannot change the main site structure, as we cannot edit the template positions.

- With template overrides, we cannot edit web assets for the whole site, our changes will be limited to the areas of the site where the override takes place

- Most important, we cannot create an override of an override. You can have only one override per element. This is very important when the template you use uses a template override for the layout you want to override.

Child templates inherit files and behavior from their parent template. That allows us to focus the development efforts on the areas of our template we want to change and use parents from the rest.

So, when we need to modify a layout from an override, we can simply create a child template from our main template and create our new override in the child template. This comes in handy when using a template from another developer that comes with template overrides.

As in Joomla!, you can have unlimited templates per site; this technique helps you to have as many overrides of the same element as you need.

Creating a child template

A basic child template consists of one XML file package in a ZIP file. So simple, so powerful. Obviously, the key here is the content of that XML file and how we add the rest of the files we need. And, of course, things get a bit more complex when we add more changes to our file.

This manifest XML file is quite like the parent template manifest file. It also resembles the other extensions' manifest files that we saw in previous chapters. Let's start creating our first child template to see how it's created. First, we need to choose a parent template to create our child. In this book, we are going to use Cassiopeia as the parent template for several reasons:

- It comes in every Joomla! installation

- Cassiopeia respects web standards, and lots of volunteers have tested it in different environments

- Cassiopeia grades very well on accessibility and usability, so it's a great starting point to create a great new template

Once we have decided to create a child template from Cassiopeia, we need to check whether the template allows us to create a child template. To see this, we go to our Joomla! site file, `templates/cassiopeia/templateDetails.xml`, and we look for the tag. The value enclosed in the tag should be 1, as per this code:

```
<copyright>(C) 2017 Open Source Matters, Inc.</copyright>
<description>TPL_CASSIOPEIA_XML_DESCRIPTION</description>
<inheritable>1</inheritable>
```

In this manifest code extract, we can see the 1 tag highlighted as we need, so we can start creating our template.

Creating a child template directly in our repository

In our code repository, we are going to add the `src/templates/cassiopeia_first/templateDetails.xml` file with the following content:

```xml
<?xml version="1.0" encoding="UTF-8"?>
<extension type="template" client="site">
  <name>cassiopeia_first</name>
  <version>1.0</version>
  <creationDate>August 2023</creationDate>
  <author>Carlos</author>
  <authorEmail>book@piedpider.dev</authorEmail>
  <copyright>(C) 2023 Piedpiper</copyright>
  <description>TPL_CASSIOPEIA_XML_DESCRIPTION</description>

  <parent>cassiopeia</parent>
  <inheritable>0</inheritable>

  <positions>
    <position>topbar</position>
    <position>below-top</position>
    <position>menu</position>
    <position>search</position>
    <position>banner</position>
    <position>top-a</position>
    <position>top-b</position>
    <position>main-top</position>
    <position>main-bottom</position>
    <position>breadcrumbs</position>
```

```
    <position>sidebar-left</position>
    <position>sidebar-right</position>
    <position>bottom-a</position>
    <position>bottom-b</position>
    <position>footer</position>
    <position>debug</position>
  </positions>

  <files>
    <filename>templateDetails.xml</filename>
  </files>

</extension>
```

In this XML file, we are defining the basic elements of our template. First of all, in the main tag, we set the `type` attribute to `extension`. A child template is a regular template, so this is the same as a regular template. We also set the template to be a frontend template with the `client="site"` attribute. Inside the tag, we add our metadata tags. In this case, as we are creating a child template, we must prefix the name of our child template with the name of our template; in our code, we are using `cassiopeia_first`.

For the rest of the metadata tags, `<version>`, `<creationDate>`, `<author>`, `<authorEmail>`, `<copyright>`, and `<description>`, we are free to set the information we want.

After adding the metadata, we have included the tag with the name of the parent template. This is important, as Joomla! will check the parent template to fill in all the files and information we do not include in our child template.

After setting the parent, we can see we configured the `inheritable` tag to 0, which indicates this template cannot have any children. This is by design, as child templates cannot have children. You may create as many child templates from parent templates as you need, but you cannot create child templates of a child template.

Once we have added the template metadata and specified the parent template, we can see the **positions** section. This section is enclosed under the `<positions>` tag, and inside it, we include all the positions available in your template to use for the modules. We can use different names for these positions; after all, we are creating a new template, and we can also add positions or remove them from the list. In any case, my advice is to keep the name for parent template positions and add the positions we need. Joomla! uses the positions in the manifest when showing available positions when publishing a module. However, to decide where to place them, we will need to include some coding in the *Adding a new module position to the template* section.

After the **positions** section, we find the **files** section. This section contains the files and folders to be installed on our Joomla! site. We are creating our child template only with the `templateDetails.xml` file, so we include it in our manifest.

This is the only file we need to create a child template, so we can package it in a ZIP file and install it in our Joomla! site through the Joomla! extension manager.

Once installed, you will be able to select this child template like any other template on your Joomla! site.

This is a very basic child template, and to be honest, it will not be very useful, as it changes nothing in the parent template configuration. We are going to improve this template in the next sections, but for now, we can see that creating this basic child template involves three steps:

1. Creating the XML.
2. Packaging the XML.
3. Installing the package in Joomla!.

This process gets a bit more complex when we want to include changes in our files, such as extra style sheets, different overrides, or more JavaScript functions.

In the next section, we are going to see how we can create a child template with just the click of a button.

Creating a child template using the Joomla! template manager

In Joomla!, we can create a child template directly from the template manager. For this, you have to log in to the administrator of your Joomla! site and go to **System | Templates**. Then, click on **Cassiopeia Details and Files** (or the analog link of the template you want to create the child template for). Finally, you click on the **Create Child Template** button. Clicking the button creates the child template and installs it on your site automatically.

Besides the `templateDetails.xml` file, Joomla! has also created the overrides folder, `templates/cassiopeia_first/html`, and the media folders:

- `media/templates/site/cassiopeia_first/css`
- `media/templates/site/cassiopeia_first/js`
- `media/templates/site/cassiopeia_first/images`
- `media/templates/site/cassiopeia_first/scss`

So, we can start adding overrides directly into these folders.

To create these folders manually, as in the previous section, we would need to create the folders in our repository structure:

- `src/templates/cassiopeia_first/html`
- `src/templates/cassiopeia_first/media/css`
- `src/templates/cassiopeia_first/media/js`

- `src/templates/cassiopeia_first/media/images`

- `src/templates/cassiopeia_first/media/scss`

Add them to the `templateDetails.xml` section:

```
<files>
    <filename>templateDetails.xml</filename>
    <folder>html</folder>
</files>

<media folder="media" destination="templates/site/cassiopeia_first">
    <folder>css</folder>
    <folder>js</folder>
    <folder>images</folder>
    <folder>scss</folder>
</media>
```

In the next section, we will see what happens to the overrides in a child template.

Overrides in child templates

When using a child template, Joomla! tries to find the files from the child template folders first, and if no file is available, it checks the file from the parent template. That applies to every resource we need to use.

So, when our parent template has an override we want to keep in our child template, we do not need to copy it again into the `html` folder of our child template. Joomla! will automatically use the override located in the parent template `html` folder.

However, when we create an override in the child theme `html` folder, it takes precedence, and Joomla! uses it instead of anything else. This is very useful to maintain our overrides on future parent template updates.

In *Chapter 10, Creating Unique Web Applications with Template Overrides*, we saw a method to create overrides of assets through the Web Assets Manager. Actually, we could only override assets using the **Web Assets Manager**. With child templates, we can create overrides of the assets without the Web Assets Manager, by creating a file in the proper media folder.

Let's see an example of this, by creating an override for the styles in the `offline.css` file. The `offline.css` file appears when we use the **Offline** mode of our Joomla! site, so first, go to **Joomla administrator** | **Global Configuration** | **Site** and enable the **Site offline** switch.

Now, when you go to the frontend of your site, you will see the default offline page of Cassiopeia.

Now, use the template manager or your code editor, and add the `media/templates/site/` `cassiopeia_first/css/offline.css` file with the following content:

```css
.logo-icon{
    display: none;
}

.header{
    background-color: #1E8d38;
    padding: 2rem;
}

.outer{
    margin: 2rem auto;
    padding: 0rem 0 2rem 0;
    border: 2px solid #1E8d38;
    background-color: #2F9E49;
    color: white;
}

.login{
    padding: 1rem 2rem;
}

.btn{
    background-color: #0d7e27;
    border-color: #0d7e27;
    color: white;
}

.btn:hover,
.btn:focus{
    background-color: #1E8d38;
    border-color: #1E8d38;
    color: white;
    outline-color: white;
}
```

This CSS code will change the appearance of the offline page, removing the Joomla! icon and switching the background color to green. As the CSS file is inside the media folder of our child template, it takes precedence over the default Cassiopeia `offline.css` file, and Joomla! uses it to generate the page.

Adding a new module position to the template

Joomla! templates can be divided into areas or positions. These positions are containers where Joomla! will place our modules and components on page load. This way, a Joomla! template knows where to place the component output or where to place the output of a module.

Earlier in this chapter, we saw that these positions are included in the `templateDetails.xml` file. Joomla! uses the positions in this manifest file to offer the available positions when editing a module. However, what's most important is to include the position in the template structure. Template positions are coded in the main file of a Joomla! template, which is the `index.php` file of the template. This is where we set up all the HTML basic structures that our template will use to create the output web page.

To make it easier to include Joomla! output content in this template structure, in Joomla!, we can use a custom HTML tag, `<jdoc:include />`.

This tag accepts several attributes:

- `type`: Indicates the kind of content from the CMS that we want to load. The main content types we can use are `head`, `component`, `modules`, and `message`. There is a link to the official *jdoc* statements documentation in the *Further reading* section of this chapter.

- `name`: This attribute only applies when we are loading a module position. It tells Joomla! the name of the module position to load.

- `style`: This attribute tells Joomla! which style or **chrome** should be used to create the output of the module.

We can use also more attributes specific to the type of content we are loading.

Let's add a new `afterfooter` position to our child template. Copy the file from your Joomla! site, `templates/cassiopeia/index.php`, into `templates/cassiopeia_first/`. Edit the file, and at the bottom of it, you might see the following code:

```php
<?php if ($this->countModules('footer', true)) : ?>
    <footer class="container-footer footer full-width">
        <div class="grid-child">
            <jdoc:include type="modules" name="footer" style="none" />
        </div>
    </footer>
<?php endif; ?>
```

Below that code, add the following code:

```php
<?php if ($this->countModules('afterfooter', true)) : ?>
    <div class="container-afterfooter afterfooter full-width">
        <div class="grid-child">
```

```
            <jdoc:include type="modules" name="afterfooter"
style="none" />
        </div>
    </div>
<?php endif; ?>
```

In this code, we first use the `countModules()` method provided by the Joomla! Framework™. This method returns the number of modules added to the `afterfooter` position. As we pass the second argument as `true`, the method only returns modules that output any content.

After detecting the content, we create a basic HTML structure to show our modules, and finally, we use the tag. For the tag attributes, we use the name `afterfooter`, which is the name of the new position, and for the style attribute, we use `none`. That will output the module with no specific styling by default. This can be changed when configuring the module in the backend, as we will see in the next section.

To test this, we can go to our Joomla! administrator area, create a new module of type `Copyright`, and assign it to the **afterfooter** position.

Let's see now how we can create different styling for our template modules.

Using different styles for the module

When checking the module configuration screen, you may find in the **Advanced** tab several options such as **Module Class**, **Header Tag**, and **Module Style**. These options change the output code of the module, such as adding a CSS class, changing the header tag, or using a different style or layout for the output.

When developing a template, we can create different **module styles** for our modules or override the ones already created. Actually, one of the attributes we set when including a module is the style we want to use by default.

Module styles are also known as **module chromes**, and we define them inside the `override` folder of our template – Specifically, inside `html/layouts/chromes/`. If you check this folder for your Cassiopeia template, you will see that there are already 2 files, `card.php` and `noCard.php`.

Let's create a module style for our child template, adding the `/templates/cassiopeia_first/html/layouts/titleCentered.php` file with the following content:

```php
<?php

use Joomla\Utilities\ArrayHelper;

$module   = $displayData['module'];
$params   = $displayData['params'];
```

```php
$attribs = $displayData['attribs'];

if ($module->content === null || $module->content === '') {
    return;
}

$moduleTag              = $params->get('module_tag', 'div');
$moduleAttribs          = [];
$moduleAttribs['class'] = $module->position . ' no-card ' .
htmlspecialchars($params->get('moduleclass_sfx', ''), ENT_QUOTES,
'UTF-8');
$headerTag              = htmlspecialchars($params->get('header_tag',
'h3'), ENT_QUOTES, 'UTF-8');
$headerClass            = htmlspecialchars($params->get('header_
class', ''), ENT_QUOTES, 'UTF-8');
$headerAttribs          = [];

$headerAttribs['class'] = 'text-center';

if ($headerClass !== '') {
    $headerAttribs['class'] = ' ' . $headerClass;
}

if ($moduleTag !== 'div') {
    if ($module->showtitle) :
        $moduleAttribs['aria-labelledby'] = 'mod-' . $module->id;
        $headerAttribs['id']              = 'mod-' . $module->id;
    else :
        $moduleAttribs['aria-label'] = $module->title;
    endif;
}

$header = '<' . $headerTag . ' ' .
ArrayHelper::toString($headerAttribs) . '>' . $module->title . '</' .
$headerTag . '>';
?>
<<?php echo $moduleTag; ?> <?php echo
ArrayHelper::toString($moduleAttribs); ?>>
    <?php if ($module->showtitle) : ?>
        <?php echo $header; ?>
    <?php endif; ?>
    <?php echo $module->content; ?>
</<?php echo $moduleTag; ?>>
```

This code is based on the noCard.php module style. With this style, we wrap the content of our module in the **module tag** chosen by the user, with the small change of centering the module title when it is shown.

After defining our namespaces, we get the module data from the $displayData array. From this array, we get three variables with all the module information:

- $module: This contains all the module information, such as the module content to show, the title, and also the module parameters
- $params: This contains all the settings that the user sets in the module configuration
- $attribs: This contains the basic attributes of the module, such as the name of the position and the name of the style to use

From these variables, we first check whether the module outputs any content and return otherwise. When the module contains information to show, then we check the module params to define the resulting HTML code.

We group the attributes of the header tag in the $headerAttribs indexed array and the attributes of the module container in the $moduleAttribs indexed array. This way, we can use the ArrayHelper::toString() method to easily generate the HTML code.

Our change in this code consists of adding the text-center class to the $headerAttribs['class'] values so that the heading is centered by the text-center CSS class from Bootstrap 5 when shown.

We can use this style when including our module, using it in the tag, as follows:

```
<jdoc:include type="modules" name="afterfooter" style="titleCentered"
/>
```

In the next section, we will see how we can distribute our child template to other sites.

Reusing child templates on different sites

Creating child templates using Joomla's Template Manager, as seen in previous sections of this chapter, is the easiest way to create our child. It might also be convenient for you to create your child template modifications and overrides directly on your Joomla! site. When we want to reuse our child in other sites, we need a way to move our changes. Luckily, we can reuse child templates on as many sites as we need; the only condition is that the site needs to have the parent template of the child already installed.

The easiest way to reuse our child template on several sites is to create an installable package. As we already have our templateDetails.xml file, we only need to package the files the proper way to create them.

There are two different folders to take into account, the main template folder and the media folder (in case you added changes to it). To make the process easier, let's copy our original child template into our code repository, and from there, we will create our package.

If your original child template is on a Joomla! site on a remote server, you would need to use FTP or a similar tool to download the files into your code repository. To make things easier in this chapter, instead of *downloading the files*, we will use the verb *copying*.

First, go to your Joomla! site templates folder and copy the content of the `templates/cassiopeia_first/` folder into our local repository at `src/templates/cassiopeia_first`.

When you have also modified or added assets to the media folder, you need to copy them. So, copy the contents of the folder from your Joomla! site at `media/templates/site/cassiopeia_first` into `src/templates/cassiopeia_first/media/`.

To create our child template package, we need to zip the `src/templates/cassiopeia_first/` folder with all its content. Also, if you check carefully, you should have inside the package the `templateDetails.xml` file, with the `html` and `media` folders.

If you have created an override for the `index.php` file or the `offline.php` files, you need to edit the `templateDetails.xml` manifest file and add them to the section accordingly, such as the following:

```
<files>
    <filename>templateDetails.xml</filename>
    <filename>index.php</filename>
    <filename>offline.php</filename>
    <folder>html</folder>
</files>

<media folder="media" destination="templates/site/cassiopeia_first">
    <folder>css</folder>
    <folder>js</folder>
    <folder>images</folder>
    <folder>scss</folder>
</media>
```

Also, you can omit any of the empty folders in this section.

This allows you to install your child template on any Joomla! site with the Cassiopeia template installed. Of course, this also works when you use a different parent template.

We have created a child template, which we can reuse on several sites, and even distribute to other Joomla! users. However, when you see the child template configuration in the Joomla! administrator, you will see that there are absolutely no parameters to configure. In the next section, we will go through adding parameters to our child template for easier configuration.

Adding parameters to a child template

So, we have no parameters to configure in the administration area of our child template. In the parent template, there are some parameters to show the logo or to choose the layout. Why is that happening? Child templates inherit the selected parameters from their parent, even though they have no parameters in the configuration area. However, as child templates are full templates, they can have their own parameters and settings, and they can actually be different from their parent template.

To add a parameter to our child template, we need to add a section to the `templateDetails.xml` file as we did with the other extensions in their manifest file. As our template does use some of the settings from its parent, it is interesting to add those parameters back to the settings. In our case, we are going to add the settings related to the logo and branding. So, edit the `src/templates/cassiopeia_first/templateDetails.xml` file and add the following code before the closing tag:

```
<config>
    <field name="brand" type="radio" label="TPL_CASSIOPEIA_BRAND_
LABEL" default="1" layout="joomla.form.field.radio.switcher"
filter="boolean">
        <option value="0">JNO</option>
        <option value="1">JYES</option>
    </field>
    <field name="logoFile" type="media" default="" label="TPL_
CASSIOPEIA_LOGO_LABEL" showon="brand:1"/>
    <field name="siteTitle" type="text" default="" label="TPL_
CASSIOPEIA_TITLE" filter="string" showon="brand:1"/>
    <field name="siteDescription" type="text" default="" label="TPL_
CASSIOPEIA_TAGLINE_LABEL" description="TPL_CASSIOPEIA_TAGLINE_DESC"
filter="string" showon="brand:1"/>
</config>
```

This code adds the section that holds the settings of our template. These fields are copied from **Cassiopeia**, our parent template, and allow us to switch the logo and define the title and a tagline for the website.

When you install the child template with these changes and enter into the configuration of the template style through **System | Template styles | cassiopeia_first**, in the **Advanced** tab, you will find these four settings to configure.

These settings have the same `name` as the settings in the parent template, and the values you choose here will override the values set in the parent template.

Now, it is time to make our child template a bit more different, so we are going to add a switch button to center the logo. To do this, edit the `templateDetails.xml` file you just edited and add the following field before the closing tag:

```
<field name="logoCentered" type="radio" label="TPL_CASSIOPEIA_FIRST_
LOGOCENTERED" default="0"
```

```
layout="joomla.form.field.radio.switcher" filter="boolean">
    <option value="0">TPL_CASSIOPEIA_FIRST_LOGO_NOT_CENTERED</option>
    <option value="1">TPL_CASSIOPEIA_FIRST_LOGO_CENTERED</option>
</field>
```

This code adds a radio where the user can choose to center the logo on the website. Now, we need to add the code to the child template that uses this setting. To do that, we edit the `src/templates/cassiopeia_first/index.php` file and place the following code after the definition of the `$wa` variable:

```
if ($this->params->get('logoCentered', false)) {
  $wa->addInlineStyle(".container-header .navbar-brand{
margin:auto}");
}
```

This code will get the saved setting for the `logoCentered` field, and if it's `true`, we use the Web Assets Manager (the `$wa` variable) to add the CSS we need to center the logo as an inline style.

When using parameters from the parent template, Joomla! uses the language strings from the parent, but when we use new parameters, we need to tell Joomla! what the translations are for these strings. In the next section, we are going to see how to add our own language strings to a child template.

Adding language files to our child template

Child templates inherit every aspect of their parents, and that also involves language files and translations. However, when we add language strings to our child template that are not included in the parent, we need to add their equivalent translations.

Following our example, we need to add some new language strings to our child template. To do so, we copy the files from our Joomla! site at `language/en-GB/tpl_cassiopeia.ini` and `language/en-GB/tpl_cassiopeia.sys.ini` into the following files, or our repository – `src/templates/language/en-GB/tpl_cassiopeia_first.ini` and `src/templates/language/en-GB/tpl_cassiopeia_first.sys.ini`. Then, we add the following lines to `src/templates/language/en-GB/tpl_cassiopeia_first.ini`:

```
TPL_CASSIOPEIA_FIRST_LOGOCENTERED="Logo position"
TPL_CASSIOPEIA_FIRST_LOGO_CENTERED="Centered"
TPL_CASSIOPEIA_FIRST_LOGO_NOT_CENTERED="Left aligned"
```

We need to copy the previous language translations so that we do not lose them. Joomla! uses a parent language file as long as the child template does not have a language file of its own. Once the child template has a language file installed on the site, Joomla! stops looking for the parent template language files and uses only the child template translations.

Finally, we need to add the recently created language files to the child template manifest so that they are installed along with our template. So, edit the `src/templates/cassiopeia_first/templateDetails.xml` file and add the following lines below the section:

```
<languages folder="language">
    <language tag="en_GB">en-GB/tpl_cassiopeia_first.ini</language>
    <language tag="en_GB">en-GB/tpl_cassiopeia_first.sys.ini
    </language>
</languages>
```

This instructs Joomla! to install the language file.

Now, after installing the template, we can see our parameter settings fully translated, and we have a child template that we can distribute to as many Joomla! sites as we need.

Summary

In this chapter, we dived into the development of a child template. We saw how this is the most basic form of a template we can develop, as it only needs one file.

We improved our child template, adding changes such as new positions and overrides to make it different from its parent template, to the point where we have created our own template to install on other Joomla! sites.

When creating overrides, we discovered how we can use child templates to override the parent template CSS and JavaScript, by simply creating the correct style sheets and JavaScript files.

Finally, we added different parameters to the template and its own language files.

This is the last chapter devoted to extension coding; in the next chapter, we will dive into testing, and we'll provide some techniques to create bug-free code.

Further reading

Joomla's official documentation has an exhaustive article about `jdoc` statements: `https://docs.joomla.org/Jdoc_statements`

Part 4:
Distributing Your Extensions

When you develop a great extension, you want the world to know about it. Why not distribute it to other Joomla! users? In this part, we cover how to test our Joomla! extensions to be sure they work as expected, even after version changes. Then, we review Joomla! security practices to always be on the safe side. Finally, we see how we have to package our extensions to release them to the world.

This part has the following chapters:

- *Chapter 12, Testing Your Extensions*
- *Chapter 13, Security Practices in Joomla!*
- *Chapter 14, Distributing Your Joomla! Extensions*

12

Testing Your Extensions

When starting any software development project, we usually focus on our current environment (at the time of writing this book, we're focusing on **Joomla! 5** and **PHP 8.2** as our environment). But as the world around us evolves, our environment keeps updating and we need to be sure that our projects work with the new requirements. We will have a new release of PHP that will be more efficient and we need to detect new issues and incompatibilities in our code. Testing our software becomes a key aspect for medium and long-term projects.

In this chapter, we will explore some options for automatically testing our Joomla! development projects. We will go from basic unit testing to more exhaustive system testing and end this chapter by introducing accessibility testing using a web browser.

After reading this chapter, you will be able to develop the tests you need for your project. This will increase the trust and confidence you have in your code.

The main topics of this chapter are as follows:

- Do I need tests?
- Including unit testing in Joomla!
- How to add system testing in Joomla!
- Testing accessibility in our extensions

Technical requirements

In this chapter, we are going to work on our coding structure as we will be adding tests to our code. So, you will need the following:

- Visual Studio Code (or a code editor of your preference)
- PHP Composer installed on your computer

You can find the code files for this chapter on GitHub at `https://github.com/PacktPublishing/Developing-Extensions-for-Joomla-5/tree/chapter12`.

Do I need tests?

In web development, we face an ever-changing environment. For instance, PHP follows a community release cycle in which we have a new PHP version every year and every major release has 3 years of security support. These new releases provide new features and code deprecations that affect our code.

If we want our software to stand the test of time, we need to keep improving it and fixing deprecations and old conventions.

We can manually test our extensions. For that, we need to replicate the environment and conditions we want to test our software in, but we can also add automatic testing to our coding process and have it done to some extent by a machine.

Manual testing is a good starting point and it's the final testing method to guarantee our extension does exactly what we want. However, as we add more testing environments and our software grows, it takes too much time to perform manual testing in all our environments.

Automatic testing has some benefits compared to manual testing:

- You can perform the same test as many times as you want in as many environments as you need.

- Automatic tests are little scripts that check that your development behaves as expected. As such, it's much funnier to write code for automatic tests than to perform manual tests.

- Writing automatic tests helps you write better code as you need modular methods that perform just one action to write a good test of them.

Testing is a whole area of software development and there are plenty of philosophies and strategies you may use to test your extension. In this chapter, we will explore the most common and useful techniques for effective testing. We'll start by learning about one of the most popular testing techniques in PHP.

Including unit testing in Joomla!

Unit testing is an industry standard that helps you guarantee the quality of your developments. Unit testing consists of testing little parts of your code. The smallest testable parts in PHP are class methods or functions. Unit tests check the logic of your code in a fast and reliable way.

When running unit tests, you do not need your whole application to be running or a connection to a database. You may run your tests directly against your code base, though you may need to set up some environment.

Unit tests should test just one specific action or result in your code. So, when you're writing your code, you need to focus and create methods that have just one result. This leads to higher-quality code. This is very helpful and has encouraged a development strategy based on testing known as **test-driven development (TDD)**.

What is TDD?

TDD consists of writing the test you want to pass and then writing the code to pass it:

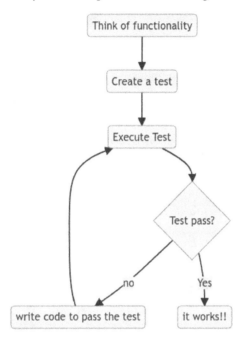

Figure 12.1 – TDD workflow

The workflow of TDD is as follows:

1.   You think of a new piece of functionality within your code.
2.   You create a test that proves the functionality works.
3.   You try to pass the test and it fails (you have no code written to pass the functionality).
4.   You write some code to pass the test.
5.   You pass the test.

This workflow is possible when you write modular code that embraces the **single responsibility principle**, which allows you to write tests for each of your methods safely. To write these tests, we use a framework called **PHPUnit**.

Installing PHPUnit

PHPUnit is the most popular framework for unit testing in PHP and it is also the unit testing framework that's used by the official Joomla! Project[SM].

We can install **PHPUnit** by using **Composer** in our repository, Let's take a look.

Installing PHPUnit through Composer

We need to have **Composer** installed globally on our computer or locally in our repository to install **PHPUnit** through Composer. The *Further reading* section provides a link to the main **Composer** website with more details according to your operating system.

Once you have installed Composer on your computer, you can use it to quickly initialize our project. First of all, from the command line, inside the main folder of your repository, execute the following command:

```
composer init
```

This will launch the `composer` initialization script. The script starts by asking questions about your project. In our case, we will use these answers:

```
Package name: piedpiper/spm
Description: A simple project management extension
Author: Carlos Cámara (carlos@hepta.es)
Minimum Stability: (click enter to use default)
Package Type: project
License: GPL v2.0
dev dependencies: phpunit/phpunit
version constraint: 8.5.32
Add PSR-4 autoload mapping: No
```

These settings generate the following `composer.json` file:

```
{
    "name": "piedpiper/spm",
    "description": "A simple project management extension",
    "type": "project",
    "require-dev": {
        "phpunit/phpunit": "8.5.32"
    },
    "license": "GPL v 2.0",
    "authors": [
        {
            "name": "Carlos Cámara",
            "email": "carlos@hepta.es"
```

```
        }
    ],
    "require": {}
}
```

Click *Enter* to confirm these settings and accept that you wish to install dependencies. This will trigger the initialization process, where a new file called `composer.json` that contains the preceding content will be created in our repository. A `vendor` folder will also be created.

The `composer.json` file contains the details of our project and the dependencies that we handled with **Composer**, while the `vendor` folder contains all the libraries in our dependencies – essentially, it's the PHPUnit framework.

Configuring PHPUnit for Joomla!

Our unit tests are little scripts that assert the responses in our main code, so we need a place to store them. For this, we are going to create a folder called `tests/Unit/`. This will be the main folder for our unit tests.

In Joomla! extension development, we commonly use variables, classes, and global definitions from Joomla! CMS™ code. This means that our extension code will rarely work outside of Joomla!. Unit tests are completely isolated from Joomla! CMS™ code, so we need to add a bootstrap file to tell PHPUnit where to look for some definitions and code. Download the bootstrap file from the repository associated with this chapter and place it in `tests/Unit/bootstrap.php`. The code will look like this:

```php
<?php
define('_JEXEC', 1);
error_reporting(E_ALL);
ini_set('display_errors', 1);
$rootDirectory = '/home/piedpiper/dev/joomla/';

if (!defined('JPATH_BASE')) {
    define('JPATH_BASE', $rootDirectory);
}

if (!defined('JPATH_ROOT')) {
    define('JPATH_ROOT', JPATH_BASE);
}
[LOTS OF EXTRA DEFINITIONS]
if (!class_exists('JLoader')) {
    require_once JPATH_PLATFORM . '/loader.php';

    // If JLoader still does not exist, panic.
    if (!class_exists('JLoader')) {
        throw new RuntimeException('Joomla Platform not
```

```
                    loaded.');
        }
}

JLoader::setup();

$loader = require JPATH_LIBRARIES . '/vendor/autoload.php';

class_exists('\\Joomla\\CMS\\Autoload\\ClassLoader');

$loader->unregister();

spl_autoload_register([new \Joomla\CMS\Autoload\
    ClassLoader($loader), 'loadClass'], true, true);

require_once JPATH_LIBRARIES . '/classmap.php';

require_once JPATH_LIBRARIES . '/namespacemap.php';
$extensionPsr4Loader = new \JNamespacePsr4Map();
$extensionPsr4Loader->load();

defined('JVERSION') or define('JVERSION', (new
    \Joomla\CMS\Version())->getShortVersion());
```

Here, we define all the environment variables we are likely to use in our extension code. In this file, we need to edit the value of the `$rootDirectory` variable in the highlighted line. This variable should store the path to a Joomla! 4 site installed on your computer.

After adding the `bootstrap.php` file, we need to tell PHPUnit to use it. To do so, we must create the `phpunit.xml` file at the root of our repository's main folder with the following content:

```xml
<?xml version="1.0" encoding="UTF-8"?>
<phpunit bootstrap="tests/Unit/bootstrap.php" colors=
  "false">
    <testsuites>
        <testsuite name="Unit">
            <directory suffix="Test.php">./tests/Unit
                </directory>
        </testsuite>
    </testsuites>
    <php>
        <const name="JPATH_BASE" value="/home/
            piedpiper/dev/joomla/" />
    </php>
</phpunit>
```

This XML file tells PHPUnit where to find our bootstrap instructions. In the section, we name our test suite `Unit` and use the `<directory>` tag to set the path to where our unit tests are located. In this case, we set it as our `tests/Unit` folder. Also, using the `suffix` property, we tell PHPUnit that all our tests will be inside files ending with `Test.php`.

In the `phpunit.xml` file, we may also define PHP constants. In this code, we are setting the `JPATH_BASE` PHP constant. In this case, defining the constant is optional. If you check the previous `bootstrap.php` file carefully, you'll see that we have some code to define this constant when it is not set.

Once we have the bootstrap file in place, we can start writing our first test.

Writing your first test

We are going to write a test for the **SPM – Customers** plugin we wrote in *Chapter 8*. In this plugin, we added a method to fix the casing for emails.

So far, we only have two requirements for the folder structure for our tests: they should be inside `tests/Unit` and the filenames should be similar to `NAMETest.php`. It will pay off if we create our tests in an orderly manner, replicating the content of the `src` folder where our code lives. So, let's start by creating the `tests/Unit/Plugin/Spm/Customers/CustomersPluginTest.php` file with the following content:

```php
<?php

namespace Piedpiper\Tests\Unit\Plugin\Spm\Customers\
  Extension;

use Piedpiper\Plugin\Spm\Customers\Extension\Customers;
use Joomla\CMS\Application\CMSWebApplicationInterface;
use Joomla\Event\Dispatcher;
use Joomla\Event\Event;

class CustomersPluginTest extends \PHPUnit\Framework\
  TestCase
{
    public function testFixCasing()
    {
        $testString = 'HELLO@PIEDPIPER';
        $testData = ['email' => $testString];

        $event = new Event('test');
        $event->setArgument('data', $testData);

        $app = $this->createStub(CMSWebApplicationInterface
```

```
            ::class);

        $dispatcher = new Dispatcher();
        $plugin = new Customers($dispatcher);
        $plugin->setApplication($app);

        $plugin->fixCasing($event);

        $resultData = $event->getArgument('data');

        $this->assertEquals(strtolower($testData['email']),
          $resultData['email']);
    }
}
```

In this code, the first thing we do is define our test namespace. This namespace matches the namespace we defined in the composer.json file (it was Piedpiper\Tests). After that, we have the folder structure where the file is located; this is the same as what was defined in the namespace.

Then, we declare the usage of our plugin class, which is at Piedpiper\Plugin\Spm\Customers\ Extension, and finally, we declare the other classes we need to use in our code.

Our class name matches our filename, and it extends the PHPUnit standard TestCase class to take advantage of all the methods it provides for testing.

Finally, our test is declared inside a method of this class. We can name this method whatever we want, but it's customary to name it after the test we want to perform.

In this method, we need to create the minimum environment for the test to run. Unit tests do not need a web server or a database as they check the logic of your code, but when running our code inside a big CMS such as Joomla!, we usually use some variables and conventions we need to replicate for PHPUnit.

Specifically, the fixCasing() method we want to test uses the plugin's $event object to get the email data, so we need to replicate this $event object and assign it the $data argument we want to test.

Next, we must instantiate the plugin class and assign the $app object. Once we have our plugin object, we must call the fixCasing() method while passing the $event variable we replicated as if we were saving a customer in the backend.

The plugin returned the fixed casing inside the data property of the $event object, so we must use the getArgument() method to retrieve it.

Finally, we must use the PHPUnit assertEquals() method to see if the initial string is in lowercase and the resulting string is the same.

This test looks pretty good. Now, we need to execute it to see if it works.

Running our first test

Once we have our tests ready, we can start testing using the `phpunit` command (which was installed after we executed `composer init`). For that, you need to go to the main folder of your repository and type the following command:

```
php ./vendor/bin/phpunit
```

If you try this right now, you will get an error because we still need to make some adjustments to the composer before we run our first test.

We need to map our test classes with their namespace because they are not included in the `bootstrap.xml` file.

Mapping classes in composer.json

Our `composer.json` file is not only a list of packages to install. This file also holds instructions on your code structure and even little scripts you can run. This helps set up some aliases and tells PHPUnit where the classes are located. So, we are going to edit the `composer.json` file. To respect the JSON structure, we need to add the following highlighted lines:

```json
{
    "name": "piedpiper/spm",
    "description": "A simple project management extension",
    "type": "project",
    "require-dev": {
        "phpunit/phpunit": "8.5.32"
    },
    "license": "GPL v 2.0",
    "authors": [
        {
            "name": "Carlos Cámara",
            "email": "carlos@hepta.es"
        }
    ],
    "require": {},
    "autoload-dev": {
        "psr-4": {
            "Piedpiper\\Tests\\": "tests",
        }
    },
    "scripts": {
        "test": "./vendor/bin/phpunit"
    }
}
```

With the `autoload-dev` configuration, we tell PHPUnit the relationship between our namespaces and the folder where the code is located. In this case, we point our `Tests` namespaces to the `tests` folder of our repository. The `scripts` setting creates a very convenient shortcut. So, when we want to run our unit tests, we just need to write the following:

```
composer test
```

This is much more convenient than writing the full path to `phpunit` every time.

Once this has been set up, we may run our test. We will get the following message:

```
Executing command (CWD): ./vendor/bin/phpunit
PHPUnit 8.5.33 by Sebastian Bergmann and contributors.

. 1 / 1 (100%)

Time: 195 ms, Memory: 10.00 MB
```

This means that our method passes the test and we are good to go. If you get a failure, then you need to recheck your code and see if there is any error that prevents the test from passing.

Unit testing is great for testing methods and the logic of our files, but by definition, it just tests small pieces of code in an isolated way. Our development projects are formed by these small units of code working together to create bigger things. So, we need a way to test our development in a more integrated way.

That's when system tests come into play. In the next section, we are going to explore how we can start creating system tests to guarantee a high-quality development product.

How to add system testing in Joomla!

System testing consists of a set of tests that check that your development works as expected, as per your design specifications. To develop system tests, you need to know how the system should work and what to expect after performing several actions in your system.

There are several methods to perform system testing. The easier to understand is manual testing. You have your testing site and you need to keep testing your development manually. This is far from ideal as you might be subject to errors and omissions in your tests. But if you are a systematic person and write down all your tests and results, it can be very effective. In any case, when you need to test against several PHP and Joomla! versions, this kind of test is highly time-consuming and not the best.

Automatic system testing is a whole subject itself and several books could be written about it. In this chapter, we are going to take the simplest way and we are going to use the **Codeception** testing framework with a minimum setup that will help us start testing quickly and effectively.

Installing Codeception

Codeception is a testing framework that's used by several PHP frameworks, including Symfony and Laravel. The Joomla! Project[SM] uses it before publishing any release. **Codeception** allows you to write your tests as a PHP program and it can translate that PHP program into an actual test with a web browser.

We can install **Codeception** using Composer, so we must go to the main folder of our repository and type the following:

```
composer require "codeception/codeception" --dev
```

The preceding code will install the testing framework in our repository folder. We also need to install the PHP browser and the `asserts` module it needs to run, so we must execute the following commands in the main folder or our repository:

```
composer require "codeception/module-phpbrowser" --dev
composer require "codeception/module-asserts" --dev
```

Once we have installed these modules, we can add the configuration file for Codeception. In the main folder of our repository, we added the `codeception.yml` file with the following content:

```
# suite config
suites:
    acceptance:
        actor: AcceptanceTester
        path: .
        modules:
            enabled:
                - PhpBrowser:
                    url: https://j4.ddev.site
                - \Helper\Acceptance

        # add Codeception\Step\Retry trait to
          AcceptanceTester to enable retries
        step_decorators:
            - Codeception\Step\ConditionalAssertion
            - Codeception\Step\TryTo
            - Codeception\Step\Retry

extensions:
    enabled: [Codeception\Extension\RunFailed]

params:
    - env
```

```
gherkin: []

# additional paths
paths:
    tests: tests/Acceptance/tests
    output: tests/Acceptance/_output
    data: tests/Acceptance/_data
    support: tests/Acceptance/_support
    envs: tests/Acceptance/_envs

settings:
    shuffle: false
    lint: true
```

In this `.yaml` file, we set the URL of our testing environment in the `url` parameter. In this file, we set `https://j4.ddev.site` as the URL of our testing site; you need to replace this with your actual URL. We configure the folder to store our tests and results in the `paths` section. In this case, I'm using the `test/Acceptance` folder as the main folder for my tests.

It's worth mentioning that in this case, **Codeception** is using a browser called **PhpBrowser**, which is a web scraper. If your project needs to test JavaScript interactions, you'll need to check if you need to install a different browser module, such as **Chromedriver** or **GeckoDriver**. There is also a fork of **PhpBrowser** that's been optimized for Joomla! sites called **Joomla Browser** that's maintained by the Joomla! Project[SM]. You can read more about it in the *Further reading* section.

Once everything has been configured, we can start writing our tests. We must add our tests inside the `tests/Acceptance/tests/` folder as this is the folder we specified in the `codeception.yml` file inside the `paths` section in the `tests` property. We need to create a php file containing a class with all our tests inside, similar to how we did with unit tests. So, let's create the `tests/Acceptance/tests/FirstCest.php` file with the following content:

```php
<?php

class FirstCest
{
    public function frontpageWorks(AcceptanceTester $I)
    {
        $I->amOnPage('/');
        $I->see('Home');
    }
}
```

In this class, we are defining one test that will check that our testing server front page works. We may use whatever class name or filename we want, but it's a good practice to use the same name for the class and the filename. It's also customary to add the `Cest` suffix to the name of the class, though it's not required.

Inside the class, we create one method per test we want to perform. These methods receive an `AcceptanceTester` object that contains the set of methods we need to run our tests. In our example, we are using the `amOnPage()` method to go to the URL of our testing site and the `see()` method to indicate a text string that should be on the page. One of the nice things about working with Codeception is that we do not need to use complex DOM specifications or paths to find elements on the page; we can use simple natural language to find the elements we want to see.

Once we have our first test method, we can go to the main folder of our repository and run Codeception with the following command in the terminal:

```
php ./vendor/bin/codecept run
```

This will output the following message:

```
Acceptance Tests (1) -------------------------------------
✔ FirstCest: Frontpage works (0.10s)
```

Here, we can see the class containing our test and the completed test. Notice that the name of the test is the name of our method formatted in natural language. This is because we named the method in camelCase format and Codeception can split the words and add required spaces.

With that, we have run our first test with Codeception, but it's of no use yet for our Simple Project Manager development. So, let's create a test that helps test our list of project features.

We could add the test as another method to our `FirstCest` class, but let's create a new class to have things more organized. Create the `tests/Acceptance/test/ProjectsViewCest.php` file with the following content:

```php
<?php

class ProjectsViewCest
{
    public function projectsViewWorks(AcceptanceTester $I)
    {
        $I->amOnPage('/index.php/spm');
        $I->seeElement('.card h2');
    }
}
```

In this test, we first go to our project view. The path should exist in our local server installation; otherwise, we will not be able to test it.

When on the page, we must look for an element of our layout using the `seeElement()` method to check the CSS path of the element.

When executing Codeception, we will see this message:

```
Acceptance Tests (2) --------------------------------------------------
------------------
✔ FirstCest: Frontpage works (0.12s)
✔ ProjectsViewCest: Projects view works (0.10s)
```

Codeception, when used with PhpBrowser, is quite powerful and you may even use it to test forms and test your site when you are logged in. Let's see how we can use it to test the backend part of our component.

Create the `tests/Acceptance/tests/AdminCustomersCest.php` file with the following PHP class:

```php
<?php

class AdminCustomersCest
{
    public function customersTableExists
      (AcceptanceTester $I)
    {
        $I->amOnPage('/administrator/index.php');
        $I->fillField('Username', 'tester');
        $I->fillField('Password', 'testerPassword12345#');
        $I->click('Log in');
        $I->amOnPage('/administrator/index.php?option=
          com_spm&view=customers');
        $I->seeElement('table');
    }
}
```

In this class, we redirect the browser to the administrator login area and we use the `fillField()` method to complete the login form. In this case, we use the form labels to match the element in the form. We could use the name of the field (case-sensitive) too. With the `click()` method pointing to the **Log in** button of the backend login form, we send the form.

After login, we redirect the browser to our customers page in the backend and we check for the `<table>` element in the page.

Running Codeception now results in the following output:

```
Acceptance Tests (3) -----------------------------------
✔ AdminCustomersCest: Customers table exists works (0.41s)
```

✔ `FirstCest: Frontpage works (0.09s)`
✔ `ProjectsViewCest: Projects view works (0.10s)`

This result shows that our tests are successful. You may notice that the time for the last test is a bit higher than for the others. This makes sense as it has more steps.

We could keep adding new tests to the site and covering all the features of our development with these functional tests. This will ensure our projects are more robust and that we will be able to test automatically for different configurations just by changing the local web server configuration.

Unit testing and system testing are great ways to develop more robust projects that are protected from changes in software updates, but when developing a web project, we also need to test other aspects, such as accessibility. In the next section, we'll see what strategies we can follow as developers to deliver accessible projects.

Testing accessibility in our extensions

When you are not familiar with accessibility, you usually think of it as something people with disabilities need. But at any time in our lives, everyone will be in a position where the environment is not right and they cannot use their senses at full potential. Think, for instance, when you are checking your mobile phone under direct sunlight or when grabbing bags and need to perform a quick route check on your device. You will need a good interface that allows you to see correctly under low contrast and with minimum interaction as you can only use one hand properly.

The myth around accessibility in web development, which is that it is very expensive to deliver an accessible product, is far from true. When you abide by current web standards and use semantic HTML in your frontend, you can achieve a high level of accessibility.

This myth probably comes from the fact that there is not a good automatic way of testing accessibility. In a web application, accessibility is meant to help humans understand a website, so only real people can do a complete accessibility test.

Also, accessibility needs to be tested in context, so on some websites, your extensions will be accessible and on other websites, they might contain accessibility errors.

Even so, semi-automatic testing is much better than no testing at all. And, as it usually happens, checking these errors and passing these tests will help you deliver a better product to your users.

Before you start testing accessibility for your extension, you need to know that passing all the tests that we are going to check in the following sections is not a guarantee of accessibility. But any accessibility error that you find while testing is an issue that you should fix to improve the accessibility of the extension.

Accessibility is a matter of how you code the resulting HTML. Therefore, we must start checking the HTML using our web browser and look at some extra tools we can install for better testing.

Testing accessibility with your browser

There are two major actors in the browser market these days: Chrome web browser and any of its derivatives (Chromium, Edge, and so on) and Firefox and any of its derivatives (Tor Browser, Pale Moon, and so on). In both families, you can find tools to automatically test the accessibility of your development.

To start testing accessibility, you need to choose your favorite web browser and open your testing site. When doing previous tests, we didn't need a specific setup for the site, but as accessibility depends on the context, you should try to make it the best context possible, so I recommend that you set default Joomla! templates for the backend (**Atum**) and frontend (**Cassiopeia**). Both templates achieve high levels of accessibility, so any errors you find will probably be related to your development.

Once you're on your testing site, you can test our projects page. So, point your browser to `https://yourtestingsite/index.php/spm` and, when you're ready, open the developers tools of your browser by clicking the *F12* key.

When using Google Chrome, you need to go to the **Lighthouse** tab of **Developer tools** and check the **Accessibility** option under the **Categories** section. When you're ready, you may click **Analyze page load**, at which point the website will be analyzed for several parameters:

Figure 12.2 – Settings to generate the Lighthouse report

Once this is complete, you will get the result of your test according to each of the categories that have been analyzed. When you click on **Accessibility**, you will see a list of issues on your page. In our case, we get this issue: **Select elements do not have associated label elements**. When you click on that element, you will see a dropdown with more details of the issue and a screenshot of the element. Also, when you hover over the details, the offending part of your page will be highlighted; you can click on it and be redirected to the specific code on the **Elements** tab.

When using Firefox, you can open its **Developer Tools** and go to the **Accessibility** tab. This is the Firefox **Accessibility inspector**. The Accessibility inspector shows two panes.

Figure 12.3 – The Accessibility tab in Firefox Developer Tools

The pane on the left contains the **Accessibility tree**, which lists your page's HTML in a tree structure, starting with the **document** tag. The pane on the right shows the properties of the checked element. Above the panes, on the left-hand side, you have three controls:

- **Check for issues**: This setting controls the problems you want to see on the accessibility tree.

- **Simulate**: This setting adjusts the color parameters of the window to any of the visual disabilities that have been configured. It's a great way to see your development in the same way as people who cannot appreciate the contrast in detail.

- **Show Tabbing Order**: This setting controls how people using only a keyboard will navigate through your page, showing the order they will be able to reach the links and buttons on your page.

In Firefox, we can also browse our projects page to test accessibility. Once you're on the `https://yourtestingsite/index.php/spm` page, open the Accessibility inspector and set **Check for issues** to **All issues**. This will replace the Accessibility tree with all the leaves of the tree presenting accessibility issues and a brief description of the issue.

Browser tools provide a minimum accessibility check. In the *Further reading* section of this chapter, you will find links to **WAVE** and **AXE**. These are a set of accessibility evaluation tools that can help you go further and analyze many more aspects of accessibility.

Besides these semiautomatic tests, there is a quick test we can perform in our web developments: **keyboard testing**. In this test, we point our browser to our projects page (`https://yourtestingsite/index.php/spm`) and then use the *Tab* key to browse the page. You should be able to reach all the links, tabs, and buttons of your site and click on them. When this is not possible, you should review your focus indicators and navigator order. The *Further reading* section provides a link with more information about this technique.

Summary

In this chapter, you learned about adding automatic tests to your development so that you have more durable code. You also learned about unit testing using PHPUnit and how to start adding unit tests to your Joomla! extensions. Then, you discovered how TDD works and learned how to add more development dependencies to your project using PHP Composer.

We focused on system testing using the Codeception framework to check that our projects behave as expected and we learned a simple and effective way to use PhpBrowser for our tests.

Finally, you learned about accessibility and how to start identifying issues in your extensions using your browser. You also learned how to do keyboard testing, which is a simple test you can start doing right away on all your developments.

So far, we have learned how to develop extensions in Joomla! and we have trusted Joomla! for security. But as developers, we need to pay special attention to this matter and create secure web applications. In the next chapter, we will learn how to enhance the security of our code.

Further reading

- You may find more information about PHPUnit and its methods at `https://www.phpunit.de`
- Composer has a great website with all the resources you need to learn more about it: `https://getcomposer.org/`
- There is a nice document about Codeception web drivers in their official documentation: `https://codeception.com/docs/modules/WebDriver`
- You can learn more about Joomla Browser by going to its GitHub repository: `https://github.com/joomla-projects/joomla-browser`
- The Codeception documentation contains all the methods that are available for working with PhpBrowser: `https://codeception.com/docs/AcceptanceTests#PhpBrowser`
- WAVE tools is a great toolkit for checking the accessibility of our web developments: `https://wave.webaim.org/`
- AXE tools also provide great help in accessibility testing: `https://www.deque.com/axe/`
- WCAG offers good introductory materials for developers who want to learn more about accessibility: `https://www.w3.org/WAI/roles/developers/`
- The Toronto Metropolitan University offers a free ebook for developers who want to know more about accessibility: `https://pressbooks.library.torontomu.ca/wafd/`
- You may find a great guide on keyboard testing on the WCAG website: `https://webaim.org/techniques/keyboard/#testing`
- There is a great article about end-to-end testing in the Joomla magazine: `https://magazine.joomla.org/all-issues/june/end-to-end-testing-with-joomla-and-cypress`

13

Security Practices in Joomla!

When developing software for the web, you'll encounter security threats. These may involve targeted attacks on your system, but more often than not, they will be random attacks with no specific target.

Joomla! is a secure platform that takes security very seriously. It has a team of expert volunteers who tackle and patch any vulnerability that might appear. But you also need to stay vigilant yourself because, as a developer, you need to be sure that your web application does not offer vulnerabilities that could be exploited.

Even though when you consider it's impossible to exploit a vulnerability in your code, you need to stay proactive and fix it. Web applications move in a complex environment with many technologies involved, so attacks might appear for unexpected reasons.

In this chapter, we will cover the most common security practices we need to follow in Joomla!. This will help you deliver secure solutions to your users.

In this chapter, we will cover the following topics:

- Fetching data from forms
- Preventing SQL injection
- Securing your assets for the future
- Hardening access to your files

Technical requirements

In this chapter, we are going to revisit the code we wrote in previous chapters, so you will need the following:

- Visual Studio Code (or a code editor of your preference)
- The code files for this chapter, which can be found on GitHub at `https://github.com/PacktPublishing/Developing-Extensions-for-Joomla-5/tree/chapter13`

Fetching data from forms

When showing information in a URL, the risk of being attacked is low. This is because the visitor has no way to send data to our site – data could be injected only by URL and Joomla! performs good cleaning on the URLs that are processed with its router.

The problem arises when we include interaction in our developments, usually adding forms to the pages. Forms are quite common, even for pages that are meant to show information such as data listings. If you remember our **Projects** view, we added a search form and pagination to easily search the projects in our database. Those features are forms. This can be seen in the following extract of the layout for the projects listing in the backend (at `src/component/admin/tmpl/projects/default.php`):

```
<form action="<?php echo Route::_('index.php?
    option=com_spm&view=projects'); ?>" method="post"
      name="adminForm" id="adminForm">
      <div class="row">
          <div class="col-md-12">
              <?php echo LayoutHelper::render('joomla.search
                  tools.default', ['view' => $this]); ?>
          </div>
      </div>

      . . .
</form>
```

In this piece of code, we can see the HTML `<form>` tags and how we call the search layout to load the filters defined in our form. This code will be translated into a text search input box with the HTML equivalent of all the filters defined in `src/component/admin/forms/filter_projects.xml`.

This view will also have a pagination section at the bottom and a select input box to change the number of items shown. All these are HTML elements that a malicious user might be tempted to modify to inject an attack into our system.

So, in your code, when receiving these values, you should never trust them completely and filter them when possible. As seen in *Chapter 4*, for project filters, we get the values at the `populateState()` method in the model. So, if you check the `src/component/admin/src/Model/projects.php` file, you may find this code:

```
protected function populateState($ordering = 'name',
    $direction = 'ASC')
{
    $app = Factory::getApplication();
    $value = $app->input->get(
                'limit',
```

```
                    $app->get('list_limit', 0),
                    'uint');
        $this->setState('list.limit', $value);
        $value = $app->input->get('limitstart', 0, 'uint');
        $this->setState('list.start', $value);
        $search = $this->getUserStateFromRequest(
                $this->context . '.filter.search',
                'filter_search');
        $this->setState('filter.search', $search);
        parent::populateState($ordering, $direction);
}
```

In PHP, the values that are passed via a form are stored in the `$_POST` global variable, but we do not use it. Instead, we use the `Input` object (called from the `app->input` property) defined in Joomla! to retrieve these values, as you can see in the highlighted lines. This is because the `Input` class provides additional cleaning and filtering. In these methods, you can see that we also include the `last` parameter, which will filter the values as unsigned integers in this case.

For the `$search` variable, you can see that we use a different method, `getUserStateFromRequest()`, that combines the current state for the variable with the value submitted in the form. This method also accepts a filter; let's add it now. Look for the following line:

```
$search = $this->getUserStateFromRequest(
                $this->context . '.filter.search',
                'filter_search');
```

Replace it with this:

```
$search = $this->getUserStateFromRequest(
                $this->context . '.filter.search',
                'filter_search',
                'string');
```

This will return a sanitized and fully decoded string in the search that's saved so that we can use it on our site.

These are the filters we can use:

- `int`: This returns an integer or an array of integers.
- `uint`: This returns an unsigned integer or an array of them.
- `float`: This returns a floating-point number (or an array of floating-point numbers).
- `boolean`: This returns a true or false value.

- `word`: This returns a string containing characters from A to Z or underscores (_). No other symbols are accepted. It's not case-sensitive.

- `alnum`: This filter returns a string with characters from A to Z and from 0 to 9 only. No symbols are accepted. It's not case-sensitive.

- `cmd`: This filter returns a string with characters from A to Z and from 0 to 9, underscores (_), periods (.), and hyphens (-). It's not case-sensitive.

- `base64`: This filter returns a string with characters from A to Z and from 0 to 9, forward slashes (/), and + or = symbols only. No other symbols are accepted. It's not case-sensitive.

- `string` or `html`: This filter (you may use any of the words) returns a regular string and removes dangerous HTML tags such as `<script>`, `<apple>`, and other tags used in attack attempts.

- `array`: This returns an array.

- `path`: This returns a clean filesystem path. It doesn't check that the path exists.

- `trim`: This returns a string without a leading or an ending white space.

- `raw`: This filter does nothing, so it just returns the value as-is.

As you can see, there are lots of filters we can use to sanitize the information we get from our forms and secure our inputs. Also, when not using a filter, misspelling the name of a filter, or using a filter not present on this list, Joomla! will apply the `cmd` filter by default.

Filtering input data before saving it to a database

In the previous section, we saw how we can filter the input data when retrieving it directly from the request. But when we used Joomla! MVC classes in *Chapter 2*, we did not need to retrieve the data directly from the request: it was some Joomla! MVC magic.

In *Chapter 2*, we learned *how to develop an edit item view for our component*. In our case, we did not have to deal with the `save` or `apply` methods because we were extending Joomla's `FormController`, which dealt with them. Internally, the controller uses the `validate()` method in the `FormModel` class, which filters and validates the data using the form filters that are configured in the form definition, as we saw in *Chapter 4*.

In *Chapter 4*, we learned how to validate the data that is received from the form by creating custom methods or using Joomla! basic validation rules, but we did not apply any filters to our data. In Joomla!, we can apply filters to the data that's sent by the form and also in the form definition, which helps secure your web application.

So, for instance, when saving our invoices, we defined our invoice form like this at `src/component/admin/forms/invoice.xml`:

```xml
<?xml version="1.0" encoding="UTF-8"?>

<form addrulepath="administrator/components/com_spm/rules">
    <field
        name="number"
        type="text"
        label="COM_SPM_INVOICE_NUMBER"
        />
    <field
        name="amount"
        type="text"
        label="COM_SPM_INVOICE_AMOUNT"
        inputmode="decimal"
        class="validate-notzero"
        required="true"
        pattern="[0-9]{1,}(\.[0-9]{1,2})?"
        />
    <field
        name="items"
        type="text"
        label="COM_SPM_INVOICE_ITEMS"
        />
    <field
        name="customer"
        type="text"
        label="COM_SPM_INVOICE_CUSTOMER"
        />
</form>
```

In this code, you may notice the validation rules we set up, but before processing the server validation rules, all these fields will be filtered using the default `string` (or `html`) filter. This filter is quite good as it removes any malicious encoding or tags, but we could make the form even more secure by adding filters for it.

So, let's add some filters to make it look like this:

```xml
<?xml version="1.0" encoding="UTF-8"?>

<form addrulepath="administrator/components/com_spm/rules">
    <field
        name="number"
```

```
        type="text"
        label="COM_SPM_INVOICE_NUMBER"
        filter="alnum"
        />
    <field
        name="amount"
        type="text"
        label="COM_SPM_INVOICE_AMOUNT"
        inputmode="decimal"
        class="validate-notzero"
        required="true"
        pattern="[0-9]{1,}(\.[0-9]{1,2})?"
        filter="float"
        />
    <field
        name="items"
        type="text"
        label="COM_SPM_INVOICE_ITEMS"
        />
    <field
        name="customer"
        type="text"
        label="COM_SPM_INVOICE_CUSTOMER"
        filter="int"
        />
</form>
```

The new `filter` attribute is highlighted here. This will apply the specific filter to the field before retrieving it from the request, so you can be sure you are handling the exact type of data you expect.

Filtering data is important for having a secure application. You must remember to always apply the most restrictive filter that assures you receive the data you expect, regardless of whether you retrieve the information directly from `input` or if you trust Joomla! Forms.

Preventing cross-site request forgery (CSRF) attacks in forms

One common web attack is **CSRF**, in which the attacker gets to inject their code into the web application through a trusted user. This might happen when an administrator does not end their session on the Joomla! site and browse a malicious site. This site might try to send data to the Joomla! site using any known form.

In Joomla!, we have a way to prevent this attack: by including a random string called **Token** in the form data. This string is then checked when the request is received, at the beginning of the controller.

In *Chapter 3*, when we added an edit form for our projects, we included this token. So, if you take a look at the `src/component/admin/tmpl/project/edit.php` file, at the end, you will see the following code:

```
use Joomla\CMS\HTML\HTMLHelper;

...

<?php echo HTMLHelper::_('form.token'); ?>
</form>
```

Here, we first declare the `HTMLHelper` class and then we use it to print the token for our form. This method will output the full `input` HTML field:

```
<input type="hidden" name="AAABBBCCCDDDEEE" value="1">
```

Here, the `name` attribute will contain the random string that will be used as a token. This random string is generated using the user ID and data from the current session, so if the user logs out or if the session expires, it's no longer valid.

Once the form has been submitted, the token is checked first thing in the method handling the data. In our case, we were extending Joomla's `FormController`, so we need to check the file inside our Joomla! installation, `libraries/src/MVC/Controller/FormController.php`. At the beginning of the `save()` method, we will find the following code:

```
    public function save($key = null, $urlVar = null)
    {
        // Check for request forgeries.
        $this->checkToken();
        ...
    }
```

This automatically checks the token.

So, when you are not extending Joomla! `FormController` classes or when you are adding your own handling methods for tasks, remember to include the logic to check the token.

Preventing cross-site scripting (XSS) attacks

XSS attacks are dangerous attacks that inject JavaScript code into the page and can lead to session stealing or impersonating another user. This attack consists of injecting JavaScript code in the URL to replace any of the variables that are passed. So, when the user loads an affected URL, the browser executes the malicious code. One simple example could be using the `https://hackedsite.`

`com?value=<script>/*+Bad+stuff+here...+*/</script>` URL, which executes the following code:

```php
<?php echo $_REQUEST('value');?>
```

In Joomla!, it's really easy to mitigate this attack – we just need to use the `$app->input->get()` method we saw at the beginning of this chapter to retrieve the values with the HTML or string filters.

Also, implementing the CSRF token we saw in the previous section protects us from this attack as the attacker cannot generate the proper token to bypass our security.

Preventing SQL injection

So far, we have secured our web application using filters and a CSRF token. And as we are using Joomla! MVC classes, which deal with lots of cleaning for us, we are pretty safe now.

A web application is as secure as the weakest of its parts, so we need to keep adding measures to prevent vulnerabilities in our development.

One of the biggest fears in web development is suffering from **SQL injection**. The classic example of this attack is when you get the data from your user and you inject it directly into your database. A typical example of vulnerable code looks like this:

```php
$userid = $_POST['userid'];

$query = "SELECT * FROM users_table WHERE userid = $userid";
```

As you can see, there is no filtering to get the `$userid` value directly from the `$_POST` superglobal, so a malicious user can send the `"1; DROP TABLE users_table;"` string. When the query is created, the result will be as follows:

```php
$query = "SELECT * FROM users_table WHERE userid = 1; DROP TABLE
users_table;"
```

When executing this query, your `users_table` will be removed.

This is a basic example with horrendous consequences. Once you are vulnerable to SQL injection, an attacker might take advantage of it to retrieve information from your database without your awareness.

In Joomla!, when using the `DatabaseQuery` class (which we have been using this whole book to interact with the database), the risk of suffering such an attack is low, especially since we are filtering all the data we receive from the user.

In any case, a low risk is higher than none, so one of the great improvements that came with the release of Joomla! 4 was the addition of **SQL-prepared statements**. This feature improves the efficiency of your database queries (especially if they are repetitive) and it practically removes the possibility of being affected by a SQL injection attack. The only downside of prepared statements is that it makes it a bit more difficult to debug SQL sentences as $query->dump();, which is used to show the database's query contents, does not work anymore.

A prepared statement is like a **template for your database queries** that the database precompiles and then fills with the proper values when executing it.

Let's go back to our frontend project model and focus on the getItem() method of the src/component/site/src/Model/Project.php file:

```
function getItem($pk = null)
{
    $id = (int) $pk ?: (int) $this->getState('project.id');

    if (!$id) {
        throw new \Exception('Missing project id', 404);
    }

    if ($this->_item !== null && $this->_item->id != $id) {
        return $this->_item;
    }

    $db = $this->getDatabase();
    $query = $db->getQuery(true);

    $query->select('*')
        ->from($db->quoteName('#__spm_projects', 'a'))
        ->where('a.id = ' . (int) $id);

    $db->setQuery($query);

    $item = $db->loadObject();

    if (!empty($item)) {
        $this->_item = $item;
    }

    return $this->_item;
}
```

In the highlighted code, we can see a SQL query that could benefit from the prepared statements. We can replace it with this code:

```
$query->select('*')
        ->from($db->quoteName('#__spm_projects', 'a'))
        ->where('a.id = :userid');
$query->bind(':userid', (int) $id);
```

As you can see, it's not a big deal – we only need to switch the direct replacement of the value with a statement (`:userid`), and then we must relate the statement with the proper value (`$id`). We can even maintain the typecasting and be sure we only inject an integer there.

Besides filtering, using prepared statements improves the security of your web application, so it's a good way of preventing vulnerabilities.

Securing your assets for the future

In *Chapter 3*, we added web assets to our component using the Joomla! Web Asset Manager and we noticed all the benefits it provides. But at some point, when you wish to make small and quick changes to your code, you might be tempted to include your styles or JavaScript directly in the HTML code of your layout files. Even more, you might feel a bit lazy and include them inside your extension folder instead of the media folder.

This might lead to exposing your extension folder to an attacker, and third-party firewall extensions installed in Joomla! might block access to these files.

Since the release of **Joomla! 5**, users can install their Joomla! files outside of the server's public folder. Linking to the direct URL of the files might be impossible in those cases.

Nowadays, adding HTML attributes such as `onclick=""` or `onchange=""` is deprecated and you should avoid them. Instead, define your events in your JavaScript files.

To prevent issues, you need to follow these rules:

- Use the Joomla! Web Asset Manager or `HTMLHelper`, as we saw in *Chapter 3*, to load your styles and scripts
- Do not include JavaScript code or events in your HTML code
- Store your fonts, images, scripts, and styles in the proper path of the media folder

This way, you will have no issues with security extensions in your development.

Hardening access to your files

Joomla! is a CMS with a powerful framework, and developing extensions for Joomla! is fun and easy thanks to all the code contributed by all the volunteers. But we should not forget that our web application in Joomla! is a collection of single PHP files working together as a whole.

Joomla! usually runs on a web server (commonly **Apache** or **Nginx**) that can execute PHP code. If you upload a custom `.php` file with some valid code to your Joomla! website and you try to access it, you will see that it works with no issues.

This also happens with the files of our extensions when you try to access them directly. Right now, if you have followed all the examples in this book, your files can be executed without Joomla!. As we are using lots of classes and libraries from Joomla!, it's very likely that, when accessed directly, you will get errors. However, these errors might offer clues to attackers, so we need to secure our files to prevent direct access to our classes.

In Joomla!, the most common way of doing this is by adding the following statement at the beginning of our files:

```
defined('_JEXEC') or die;
```

When you try to access any file with this statement, the web server will check if the _JEXEC constant is defined and it will stop execution otherwise.

The _JEXEC constant is defined by Joomla! at the beginning of its execution cycle to guarantee that our PHP files will only be used within Joomla!.

In the event you need a custom entry point for your web application, the preferred method is to create a controller in your component that handles it. In this case, you need to put the proper authentication methods in place so that your entry point cannot be exploited.

Using the JED Checker extension

In the next chapter, we will see what entails distributing our extension, but it's valuable to mention the **JED Checker** extension here.

JED Checker is a Joomla! extension that automatically checks the code of your extension for problems that prevent its submission to the **Joomla! Extensions Directory**™.

It's really easy to use and even if you do not plan to upload your extension to the Joomla! Extensions Directory, it provides useful information about your code that you might have missed.

To use JED Checker, follow these steps:

1. First, you need to install it on a Joomla! site (it does not need to be your testing site; any Joomla! site will do). To install it, go to the backend of the site, click **System**, and in the **Install** section, click **Extensions**.

2. Now, in the installer, click the **Install from Web** tab, and in the search area, type JED Checker. You will see the **JED Checker** extension, as per *Figure 13.1*.

3. After clicking on the magnifier button, the JED Checker will appear. Click on the extension name and then on the **Install** button.

4. Once installed, go to **Components | JED Checker** from the side menu; you will see a little form where you have to upload a ZIP package that contains your extension code.

5. Create the package and click on **Submit**. After uploading the file, click on the **Check** button; you will see the results for your extension.

As shown in *Figure 13.1*, on the left-hand side, the different areas are checked and there's a little badge stating the number of issues and a color indicating the severity of the issue:

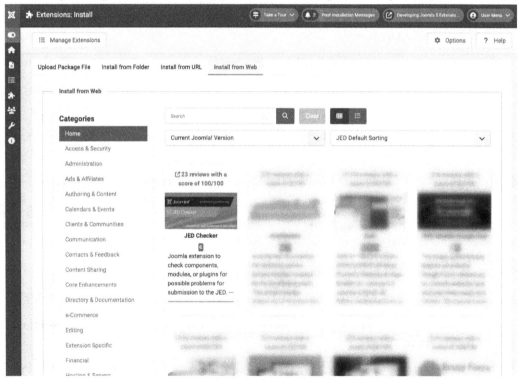

Figure 13.1 – JED Checker shown in the Install from Web tab of the Joomla! Extensions installer

We will focus on the following issues shown in the report, as shown in *Figure 13.2*:

- **PHP Files missing JEXEC security**: This check tells you how many of your files do not have the defined('_JEXEC') . or die; statement at the beginning of them. The report should show no files affected by this issue.

- **Joomla! Framework™ deprecated and unsafe**: This check informs you of deprecated or unsafe code in your extension. Ideally, there should be no deprecated code, but it might not be an issue. Unsafe code, on the other hand, should be fixed.

- **JAMSS - Joomla! Anti-Malware Scan scripts**: In this section, the checker runs a script that detects malware in the files. If you see any file in this section, it means you are using files that contain malware, so you must review them and fix or remove them. To ensure you have a safe extension, this section must report no files:

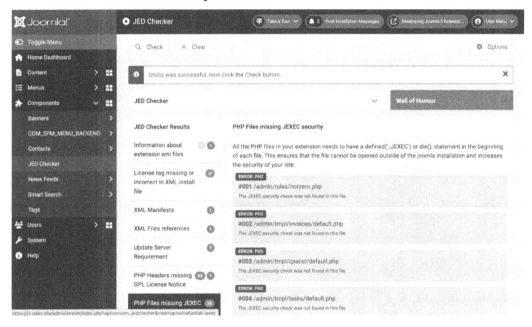

Figure 13.2 - JED Checker report for our component before applying security fixes

With that, we can summarize this chapter.

Summary

Joomla! is a secure platform with a robust framework that allows us to deliver safe applications to our users. But as with any other tool, if we do not pay attention to the details, we might include vulnerabilities in our code.

In this chapter, we learned about important security practices that allow for safer coding in Joomla!. First, we learned how to filter the requests we receive in our extension through the entry points we defined in our component. Then, we focused on how to secure our queries to the database using prepared statements and also casting our values to the specific types. Finally, we provided some tips to handle our static assets securely, looked at how to prevent random access to our PHP files, and learned how to automatically check our extensions using the JED Checker component.

With that, we have developed a fully equipped project manager, added automatic tests, and hardened ourselves against vulnerabilities. In the next chapter, we will look at all the things we need to consider when releasing to the world.

Further reading

- There is an extensive article about CSRF attacks on Wikipedia: `https://en.wikipedia.org/wiki/Cross-site_request_forgery`

- You may contribute to and find more information about JED Checker by going to its GitHub page: `https://github.com/joomla-extensions/jedchecker`

14
Distributing Your Joomla! Extensions

In the previous chapters, we developed a great extension for simple project management. We worked a lot and developed a component, some plugins, a module, some overrides, and even a child template. That's a lot of work to keep to yourself, so you probably want to release it to the world.

In this chapter, you will learn how to prepare your extension so that you can publish all the steps you need to follow to release it to the world, and even how to get paid for it.

By the end of this chapter, you will know how to create a distributable package with your development that can be installed on as many sites as possible. You will also know how to handle the database changes automatically and how to perform advanced tasks when installing your packages. Finally, you will see how easy it is to add a paywall to your extension and limit downloads to people after the paywall.

These are the topics we will cover in this chapter:

- Creating a package for your extensions
- How to manage database changes on your extensions
- How to execute advanced tasks on extension install
- Setting up an update server
- Adding a paywall to your extension download

Technical requirements

In this chapter, we will be creating the package files to distribute our extensions, so you will need the following:

- **Visual Studio Code** (**VS Code**) (or a code editor of your preference)
- The code files for this chapter, which can be found on GitHub at `https://github.com/PacktPublishing/Developing-Extensions-for-Joomla-5/tree/chapter14`

Creating a package for your extensions

In Joomla!, extensions are distributed in the form of packages. These packages consist of a compressed file (usually in the `.zip` format), which holds all the extension files, and a manifest file, which contains instructions for Joomla! on how to place the files inside Joomla!.

In *Chapter 2*, we created our first package for the `com_spm` component. To create this `.zip` file, we just compressed the contents of the `src/component` folder. That worked because we had the manifest file (`src/component/spm.xml`) placed in the main folder of the ZIP package. Let's look at the different parts of our manifest file. Open the `/src/component/spm.xml` file; you will see the following lines at the beginning and the end of the file:

```
<? xml version="1.0" encoding="utf-8" ?>
<extension type="component" method="upgrade">

...

</extension>
```

In these lines, we declare the XML standard we are using and the type of extension to install. In the manifest file, the order of the sections is not important. The common practice is to include the metadata at the beginning of the file:

```
<name>COM_SPM</name>
<author><![CDATA[Carlos Cámara]]></author>
<authorEmail>carlos@hepta.es</authorEmail>
<authorUrl>extensions.hepta.es</authorUrl>
<creationDate>2022-07-21</creationDate>
<copyright>(C) 2023 Piedpiper Inc.</copyright>
<license>GNU General Public License version 2 or later; see
  LICENSE.txt</license>
<version>0.1.0</version>
<description><![CDATA[COM_SPM_DESCRIPTION]]></description>
```

This metadata does not affect your extension's behavior, but it is important to let your user learn more about the extension. Author information will be displayed in the **Manage extensions** listing and adding a tag with proper information will help a lot of your users learn more about your extension.

Below the metadata information, you may find the `namespace` tag, which contains the namespace of our extension:

```
<namespace path="src">Piedpiper\Component\Spm</namespace>
```

This tag helps Joomla! add your namespace to a map of classes used in the framework. This map is created inside Joomla's `cache` folder in the main folder of your Joomla! installation.

After this important tag, we have the `<administration>` section:

```
<administration>
    <files folder="admin">
        <folder>forms</folder>
        <folder>services</folder>
        <folder>src</folder>
        <folder>tmpl</folder>
        <file>access.xml</file>
        <file>config.xml</file>
    </files>
    <menu link="option=com_spm" img="class:default">
      COM_SPM_MENU_BACKEND</menu>
    <submenu>
        <menu link="option=com_spm&amp;view=projects"
          img="default">
              COM_SPM_PROJECTS
        </menu>
        <menu link="option=com_categories&amp;
          view=categories&amp;extension=com_spm"
            img="default">
              COM_SPM_PROJECT_CATEGORIES
        </menu>
        <menu link="option=com_spm&amp;view=tasks"
          img="default">
              COM_SPM_TASKS
        </menu>
        <menu link="option=com_spm&amp;view=invoices"
          img="default">
              COM_SPM_INVOICES
        </menu>
    </submenu>
</administration>
```

The `<administration>` section informs Joomla! of the actions it needs to take to accommodate our extension in the backend of the site. In this case, we start by adding a subsection. In the `<files>` section tag, we add the `folder` attribute, which contains the name of the folder inside your package that contains the backend files and folders of your component. The subsection helps Joomla! create the administrator folder of your component and it accepts these tags:

- `<folder>`: With this tag, you indicate the name of the folder in your package that is going to be copied into the administrator area of your component
- `<file>`: This tag indicates the name of a file that will be copied into the administrator area of your component

It's important to note that when creating your package, you should replicate what the administrator folder of your component will look like. Otherwise, you will be adding unnecessary complexity to the structure.

After declaring our file structure, our manifest file declares the menu item for our component in the backend. We must use the `<menu>` tag to declare the main entry point of our component:

```
<menu link="option=com_spm" img="class:default">
  COM_SPM_MENU_BACKEND</menu>
```

In this tag, we accept a couple of attributes:

- `link`: This tells Joomla! the route to our component in the backend. We do not have any SEF in the backend, so we should indicate the full URL path to the default view of our component. Usually, adding the `option=com_COMPONENTNAME` value will be enough, but you could add the `view` variable to the URL path.
- `img`: This parameter indicates the name of a CSS class to add an icon to your URL.

Immediately after the `<menu>` tag, we have the section where we can add other links to our component areas:

```
<submenu>
    <menu link="option=com_spm&amp;view=projects" img="default">
            COM_SPM_PROJECTS
    </menu>
    <menu link="option=com_categories&amp;
      view=categories&amp;extension=com_spm" img="default">
            COM_SPM_PROJECT_CATEGORIES
    </menu>
    <menu link="option=com_spm&amp;view=tasks"
      img="default">
            COM_SPM_TASKS
    </menu>
```

```
<menu link="option=com_spm&amp;view=invoices"
  img="default">
        COM_SPM_INVOICES
</menu>
</submenu>
```

When your component has different areas, you can add this submenu. It will be shown when the user clicks on the link to our component. We can also use the `<menu>` tag to add links to the submenu.

As we are writing the links in an XML file, we need to pay attention and respect the XML writing convention and use HTML entities to write special characters such as &.

Once defined, we can start with the site's `files` section. In this case, we will use the `<files>` tag to declare the file structure in the frontend area of our component:

```
<files folder="site">
    <folder>src</folder>
    <folder>tmpl</folder>
</files>
```

This section works exactly like the section we defined in the area. In the `folder` tag, we declare the name of the folder inside our archive package, which contains our folder structure for the frontend part of the component.

For the `<media>` tag, the code could be as follows:

```
<media folder="media" destination="com_spm">
    <folder>css</folder>
    <folder>js</folder>
    <filename>joomla.asset.json</filename>
</media>
```

This tag works the same as the `<files>` tag, but instead of moving the files into the front end of the component, it moves them to a subfolder in the `media` folder. This subfolder is defined in the `destination` attribute.

When Joomla! receives the package, it uncompresses it in Joomla's temporary folder (usually located in the `tmp` folder inside the root of our Joomla! installation). Then, it reads the manifest file and follows the instructions to accommodate the package on our site.

Managing versions in your extension

In all our manifest files, we have defined the version of the extension we will install. This is important because Joomla! needs to know the exact version of the installed version when checking for updates.

The common practice in Joomla! is using **Semantic Versioning** (**SemVer**). This way of adding versions to your extension provides more information to the user about what has changed in the extension.

In SemVer, software versions are created using three numbers – *Major.Minor.Patch*:

- *Major*: This number indicates big changes in your software, which means problems and incompatibilities will appear on other software that uses your extension API
- *Minor*: This number indicates adding functionality or a feature that does not affect the current usage of your extension API
- *Patch*: This number indicates that you are submitting bug fixes that present no issues with software using lower versions in the same minor branch

In our SPM extension, we started with release 1.0.0, so we can use SemVer easily by respecting the different uses of the numbers. For instance, we could increase the minor version number at every chapter so that we end up with version 1.14.0.

In any case, it's important to add version numbers to our releases, especially when we release them to the world.

Packaging all the extensions into one file

In this book, we have developed several extensions to provide more features to our SPM, and we have learned how to create individual packages for each extension. When delivering a package to our users, we could send them one package for the component, another for the module, and some of them for each of the plugins in our project. Some developers do it like that, but it's not very convenient for the user.

In Joomla!, we cannot mix different types of extensions in the same manifest XML, but we have a **package** extension we can use to pack all our extensions in the same package and provide that only package to the user.

A package extension consists of an XML manifest file and the file packages of all the extensions we want to include in our package. Let's create the package for our SPM by creating the `src/package/pkg_spm.xml` file with the following content:

```
<?xml version="1.0" encoding="UTF-8" ?>
<extension type="package" method="upgrade">
    <name>Simple Project Manager</name>
    <packagename>spm</packagename>
    <author>Carlos Camara</author>
    <authorUrl>https://developingj5extensions.com/</authorUrl>
    <creationDate>2023-11-01</creationDate>
    <copyright>Copyright Piedpiper - 2022- 2023</copyright>
    <license>GNU General Public License version 2; see
      LICENSE.md</license>
```

```
    <version>1.0.0</version>
    <packager>Carlos Camara</packager>
    <packagerurl>https://developingj5extensions.com/
       </packagerurl>
    <description>Simple Project Manager package
       </description>
    <scriptfile>pkg_script.php</scriptfile>
    <blockChildUninstall>true</blockChildUninstall>
    <files folder="packages">
        <file type="component" id="com_spm">
          com_spm.zip</file>
        <file type="plugin" id="spm" group="webservices">
          plg_webservices_spm.zip</file>
        <file type="plugin" id="spm" group="content">
          plg_content_spm.zip</file>
    </files>
    <variant>full</variant>
</extension>
```

This manifest file is very similar to the previous ones, but there are some new tags and properties that we need to address:

- <packagename>: This tag indicates the name of the package. It should define the content of the package and it must be the same as the manifest filename without the pkg_ prefix. In our case, this spm.

- <packager> and <packagerurl>: These tags define the author of the package (it might not be the same as the developer of the extensions).

- <scriptfile>: This works similarly to how it does with individual extensions, but it should be named with the pkg_ prefix.

- <blockChildUninstall>: Installing a package in Joomla! is just a convenient way of installing several extensions. Setting this parameter to 1 prevents users from uninstalling extensions of the package individually.

- <file>: The file tag in the package manifest accepts the type attribute to indicate the type of package we are installing and id to indicate the name of the extension to install.

When adding plugins to the package, we must also include the group plugin.

> **Important note**
> Please note that the id attribute must be the same as the entry in the #__extensions table, which is the same as the name we set in the attribute of the extension.

Once we have defined the package manifest, we can create a ZIP package containing it and the extensions we want to install with it.

How to manage database changes on your extensions

When creating our main component, we had to create database tables to store our data manually in the database. This is not the best way to deliver a proper component to the world, especially since Joomla! allows us to create our database tables automatically on component installation.

To make Joomla! create our tables, we need to provide it with a SQL command. So, let's add the `src/component/admin/sql/install/mysql/install.sql` file and copy the content of the `mock-data/src/database.sql` file:

```
CREATE TABLE IF NOT EXISTS '#__spm_projects' (
    'id' int(11) UNSIGNED NOT NULL AUTO_INCREMENT,
    'name' VARCHAR(255) NOT NULL,
    'alias' VARCHAR(255) NOT NULL,
    'description' TEXT,
    'deadline' DATETIME,
    'category' INT(11),
    'created' DATETIME DEFAULT NOW(),
    'modified' DATETIME DEFAULT NOW(),
    'created_by' INT(11)  NOT NULL ,
    'modified_by' INT(11)  NOT NULL ,
    PRIMARY KEY ('id')
    ) ENGINE=InnoDB;

CREATE TABLE IF NOT EXISTS '#__spm_tasks' (
'id' int(11) UNSIGNED NOT NULL AUTO_INCREMENT,
    'title' VARCHAR(255) NOT NULL,
    'alias' VARCHAR(255) NOT NULL,
    'description' TEXT,
    'deadline' DATETIME,
    'state' INT(3) NOT NULL,
    'project' INT(11),
    'created' DATETIME DEFAULT NOW(),
    'modified' DATETIME DEFAULT NOW(),
    'created_by' INT(11)  NOT NULL ,
    'modified_by' INT(11)  NOT NULL ,
    PRIMARY KEY ('id')
    ) ENGINE=InnoDB;

CREATE TABLE IF NOT EXISTS '#__spm_customers' (
```

```
    'id' int(11) UNSIGNED NOT NULL AUTO_INCREMENT,
    'firstname' VARCHAR(255) NOT NULL,
    'lastname' VARCHAR(255) NOT NULL,
    'email' VARCHAR(255) NOT NULL,
    'company_name' VARCHAR(255) NOT NULL,
    'company_id' VARCHAR(255) NOT NULL,
    'company_address' VARCHAR(255) NOT NULL,
    'phone' VARCHAR(25) NOT NULL,
    'user' INT(11),
    'created' DATETIME DEFAULT NOW(),
    'modified' DATETIME DEFAULT NOW(),
    'created_by' INT(11)   NOT NULL ,
    'modified_by' INT(11)   NOT NULL ,
    PRIMARY KEY ('id')
    ) ENGINE=InnoDB;

CREATE TABLE IF NOT EXISTS '#__spm_invoices' (
    'id' int(11) UNSIGNED NOT NULL AUTO_INCREMENT,
    'items' TEXT NOT NULL,
    'number' VARCHAR(25) NOT NULL,
    'amount' FLOAT DEFAULT 0.0,
    'customer' INT(11),
    'created' DATETIME DEFAULT NOW(),
    'modified' DATETIME DEFAULT NOW(),
    'created_by' INT(11)   NOT NULL ,
    'modified_by' INT(11)   NOT NULL ,
    PRIMARY KEY ('id')
    ) ENGINE=InnoDB;
```

These are the SQL commands we can use to create our tables in a MySQL or MariaDB database engine, as we saw in *Chapter 1*. Now, we can include the `<install>` section in our manifest file, under the `<extension>` section, as follows:

```
<extension>

...

<install>
    <sql>
        <file driver="mysql" charset="utf8">
            sql/install/mysql/install.sql</file>
    </sql>
</install>
</extension>
```

```
...

</extension>
```

This directive tells Joomla! to use the `install.sql` file we just defined when using the `mysql` database's `driver`. As Joomla! supports MySQL and PostgreSQL, you need to define the SQL instructions specific to each database engine. If you only want to consider one of the database engines, you just need to provide one of the files. In Joomla!, to provide better support for multilinguals, by default, we use the **UTF-8** charset, so we set it in the `charset` attribute to clarify this.

These instructions will only execute on the extension installation routine. When you want to add changes to the database after updating your extension, you need to define a different set of instructions.

How to change your database structure by updating your extensions

It's very common to add changes to your database structure when adding more features to your component. In these situations, we need to inform Joomla! which changes it needs to perform in the database.

To do this, we can use the `<update>` tag in the manifest file:

```
<extension>

...

<update>
    <schemas>
        <schemapath type="mysql" charset="utf8">
        sql/updates/mysql</schemapath>
    </schemas>
</update>

...

</extension>
```

In this case, we use different tags, but the meaning and scope are the same. Instead of the `<file>` tag with the `driver` attribute, we use the `<schemapath>` tag with the `type` attribute, indicating the type of database we target.

The `<schemapath>` tag does not point to a specific file but to a specific folder in our extension package. To include the update instructions, you should create a file with the instructions. But before we get into that, you must understand how database versions work in Joomla!.

The database version is not related to the extension version number, so you may start with the version number you want, regardless of the version number of your extension. But when adding MySQL updates, Joomla! must know what changes are performed on each update. Presumably, your extension updates and changes to the database will be sequential and the result of one change will depend on the database structure of the previous release. This means that with each version, you are changing the database while assuming the user is in the last version of the extension. What happens when the user skips several versions involving database changes on each? In that case, Joomla! needs to perform the skipped changes before applying the latest changes in the database.

Joomla! stores the database version number as soon as it detects any file in the folder defined in the section, so if we add the `src/component/admin/sql/updates/mysql/1.0.0.sql` file, Joomla! will recognize this file as the original database version and will record the database schema version as 1.0.0. On your next component update, Joomla! will look into the folder and when it finds a different version file, let's say 1.0.1, it will update the component schema version to 1.0.1.

When the installed extension provides a `2.0.0.sql` file, Joomla! will execute the changes from files 1.0.2, 1.0.3, 1.1.0, and so on in order, until it gets to `2.0.0.sql`, which will be the last executed file. This way you can be sure that, no matter from which version your user updates the extension, Joomla! will apply all the changes in the right order.

For the SPM extension, we did not add a **status** field for the database. In some countries, once you create an invoice, you cannot modify it, or you might get in trouble with the government. Let's include the status field to reflect when the invoice is a **draft** or it's **final**.

In our extension, let's start defining the MySQL updates by copying the `src/component/admin/mysql/install/mysql/install.sql` file into the `src/component/admin/sql/updates/mysql/1.0.0.sql` file. This way, we guarantee that the first schema version has the same structure as the database scheme we are using at `install`.

Then, we can perform our change by creating the `src/component/admin/sql/updates/mysql/1.0.1.sql` file with the following content:

```
ALTER TABLE '#__spm_invoices' ADD 'status' VARCHAR(5) NOT
NULL DEFAULT 'draft' AFTER 'id';
```

This SQL code adds a new column to the `invoices` table to store the `final` or `draft` values, with these being the latest and the default values.

Now, when we upload our extension to Joomla!, the database schema for the SPM component will be updated to version 1.0.1 automatically. If the database changes cannot be executed, Joomla! will show a warning to the user after installation and when accessing the **System | Manage Database** section of the administrator area, you will see the database for the component that needs to be updated.

Cleaning the database on uninstall

In Joomla!, we can also define some SQL commands to be executed when the user uninstalls our extension. This setup is meant to remove the database tables we created when installing our component.

To add these instructions, we must declare the `<uninstall>` section in the `src/component/spm.xml` manifest file with the following lines:

```
<uninstall>
    <sql>
        <file driver="mysql" charset="utf8">
          sql/install/mysql/uninstall.sql</file>
    </sql>
</uninstall>
```

We must also add the following code to the `src/component/admin/sql/install/mysql/uninstall.sql` file:

```
DROP TABLE '#__spm_projects';
DROP TABLE '#__spm_tasks';
DROP TABLE '#__spm_customers';
DROP TABLE '#__spm_invoices';
```

Now, when we uninstall the SPM component, these tables will be removed from our database and all the information they contain will be lost. When adding this feature to your component, it's a good idea to inform your users before performing the uninstall so that they can back up the information.

We can now handle lots of database changes when installing, upgrading, or even removing our extension. Now, let's learn how to make other changes when managing the extension.

How to execute advanced tasks on extension install

Joomla's database update management is advanced, but sometimes, it's not enough for our needs and we need to perform custom checks and tasks when installing our extensions.

We can specify a PHP script to perform custom tasks when installing our extensions. As a good example, let's add a PHP check to our `install` extension and enable our plugins automatically after installing them.

To do this, edit the `src/component/spm.xml` component manifest file and add the `<scriptfile>` tag to the following section:

```
<extension>

    . . .
```

```
<scriptfile>script.php</scriptfile>

...

</extension>
```

With that, we've instructed Joomla! to look for the `script.php` file in the main folder of our package and execute the instructions it finds there.

Next, create the `src/component/script.php` file with the following content:

```php
<?php

defined('_JEXEC') or die;

class Com_SpmInstallerScript
{
}
```

The `script.php` file contains a PHP class that does not extend to any other class or technically implements any interface.

Joomla! will now look for this file and look for some specific methods in the class when installing the extension. These methods will be executed at different steps of the installation process. These are the methods:

- `preflight($type, $parent)`: This method is executed before running any changes on Joomla!. The `$type` variable indicates the action we are executing: `install`, `update`, or `discover_install`. The `$parent` variable is the installer object.

- `install($parent)`: This method is executed when the extension files have been updated and the extension database structure has been upgraded (following the `schemapath` section's file instructions). It receives the installer object as a parameter.

- `uninstall($type, $parent)`: This method is executed after removing the files of the extension and after executing the section's SQL instructions.

- `update($parent)`: This method receives the installer object as a parameter, and it is only executed when installing an update of the extension.

- `discover_install($parent)`: This method is similar to the `install()` method, and it's only triggered when you are using the **Discover** installation in the Joomla! extension installer.

- `postflight($type, $parent)`: When we get to this method, the extension has been fully installed and Joomla's #__extensions table has been updated with the new version. It's mainly used to show custom messages to the user.

Let's start adding a PHP version check on the extension install. This is a customary practice as our extensions will be developed and tested with one PHP version in mind. So, to be sure the user is not using an old PHP version that might pose issues, we must check the PHP version used to run the site before installing the extension.

This PHP check must be done before installing the extension in Joomla!; otherwise, we risk breaking the user's site. So, we must add the `preflight()` method to the class with the following content:

```php
public function preflight($type, $parent)
{
    $minimumPhp = "8.1.0";

    if (version_compare(\phpversion(), $minimumPhp, '>=')) {
        return true;
    }

    return false;
}
```

In this code, we define the minimum version of PHP we support in our extension, and then we use the `version_compare` PHP function to check if the current PHP version is greater than or equal to our minimum supported version. When the version matches our minimum, we return `true`, and the installation continues. When the site does not meet the minimum requirement, we return `false`. Returning `false` in this method stops the installation process.

Let's create the `src/package/script.php` file with the following content:

```php
<?php

\defined('_JEXEC') or die;

use Joomla\CMS\Factory;

class Pkg_SpmInstallerScript
{
    public function preflight($type, $parent)
    {
        $minimumPhp = "8.1.0";

        if (version_compare(\phpversion(), $minimumPhp,
            '>=')) {
            return true;
        }
```

```
                return false;
        }
}
```

Again, this is a simple PHP class named `Pkg_SpmInstallerScript` that follows a naming convention. We are using the same `preflight()` method that we wrote for our component. This makes sense – when we need a minimum version of PHP for the component, we should also require it for the package. In this script, we will require some of the Joomla! methods, so we have added the required namespaces.

We also want to enable our web service and content plugins on install, to make it easier for the user to use the component out of the box. We could add an installation script to each of the plugins to make them independent of the package installation, but this is more useful and powerful when you have several plugins installed at the same time, so we will add this script to the package.

Now, we must add our `postflight()` method with the following code:

```
public function postflight($type, $parent)
{
    $onlyOnInstall = ['install', 'discover_install'];

    if (!in_array($type, $onlyOnInstall)) {
        return true;
    }

    $db = Factory::getContainer()->get('DatabaseDriver');
    $query = $db->getQuery(true);
    $query->update($db->quoteName('#__extensions'));
    $query->set($db->quoteName('enabled') . ' = 1');
    $query->where('( ' . ($db->quoteName('name') . ' = ' .
      $db->quote('plg_webservices_spm'))
            . ' OR ' . ($db->quoteName('name') . ' = ' .
                $db->quoqte('plg_content_spm')) . ' )');
    $db->setQuery($query);
    $db->query();


}
```

In this `postflight` method, we first check we are installing our package. We do not want to mess up user configuration and enable a plugin that has been disabled! Then, we get a database object to update the `#__extensions` table and set our plugins as enabled with a simple query.

We do not have information on the status of the plugins in the `$parent` method, so we need to get the right record using the `where` statement.

Enabling plugins on package `install` is very convenient for our users, and using the installation script helps us automate lots of tasks that will make their lives easier. But one of the best features we could add to our extensions is enabling live updates to allow them to update to new releases directly from their backend. In the next section, we will learn how to enable this feature using an **update server**.

Setting up an update server

When you develop extensions for Joomla!, commercially or for fun, you want people to use the latest release of your extension. Constant updates of your extensions warrant you are offering the best experience to your users with the latest improvements and features, and it also ensures the security of your users' websites as you will probably keep up with the latest PHP versions and fix any known vulnerabilities in your code.

But whenever you update your extension code, you should inform your users about the new release and provide a download package they can install on their sites. This is very inconvenient for you as you need to set up a whole information network. However, it's also inconvenient for your users as they will need to upload the new releases to update their sites.

In Joomla!, we can push new release notifications to our users easily by setting up an `update` server on our websites.

The `update` server for our extension consists of an XML file declaring release information for our extension. This file must be public and Joomla! should be able to directly access it from a URL. We are going to create our `update` server in the same Git repository, so we will create the `update_server/updates.xml` file with the following content:

```xml
<?xml version="1.0" encoding="utf-8"?>
<updates>
    <update>
        <name>Simple Project Manager Package</name>
        <description><![CDATA[A simple project manager
          extension]]></description>
        <element>pkg_spm</element>
        <type>package</type>
        <version>1.0.0</version>
        <maintainer>Carlos Camara</maintainer>
        <maintainerurl>https://developingj5extensions.com
          </maintainerurl>
        <client>administrator</client>
        <infourl title="New release of SPM package">
          https://github.com/</infourl>
        <downloads>
            <downloadurl type="full" format="zip">
              https://github.com/</downloadurl>
```

```
        </downloads>
        <sha256></sha256>
        <tags>
            <tag>stable</tag>
        </tags>
        <targetplatform name="joomla"
          version="4\.[01234]|5\.0" />
        <php_minimum>8.1.0</php_minimum>
        <supported_databases mysql="5.7.0" mariadb="10.2"
          postgresql="9.2" />
    </update>
</updates>
```

This XML file follows the same rules as the manifest files we have looked at in this book. The main section contains all the possible updates for our extension. Each update is enclosed between an `<update>` tag. We must define the following tags:

- `<name>`: The name of the extension to update.

- `<description>`: A short description of the extension.

- `<element>`: The installed name of the extension. We are creating the `update` server for the package, so we use the package name.

- `<type>`: This defines the type of extension. Here, we are using `package`.

- `<version>`: The version number for our package.

- `<maintainer>`: The name of the author of the package (optional).

- `<maintainerurl>`: The URL of the author of the package (optional).

- `<client>`: This tag indicates the target area of Joomla!. For packages and components, it's set to `administrator`. For plugins, you should set it to `site`, and for modules and templates, you must specify the proper value (`administrator`) for backend modules and templates and `site` otherwise. The default value is `administrator`, and not adding the right value will result in no updates showing.

- `<inforurl>`: This tag is optional and lets you add a URL with information about the update.

- `<downloads>`: This tag defines the downloads section for the update.

- `<downloadurl>`: This tag defines the URL where Joomla! will download the `update` package. It accepts the `type` attribute, indicating whether it's an `upgrade` package with just the minimum changes or a `full` package with the full component. It's usually set to `full`. It also accepts the `format` attribute with the file format for the `upgrade` package. For maximum compatibility, I recommend using `zip`.

- `<sha256>`: This tag is optional, and it indicates the file checksum value of the package. This increases the security of the download as Joomla! will check the downloaded file before upgrading.

- `<tags>`: This tag is optional and defines a new section where you can add tags relevant to the update. They are mainly used to determine the stability of the package and use the `dev`, `alpha`, `beta`, `rc`, and `stable` keywords. If no stability is set, Joomla! assumes it's `stable`.

- `<targetplatform>`: With this tag, you set the platform and version the update is developed for. For the `name` attribute, you can only use `joomla`, and for the `version` attribute, you can use a single version or a regular expression to set several versions. In any case, this is only valid when you target several versions of Joomla! with the same file. If you need different update packages for different Joomla! versions, you should define a new full `<update>` section pointing to the right file.

- `<php_minimum>`: This sets the minimum PHP requirement for the component. When Joomla! checks for new updates, if the installation does not meet the minimum PHP requirement, it shows a message to the user and does not allow the update.

- `<supported_databases>`: This tag sets the minimum database requirements. It accepts three attributes – `mysql`, `mariadb`, and `postgresql` – indicating the minimum version of each database server.

Once we have an `update` server, we must add it to our extension manifest file so that Joomla! adds it to the update sites table and checks for updates of the package.

Adding this `update` server to the manifest file requires that we edit the `src/package/pkg_spm.xml` manifest file and add the following section:

```
<extension>

    . . .

    <updateservers>
        <server type="extension" priority="2" name="Simple
        Project Manager Updates">https://
            raw.githubusercontent.com/PacktPublishing/
                Developing-Extensions-for-Joomla-5/chapter14/
                    src/update_server/updates.xml</server>
    </updateservers>
</extension>
```

In the `<server>` tag, we use the `type` attribute with the `extension` value to indicate it's a unique extension (remember that an extension package is an extension itself). Then, we can define a `priority` attribute. This attribute is used if there are several `update` servers for the package. The one with lower priority prevails. Finally, we include the attribute for the extension's `name`; the value of the tag will be the URL of the XML file.

After these XML definitions, when we add a new update to our `update` server, Joomla! will check it and notify the user about the new release.

After setting the `update` server and adding it to the package manifest file, we can offer regular updates to our users easily and be ready to publish our extension for the world to enjoy.

Adding a paywall to your extension download

Joomla! supports commercial developers and provides some features to make it easier to set up a business developing extensions for Joomla!. One of the latest additions to the core is the support for **download keys** when requesting updates.

Download keys are usually an alphanumeric string format and permit you to download updates of your extensions. This is very convenient for users as they can use the live update feature for the extensions. Regarding developers, they can control who can download their extensions.

These download keys must be added to the extension live update download link so that when a user requests the download, it will be granted if the key is valid and denied otherwise.

The way to consider download keys in your Joomla! extension is by adding a new section to your manifest XML. So, let's edit the `src/package/pkg_spm.xml` file and add the following tag:

```
<dlid prefix="spm_key=" suffix="&amp;customer=1"/>
```

When Joomla! finds this tag on extension installation, users can add a download key to the **Update sites** area for the installed extension.

Once the download key has been set, Joomla! uses the `prefix` and `suffix` attributes, along with the download key introduced by the user, to generate the download URL for the package in the form of `https://developingj5extensions.com/package-download?spm_key=DOWNLOAD_KEY&customer=1`.

So, Joomla! appends the *prefix + download key + suffix* indicated to the download URL and the download request will have a key parameter that you can use to allow or deny the download.

In any case, you may leave both attributes (`prefix` and `suffix`) empty and only the download key parameter will be added.

This way, setting up a paywall and generating download keys for your customers is the only thing you need to do to add a download paywall to your extension. There are several options to do it, depending on the marketing approach and involvement you want.

Summary

In this chapter, we learned how to put together all the work we have done in this book and create a package to distribute our extensions to the world.

We learned how to push changes to the user database structure to add new features or fix existing bugs. Joomla! helps a lot with this as it provides proper tags and mechanisms so that we can focus on the database code.

Finally, we learned how to create an update server to notify users about new releases and how to protect extension updates behind a paywall just using Joomla! code.

After all these chapters, I hope you found this content helpful and that you have a grasp of the basics regarding how to develop Joomla! solutions for your next projects.

In this book, we tried to provide a guide for extension development as close as possible to Joomla's coding standards and architecture in the simplest way possible. A great way to learn more about Joomla! extension development is going to GitHub and helping with Joomla! issues.

Joomla! is a community-driven project and the community will help you with your issues and questions in the Joomla! forum.

See you in the community!

Further reading

- Joomla's documentation about manifest files is really descriptive: `https://docs.joomla.org/Manifest_files`

- You can read more about SemVer on its site: `https://semver.org/`

- The Joomla! documentation provides a great article that specifies all the details regarding the Joomla! update server file: `https://docs.joomla.org/Deploying_an_Update_Server#Supporting_Tools`

Index

A

A/B testing 209
Access Control List (ACL) **104, 136**
  adding, to component categories 117
  adding, to components 105
  adding, to custom fields 122, 123
accessibility
  testing, in extensions 251
  testing, with browser 252, 253
accessiblemedia field type
  using 92
Access Level Configuration (ACL) 44
access levels
  viewing 106
action buttons 43
Active Record pattern 47
Advanced tab
  adding, to module configuration 157, 158
advanced tasks
  executing, on extension install 280-283
alternative layout
  adding, for module 214
  creating 213
alternative menu item
  adding, for component view 213, 214
Apache 265

assets
  adding, to overrides 216
  disabling, in overrides 216
  loading, with HtmlHelper 67, 68
  overriding, with Web Assets Manager 215
  registering, with JSON file 65, 66
  securing, for future 264
Atum 252
authorization methods
  basic authorization 134
  Joomla! token authorization 134
automatic system testing 246
automatic testing
  benefits 238
AXE 253

B

backend templates 208
basic authorization 134
Before Execute event 190
Bootstrap 5 61, 63
browser
  accessibility, testing with 252, 253

C

Cassiopeia 231, 252
categories
    custom properties 113-117
    using, in components 110, 111
category management 104
category service 115
child templates 219
    creating 220
    creating, directly in repository 221-223
    creating, with Joomla! template manager 223
    language files, adding to 232, 233
    need for 220
    overrides 224, 225
    parameters, adding to 231, 232
    reusing, on different sites 229, 230
Chromedriver 248
classes
    mapping, in composer.json 245, 246
CLI applications
    advantages, over regular web
        applications 186
client side
    user input, validating on 97-99
CLI messages
    internationalizing 195-199
Codeception 246, 247
    installing 247-250
Command-Line Interface
    (CLI) 105, 185, 186
complex translations
    adding 126, 127
component categories
    ACL, adding to 117
    customizing 112
component database structure
    defining 10, 11

component file architecture 26
    admin folder 26
    site folder 26
component repository structure
    creating 31
components 4
    ACL, adding to 105
    categories, using in 110, 111
    characteristics 5
    CSS, adding to 61, 62
    custom actions, defining for 109, 110
    custom fields, using in 118-120
    friendly URLs, adding to 77-80
    frontend item view, developing for 68, 69
    frontend list view, developing for 54, 55
    GET endpoint, adding to 141, 142
    JavaScript, adding to 61-63
    multilingual capabilities, using in 124-126
    permissions configuration, adding 106-108
    permissions, honoring in
        extensions 108, 109
    POST endpoint, adding to 142, 143
    request handling 140
    SEF URLs, translating into variables for 81
    styles, adding to 63
    Web Service API, adding to 136
component's backend
    building 26
    services folder 27, 28
    src folder 28
    tmpl folder 31
component view
    alternative menu item, adding for 213, 214
    template override, creating for 210-212
Composer 240
    PHPUnit, installing through 240, 241
console plugin group 189
Content Management System (CMS) 3, 103

content plugin 165
  creating 170-177
createCRUDRoutes() method
  using, to add Web Service endpoints 138
Cron Job 186
Cron tasks 187
cross-site request forgery (CSRF) attacks
  preventing, in forms 260, 261
Cross-Site Scripting (XSS) attacks 49
  preventing 261
CSS
  adding, to component 61, 62
cURL 131
custom actions
  defining, for components 109, 110
custom endpoint requests
  adding, to Web Service 139, 140
Customer entity 6
  actions 7
Customer Relationship Manager (CRM) 120
customer's plugin
  creating 180-183
custom fields 105, 117, 118
  ACL, adding to 122, 123
  displaying, in views 120-122
  using, in components 118-120
custom form field types
  defining 93-95

D

data
  fetching, from forms 256-258
  reading, from Web Service 141, 142
  writing, from Web Service 142, 143
database
  changes, managing on extensions 276-278
  cleaning, on extension uninstall 280

mock data, importing into 21, 22
  relationships, reflecting in 14-16
  tables, creating in 16-18
Database namespace 188
database structure
  modifying, by updating extensions 278, 279
database tables
  adding, for entities 12, 13
  extra information columns, adding to 13, 14
  select options, creating from 92, 93
dbadminer 18
Dependency Injection
    Container (DIC) 27, 148
download keys 287
DRY (Don't Repeat Yourself) principle 150

E

edit item view, for component
  controller, adding to project entity 48
  developing 41, 42
  forms folder, creating 46, 47
  layout, creating 48, 49
  manifest file modifications 49
  model, adding to retrieve and
    save data 44-46
  project data, getting from database 47
  project view, creating 42-44
  testing 51
Editor form field type
  using 91, 92
endpoints 130
entities 5
  actions 7
  Customer 6, 7
  database tables, adding for 12, 13
  defining 6
  finding 6

Invoice 6, 8
Project category 8
Project Category 7
Projects 6, 8
Task 7, 8
equals rule 100
Extension 188
extension download
  paywall, adding to 287
extension install
  advanced tasks, executing on 280-283
extensions 270
  accessibility, testing in 251
  database changes, managing on 276-278
  package, creating for 270-273
  packaging, into one file 274, 275
  updating, to modify database
    structure 278, 279
  versions, managing in 273, 274

F

Faker PHP library 19
files
  access, hardening to 265
Finder plugin 165
Firefox Accessibility inspector 252
FontAwesome
  URL 34
forms
  cross-site request forgery (CSRF)
    attacks, preventing in 260, 261
  data, fetching from 256-258
  defining 84
friendly URLs
  adding, to component 77-80
  parameters, translating into 80

frontend item view
  developing, for component 68, 69
  layout, adding for item detail 72, 73
  menu item, adding for 73-75
  model, adding for 69-71
frontend list view
  adding, for list of projects 56, 57
  coding 55
  data, obtaining to show 57-59
  developing, for component 54, 55
  DisplayController, adding 55, 56
  template, adding to lay out data 59-61
frontend templates 208

G

GeckoDriver 248
GET endpoint
  adding, to component 141, 142
Global Configuration 135

H

HtmlHelper
  assets, loading with 67, 68
HTTP requests, in Web Service
  DELETE 130
  GET 130
  PATCH 130
  POST 130

I

input data
  filtering, before saving to database 258-260
Invoice entity 6
  actions 8

J

JavaScript
adding, to component 61-63
JED Checker extension 265
using 265-267
Joomla! 3
minimum component, testing 34
namespaces 28
PHPUnit, configuring for 241-243
plugins 164, 165
URL 4
Joomla! 5 237, 264
Joomla!.assets.json file
used, for loading projects.css 66, 67
Joomla Browser 248
Joomla! categories
benefits 113
disadvantages 113
Joomla! Category Manager 112
Joomla! CLI 187, 188
commands 188
generic options 189
Joomla! CLI command
adding, to Joomla! 189-193
parameters, adding to 199-202
Joomla! database 11, 12
Joomla! ecosystems
actions 107
Joomla! Extension Directory™ 265
Joomla! forms
fields, receiving in model 88, 89
filter form, displaying in projects list 87
general options, adding to extensions 84, 85
individual items, editing 89
options form, displaying in component 86

search and filter capabilities,
adding to listings 86, 87
Joomla! modules
caching 158, 159
Joomla! template 208
files 208, 209
new module position, adding to 226, 227
Joomla! template manager
used, for creating child template 223
Joomla! token authorization 134
Joomla! views
template override, creating for 210
Joomla! Web Service API
using 132
JSON file
used, for registering assets 65, 66
JSON response, objects
data 133
links 133
meta 133

K

keyboard testing 253

L

language files
adding, to child template 232, 233
Launch Joomla service
URL 34
list view, for component
adding, for projects data 35, 36
developing 35
model, adding to projects view 36-40
projects list, showing 40, 41

M

manifest file
<administration> tag 33
<description> tag 33
<files> tag 34
<Menu> tag 34
<namespace> tag 33
<version> tag 33
creating 32, 33
creating, for plugins 168, 169

manual testing 238

menu item
adding, for views 73-75
options, adding to 75, 76

minimum component
testing, on Joomla! 34

mock data
benefits 18
content, defining of 18
generation, automating 19-21
importing, into database 21, 22
tips 18

model
adding, for frontend item view 69-71

Model-View-Controller (MVC)
pattern 28, 54

module
alternative layout, adding for 214
helpers, using 150, 151
layout, adding 152
manifest, writing for 152, 153
template override, creating for 212

module chromes 227

module configuration
Advanced tab, adding 157, 158
customers parameter 154
maximum projects to show parameter 154

ordering parameter 154
parameters, using 154-156
saved parameters, using in code 159-162

module file structure 148
provider code, creating 148-150

module styles 227

module tag 229

multilingual capabilities 105
using, in components 124-126

MySQL prepared statements 81

N

namespaces 28
Nginx 265

O

onContentPrepare event 167
overrides
assets, adding to 216
assets, disabling in 216
in child templates 224, 225

P

package
creating, for extensions 270-273

package extension 274

parameters
adding, to child template 231, 232
adding, to CLI command 199-202
translating, into friendly URL 80

paywall
adding, to extension download 287

PHP 8.2 237
PhpBrowser 248
PHP cURL 131

phpMyAdmin 4, 18
PHPUnit 239
  configuring, for Joomla! 241-243
  installing 240
  installing, through Composer 240, 241
plugins 163, 164
  adding, to component 178, 179
  calling, from components 165-167
  file structure 168
  folder structure 168
  groups 164, 165
  manifest file, creating for 168, 169
  template override, creating for 212, 213
POST endpoint
  adding, to component 142, 143
Project category entity 7
  actions 8
projects.css
  loading, with Joomla!.assets.json file 66, 67
Projects entity 6
  actions 8

R

relationships 5
  defining 9, 10
  reflecting, in database 14, 16
request
  handling, in components 140
REST 130

S

scheduled tasks 187
SEF URLs
  translating, into variables for components 81
select options
  creating, from database tables 92, 93

Semantic Versioning (SemVer) 274
Semantic Versioning Specification
  URL 33
server side
  user input, validating on 99-101
services folder 27, 28
Simple Project Manager 29
single responsibility principle 239
SOAP 130
SQL injection
  preventing 262-264
SQL-prepared statements 262
src folder 28
  Controller folder 29, 30
  Extension folder 29
  namespaces 28
  View folder 30, 31
standard Joomla! Form fields
  using 90, 91
styles
  adding, to component 63
subform field type
  using, ways 95-97
Symfony console
  output tags 194, 195
SymfonyStyle methods 194
system testing 246, 251

T

tables
  creating, in database 16-18
Task entity 7
  actions 8
template modules
  styling 227-229

template override 209
    creating, for component view 210-212
    creating, for Joomla! views 210
    creating, for module 212
    creating, for plugin 212, 213
    use cases 209, 210
test-driven development (TDD) 239
    workflow 239
tests 238
    running 245
    writing 243, 244
Token 260

U

unit testing 238, 246, 251
update server 284
    setting up 284-287
user groups 106
user input
    validating, on client side 97-99
    validating, on server side 99-101
User - Joomla API Token plugin 135
UTF-8 charset 278

V

versions
    managing, in extension 273, 274
views
    custom fields, displaying in 120-122
Visual Studio Code
    URL 4

W

WAVE 253
Web Asset Manager 63, 64, 224
    advantages 64
    assets, overriding with 215
Web Service 130
    custom endpoint requests adding to 139, 140
    data, reading from 141, 142
    data, writing from 142, 143
Web Service API 105, 130
    adding, to component 136
    consuming 131, 132
    permissions 135
Web Service endpoints
    adding, createCRUDRoutes() used 138
Web Service plugin
    developing 136, 137
Web Services - Contact plugin 135
Web Services type 165

Packtpub.com

Subscribe to our online digital library for full access to over 7,000 books and videos, as well as industry leading tools to help you plan your personal development and advance your career. For more information, please visit our website.

Why subscribe?

- Spend less time learning and more time coding with practical eBooks and Videos from over 4,000 industry professionals

- Improve your learning with Skill Plans built especially for you

- Get a free eBook or video every month

- Fully searchable for easy access to vital information

- Copy and paste, print, and bookmark content

Did you know that Packt offers eBook versions of every book published, with PDF and ePub files available? You can upgrade to the eBook version at packt.com and as a print book customer, you are entitled to a discount on the eBook copy. Get in touch with us at customercare@packtpub.com for more details.

At www.packt.com, you can also read a collection of free technical articles, sign up for a range of free newsletters, and receive exclusive discounts and offers on Packt books and eBooks.

Other Books You May Enjoy

If you enjoyed this book, you may be interested in these other books by Packt:

Implementing Atlassian Confluence

Eren Kalelioğlu

ISBN: 978-1-80056-042-0

- Create, organize, and manage sustainable content on Confluence while enhancing collaboration
- Learn effective team collaboration techniques to boost productivity and efficiency
- Grasp the essential principles of scaling Confluence to meet your organizational needs
- Configure Confluence as a hub for external systems
- Use Jira Service Management and Confluence together
- Integrate Confluence with tools such as Google Workspace, Slack, Jira, and Teams for a seamless workflow
- Enhance Confluence by adding and personalizing new functionalities for your unique requirements

Drupal 10 Development Cookbook - Third Edition

Matt Glaman, Kevin Quillen

ISBN: 978-1-80323-496-0

- Create and manage a Drupal site's codebase
- Design tailored content creator experiences
- Leverage Drupal by creating customized pages and plugins
- Turn Drupal into an API platform for exposing content to consumers
- Import data into Drupal using the data migration APIs
- Advance your Drupal site with modern frontend tools using Laravel Mix

Packt is searching for authors like you

If you're interested in becoming an author for Packt, please visit authors.packtpub.com and apply today. We have worked with thousands of developers and tech professionals, just like you, to help them share their insight with the global tech community. You can make a general application, apply for a specific hot topic that we are recruiting an author for, or submit your own idea.

Share Your Thoughts

Now you've finished *Developing Extensions for Joomla! 5*, we'd love to hear your thoughts! Scan the QR code below to go straight to the Amazon review page for this book and share your feedback or leave a review on the site that you purchased it from.

https://packt.link/r/1804617997

Your review is important to us and the tech community and will help us make sure we're delivering excellent quality content.

Download a free PDF copy of this book

Thanks for purchasing this book!

Do you like to read on the go but are unable to carry your print books everywhere?

Is your eBook purchase not compatible with the device of your choice?

Don't worry, now with every Packt book you get a DRM-free PDF version of that book at no cost.

Read anywhere, any place, on any device. Search, copy, and paste code from your favorite technical books directly into your application.

The perks don't stop there, you can get exclusive access to discounts, newsletters, and great free content in your inbox daily

Follow these simple steps to get the benefits:

1. Scan the QR code or visit the link below

https://packt.link/free-ebook/9781804617991

2. Submit your proof of purchase

3. That's it! We'll send your free PDF and other benefits to your email directly

www.ingramcontent.com/pod-product-compliance
Lightning Source LLC
Chambersburg PA
CBHW080624060326
40690CB00021B/4806